3011

D1631223

8ut

Reconnecting

Other books by Joseph J. Luciani, Ph.D.

Self-Coaching: The Powerful Program to Beat Anxiety and Depression

The Power of Self-Coaching: The Five Essential Steps to Creating the Life You Want

Reconnecting

A Self-Coaching Solution to Revive Your Love Life

JOSEPH J. LUCIANI, PH.D.

WILEY

John Wiley & Sons, Inc.

Published by John Wiley & Sons, Inc., Hoboken, New Jersey
Published simultaneously in Canada

For general information about our other products and services, please contact our Customer Care Department within the United States at (800) 762-2974, outside the United States at (317) 572-3993 or fax (317) 572-4002.

Wiley also publishes its books in a variety of electronic formats. Some content that appears in print may not be available in electronic books. For more information about Wiley products, visit our web site at www.wiley.com.

Library of Congress Cataloging-in-Publication Data:
Luciani, Joseph J.
Reconnecting: a self-coaching solution to revive your love life/Joseph J. Luciani.
    p. cm.
Includes index.
ISBN 978-0-470-32505-6 (cloth)
    1.   Man-woman relationships. 2. Couples—Psychology. 3. Self-talk. I. Title.
HQ801.L829 2009
646.7'8—dc22
                                                                        2008055870

Printed in the United States of America

10 9 8 7 6 5 4 3 2 1

To Karen:

When we first met on that frozen pond almost a half century ago, we were just kids—two star-cross'd lovers. Today after thirty-seven years of marriage and a lifetime of love, I feel this book needs to be dedicated to you. And to us.

Contents

PART TWO

Catalytic Self-Coaching
Working with Your Partner

Acknowledgments

In writing this book, I've looked to my own past relationships for guidance and inspiration. I owe a debt of gratitude to the following wonderful people for shaping my perceptions and understanding of love, intimacy, and life's true meaning.

I begin with my patients and all the wonderful people who have joined my Self-Coaching community at www.self-coaching.net. I want to thank you, not only for your ongoing support, but for being the catalyst behind this project.

I'd like to thank my agent, Jean Naggar, for her unwavering faith in me and my message. Jean was truly instrumental in encouraging me to undertake this project, my fourth book in my Self-Coaching series. Jean's guidance and friendship over the years have proven to be invaluable in my literary development. I feel fortunate to have worked with her and her talented, supportive, and wonderful staff, Jennifer Weltz, Alice Tasman, Mollie Glick, Jessica Regel, and Marika Josephson.

Special appreciation and thanks go to my editors at John Wiley & Sons, Tom Miller and Christel Winkler. From the very beginning, Tom has given me the confidence to believe that I can be a successful author. I know I'm in good hands when working with Tom's X-ray intuition and literary instincts and judgment. For Tom, taking a manuscript, tweaking it, and turning it into something truly inspired seems almost effortless.

Thank you, Tom, not only for being my mentor and friend, but for being such an essential part of my journey with John Wiley & Sons. And thank you for believing in this project.

Jane Rafal and I have worked together for many years. Jane was the first person to convince me that I could be a writer. Her unwavering support, encouragement, and friendship are major reasons why I go on authoring new books. Under her editorial tutelage, my writing skills have become more refined over the years, in spite of my initial misgivings. Her talents go far beyond merely offering sage editorial advice—she's my coach, friend, and mentor in all things related to writing. Most importantly, Jane is simply a wonderful person. I don't know what I'd do without her.

Special thanks go to Justine Banas for her critical read-through of this project along with her ongoing suggestions and insightful feedback. Justine's editorial talents and intuitive psychological understanding were pivotal to this book's evolution. Justine has been a valuable resource, friend, cheerleader, and confidante in helping me see the forest for the trees (and then some).

I'm humbled by the knowledge that my mother, who battled all odds this past year and decided to survive, will get to read this book. Thank you, Mom, for the lifetime of love you've given me. To my mother-in-law, "Grandma" Joan, thank you for letting me know that happiness is a choice. You're an inspiration to us all. To my cousins Celeste Galdieri, Cathy Mangano, and Tom Carrino, I was never an only child with you guys around. Thank you for always believing in me and sharing my ambitions. To my wife's Girls' Night crew, Eileen Tepe, Ginny Torre, cousin Celeste, and Maryann Hardy, thank you for allowing me to share some laughs with you every Monday night. To my brother-in-law Ron York and his wife, Pricilla, I want to thank you for always being excited for me and for my writing. Special thanks to Ron for helping me recharge my batteries at our Giants Stadium tailgates. Alex Locatelli, my lifelong friend, lawyer, college roommate, and confidant—I'm blessed to have such a loyal friendship. Warmest thanks to Alan and Nan Gettis, best friends to my wife and me, for the love, laughs, closeness, and support we've shared through so many unforgettable years and times. Very special thanks to Deborah Mengrone for all her valuable support, encouragement, and unwavering belief in this project. To my Sanibel cousins Stan (Beaver) and Lisa Stasi, thank you for all the sunsets we've shared, the many laughs, and your gracious hospitality. To Anne Baretta for always looking to spread the Self-Coaching word, but mostly for her valued loyalty and friendship. To my yoga instructor and dear friend Perinkulam Ramanathan, who continues to allow me to reach deeper into my life experiences. Rama's influence and loving heart permeate this entire project. *Om Shanthi.*

I would like to thank my cocreator of the M3 Lifestyle program (www.M3Lifestyle.com), Mohey Elsayed, for working with me to extend my psychology of empowerment to the fitness and health community. I would also like to thank Bill Herndon of One Source Media for including "Dr. Joe" as the on-site psychologist in the TV pilot *Almost Famous*. These experiences challenged me to develop a more evolved understanding of motivation, which I've been able to use as a source of inspiration for this book.

My son, Justin, who is now involved in his burgeoning entrepreneurial business, www.wdezine.com and www.healthycommons.com, continues to amaze me with his creativity and determination. Justin has a great heart and a great mind; I see him as a courageous voyager seeking life's adventures and discoveries. My daughter, Lauren, is about to begin her career as a schoolteacher. Lauren's outward beauty is only a metaphor for the inner beauty, optimism, and passion that lie within—she will captivate her students as much as she captivates me. Thank you, Lauren and Justin, for helping me understand how much love matters to me. You guys are my raison d'être.

Lastly, I turn to my wife, Karen. There's a picture on my den wall of two teenagers holding hands, leaning up against an old Chevy parked in back of Fort Lee High School. Many years ago when that picture was taken, I knew somehow that our lives would inexorably be intertwined, then, now, and always. I'm blessed to have had a lifetime to recognize the depths of our relationship. Who I am today is indistinguishable from who *we* are today—thank you for giving me a reason to write this book.

PART ONE

The Self-Coaching Phase

Working without Your Partner

1

Can I Really Save My Relationship?

Becoming a Catalyst

Catalyst: *an agent that causes change or action*

Suffering without hope is intolerable. Sometimes after hours, in the quiet of my office, I can still hear the anguished voices:

"Don't you realize that your need to watch porn every time we make love makes me feel so cheap? I feel rejected when you watch other women. Don't I turn you on anymore?"

"Stop pretending there's no problem. You can't even look at me anymore. It feels like we're on different planets, different worlds apart . . . What happened to us? Is it me? I just don't understand."

"You've become so nasty; you're not the person I married. I honestly think you hate me. I can't go on feeling this miserable."

"How could you do this to me? How could you sleep with her? Obviously you have no respect for me or our relationship. Believe me, if I had a gun in my hand right now, I think I would use it on you! Or her!"

"I'm so confused. I just don't know if I love you anymore. Maybe a separation would help. It's not that I don't care about you . . . I just need time. I can't take the constant bickering . . . I just can't take it. I'm sorry . . . so sorry. It's not you, it's me."

All of these statements came from couples I've counseled, and, as you might suspect, they represent a small fraction of the different notes that make up the sad song of relationship chaos. Since you're reading this book, you too are probably suffering and looking for relief. I wrote this book to give you hope. But hope by itself is too passive, too uncertain . . . so, more than hope, this is a book about change. Positive change.

If you've ever felt like any of the patients quoted above, or whatever concerns you may have about your relationship—however confused, bogged down, or distraught you may feel at this moment—I want you to know that there's a realistic solution: a Catalytic Self-Coaching solution that doesn't require anything more than an open mind and a willingness to explore the riddle that your relationship has become.

So if you're in a problem relationship—one that's slipping, becoming more troubled, less loving, and more confused—I have one question for you: how come you're the one reading this book and not your partner? Don't make any excuses; the simple truth is that *you're* the one who decided to do something about your struggling relationship. Not your partner. And you are the reason I wrote this book. Sure, in a better world, it would be great if you *and* your partner would share the responsibility for change. But in the real world, most struggling relationships become asymmetrical; one partner becomes the problem solver and the other the problem avoider. (You may be tempted to see your partner as the "problem maker," but for now, try to suspend this belief until we discuss the dynamics of your relationship.) Since you're doing the reading right now, let's designate you as the problem solver. And if your partner isn't happy with this designation, then by all means share the book—having two problem solvers in one relationship is great. But as you're about to find out, it's not a necessity either!

From the start, let's face one undeniable law of relating: struggle does not take place in a vacuum. Every struggle involves two partners with two unique perceptions. And every solution includes two partners with one shared perception. This book makes no claim that you can fix or change your partner; only your partner can do that. What I can promise is that you can become a catalyst for getting your less than cooperative partner to join you in a meaningful healing process, even if you have to start this process alone.

As I mentioned earlier, if you're reading this book, chances are you've voluntarily assigned yourself the role of problem solver. If you're willing to accept this as a necessary, albeit temporary, burden, then this book can help. But don't look at this undertaking as a burden. Instead, try to see it as an attempt to protect your investment. Whatever your reason—whether it's children, years together, shared assets, pets, or fear of dissolving the relationship and facing the unknown—I think you'll agree that you have much more to gain if things work out than if they don't. And let's face it, does it really matter who initiates the process if in fact you wind up reclaiming the love you've lost? It's not a contest, it's your life.

Pain: The Bright Side

Although your situation is unique, all relationship struggles have one thing in common: pain. It doesn't matter if you're feeling unloved, unable to love, abused, neglected, or just plain confused—pain is pain! And it stinks! But there is a bright side; pain can be a great motivator. Whether it's going to the dentist to finally get that long-needed root canal taken care of or spending the money to replace those worn-out running shoes that leave you limping after every workout, pain instigates change.

Misconception 1: In a Struggling Relationship, Only One Partner Suffers

You might assume that since you're the only one who actually wants to do anything to save your relationship, at least for the moment, you must be suffering more than your partner. Not true. Just because your partner may not be showing any outward signs of pain or distress, don't think there isn't a fire burning in the cellar.

It's not unusual for a struggling partner to bury his or her feelings in insulating-avoidant behavior. This can include emotional withdrawal, excessive diversion (TV, compulsive hobbies, and so on), flirtations and affairs, overeating, substance abuse, workaholism—in fact, just about anything that masks the pain and conflict by creating a buffer of distraction or distance. For other partners, the problem isn't avoidance. It's violence. The flip side of avoidant behavior is hostile-aggressive behavior. This category includes such distasteful behavior as yelling, nastiness, obnoxiousness, physical and psychological abuse, passive aggressiveness, and demeaning, hurtful personality attacks.

Whether it's aggressive or passive, avoidant or insulating, the motor that drives this shabby behavior is pain. Although you and your partner may experience and express your pain differently, in a stumbling relationship, no one is spared. Pain is an equal-opportunity experience.

Misconception 2: You're Unloved

Another equally common misconception is that an uncooperative, seemingly unaffected, avoidant, or aggressive partner doesn't love you. (I'll be defining love in a later chapter.) Although some behavior, such as aloofness, lack of concern, or any form of hostility, may leave you convinced that things are hopeless, this may be far from the truth. Avoidant and aggressive behavior typically has nothing to do with lack of love and everything to do with your partner's attempts to sidestep vulnerability. Let's face it, if instead of being loved you expect to be rejected, you're going to do what comes naturally—protect yourself. It's human nature. You are not going to risk the emotional vulnerability inherent in loving if you don't feel safe. Neither is your partner.

Control: The Bottom Line

Understanding your relationship struggle doesn't need to be complicated, not when you are able to identify the root of all strife. The driving biological forces in nature are said to be the avoidance of pain and the seeking of pleasure. I'd like to add another equally compelling drive to this list: we humans abhor losing control and do whatever we can to regain it. From the time we are infants, we meet chaos with a reactive attempt to control the situation. The Moro reflex, which is present for a brief period after birth, demonstrates this natural instinct. If an infant falls rapidly, the child's arms and legs will mimic the grasping response of a young monkey clinging to its mother as she climbs through the trees. From an evolutionary standpoint, this is known as a vestigial behavior pattern— one that reflects our evolutionary past. From our first moments on earth, we have instinctively responded to danger by protecting ourselves from harm and trying to regain control.

I mention all this so you can understand the powerful forces at work when people feel threatened. Whether the threat is real or imagined makes no difference. If you *feel* threatened, abandoned, neglected, or unloved, you will do what comes naturally—you will try to gain control over those chaotic feelings. Sometimes you may do it constructively by talking, discussing, and trying to resolve the problem. Sometimes you may do it destructively, by avoiding, attacking, or otherwise protecting yourself from perceived harm. Destructive or constructive, you're only trying to feel less out of control.

When there's turbulence in a relationship, each partner tries reflexively to regain some control over the floundering situation. Every relationship struggle reflects some combination of three basic controlling strategies. Depending on the degree of security or insecurity, each partner will adopt one of these reactions:

1. **Constructive.** Trying to talk, understand, or get some help.

2. **Avoidant.** Retreating into a turtle shell of protection and avoidance.

3. **Aggressive.** Becoming hostile and aggressive: "If I push you away, you can't hurt me."

The optimum approach for resolving problems and reclaiming love is for both partners to be constructive—a constructive-constructive approach. A mutually constructive approach is the eventual goal of this book. Unfortunately, we don't always begin with the optimum.

When neither partner can be constructive, and instead both of them wind up embroiled in patterns of avoidance or aggression, they're more likely to find themselves talking to a divorce lawyer than to each other. Why? Because in these three defensive combinations, avoidant-avoidant, avoidant-aggressive, aggressive-aggressive, there's very little room for healing. Both partners are backed into their mutually exclusive corners, shielding themselves from harm and clearly not able to trust or love.

When at least one partner takes a constructive, Catalytic Self-Coaching approach, even if the other one is aggressive or avoidant, a positive resolution is not only possible, it's likely. I come back to you, the designated problem solver, or, as I'll begin referring to you throughout the book, the *catalytic partner*. Since you're doing the reading, then by definition, you are engaging in a constructive approach. Regardless of your partner's attitude, as long as you are employing a constructive approach, Catalytic Self-Coaching becomes an option.

Eyes Wide Open: Seeing Both Sides

In over thirty years of working with couples, I've seen time and again that there are always two sides to a story. I can't think of a time when one partner came into a session admitting, "It's all my fault. I'm a terrible, uncaring lout and I'm the sole reason we're having trouble!" Stop thinking that your job is to show your partner the proverbial light, the truth, or the reality. Instead, start recognizing that there are two lights, two truths, and yes, two realities.

I can hear you now: "What, are you saying I should excuse my husband's rotten, obnoxious behavior?" No, not excuse it, but you will need to understand it; just as your obnoxious husband might need to understand why you're less than receptive to his romantic overtures. From this point on, don't judge your partner's behavior by what you see or feel; try instead to recognize that what motivates and drives destructive behavior is the instinctual attempt to gain control. Another way of saying this is that you need to know that your partner—for whatever reason—is feeling out of control and just doing what comes naturally: defensively trying to survive.

I'm reminded of a TV set we had when I was a child. It had a two-inch screen (this was an early 1950s vintage set) with a four-inch magnifying glass. Although the magnifying glass gave you a more expansive view, it also distorted the images. This is what happens with defensiveness. You may think you're seeing the bigger, clearer picture, when in fact what you're seeing isn't accurate, it's a distorted view. Only by removing defensiveness, which like my TV has a magnifying and distorting effect on your problems, can you begin to start seeing the real picture. At first you may be squinting to see what's going on, but in time, without distortion, you'll move up to a sixty-inch, widescreen view of what needs to be done.

Why Is Change So Hard?

Newton's first law of motion states that objects at rest tend to stay at rest and objects in motion tend to stay in motion. In other words, objects—and people—tend to keep on doing what they're doing. The tendency to resist change, or inertia, is completely natural. Since you're in a struggling relationship, no one has to tell you the meaning of the word *stuck*. Being stuck is having relationship inertia.

Let's cut to the chase. This is a book about change, about overcoming your relationship inertia with or without your partner's help. There are many reasons why people change. I'm sure you've known people who have lost weight, stopped smoking, started exercising, and become better partners; people who have actually changed. I'm equally sure you know people who have plodded along in endless ruts of "I just can't lose weight," "I don't follow through on my exercise," or "My wife and I haven't had sex in five years." For over thirty years it's been my job to figure out why some relationships thrive and become lifelong successes, while others are filled with personal unhappiness, inadequate communication, faulty perceptions, and broken hearts. Why do some people manage to change while others don't? What's the secret? The secret is that there is no secret. But as with any riddle, if you can't see the solution, can't understand it or employ it, it might as well be a secret.

If you're about to become the catalyst for change in your relationship, you're going to have to answer this riddle. I'm going to show you how to do that by teaching you why people change, what specifically in your relationship has to be changed, and how you can use coaching to achieve change. Understand these three components of change—the why, what, and how—and you'll be in a position to do some serious coaching. The *what* and the *how* of changing your relationship will be dealt with extensively in upcoming chapters. For now, I'll begin your Catalytic Self-Coaching education by introducing you to *why* people change.

Why People Change

People and computers share many similarities. One of them is related to what in the computer world are called cookies. A cookie is a small file that a Web site embeds in your computer to store information about you (such as Web pages you've visited, items you've put into an online shopping cart, your user name, password, and so on). The Web site retrieves this information to identify you (or your preferences) in the future. Essentially, your computer gets to know your Web browsing habits and learns to anticipate your Internet behavior. This is efficient.

Like computers with embedded cookies, humans are programmed with biological cookies called habits. The ability to form habits is a valuable part of our human programming that allows us to become more efficient organisms. When we do something long enough, we begin to shift from intentional behavior to a more automatic, reflexive kind of behavior. If you want to see a demonstration of this phenomenon, reach down and tie your shoe. Your hands tie the knot with practiced precision and speed; this is habit.

Habits serve us in many ways. For one, they make us more efficient. Imagine if every time you bent over to tie your shoe you had to think about which hand crosses over the other. Whether you're driving a car, touch-typing at a computer, or even walking up or down steps, your habits allow you to move and flow more easily through your life. Habits can be helpful, but they can also cause problems. Overeating, gambling, insecurity, worry, obnoxiousness, stubbornness, and defensiveness are also habits, habits that can alter the course of your life and your relationships.

The problem with changing any habit is that the change usually causes some degree of discomfort. When we depart from the familiar we enter a world of uncertainty, frustration, or even fear. If you want to feel some frustration, try switching your hands the next time you tie your shoe, comb your hair, or brush your teeth. Earlier in this chapter, I mentioned that human beings like feeling in control. Since change entails a departure from behavior that has become comfortable and familiar—but not necessarily constructive—it's not uncommon to feel an initial loss of control with these efforts, at least until the new behavior is acquired. In order for someone to want to leave their comfort zone and accept any loss of control, there needs to be enough of an incentive.

Think of it as a tipping point. When the incentive-energy becomes greater than the inertia-energy, change occurs. In a relationship, for example, if your partner feels that being more open and expressive is going to be well received (incentive-energy), there's a likelihood that change will be considered. If, on the other hand, your partner feels that opening up and being more expressive might be used against him or her (inertia-energy), the likelihood of change is minimal. The formula looks like this:

Incentive-energy > inertia-energy = change
Inertia-energy > incentive-energy = no change

It all boils down to your partner asking, "Why risk change if the payoff isn't worth it?" The operative word here is *risk*. In most situations, change entails a willingness to embrace risk. In order for you to convince your partner to risk change, you're going to have to demonstrate that:

- There is a high probability that change will improve the situation.
- Change is realistic and obtainable.
- The risk involved in change is acceptable.

Since humans are survival machines, your partner is not going to lower his or her defenses without first feeling sure of surviving the proposed change. It's common sense. We change when we feel we have a legitimate chance of success, or a better life, or the prospect of becoming happier. We don't change when we feel this is unlikely or too risky.

The Go, No-Go Threshold

Everyone has a threshold for change, which depends on the severity of one's insecurity. It's a kind of go, no-go point, at which a shift from inertia to action can occur. I'm reminded of a water-propelled plastic rocket I had when I was a kid. You filled the rocket with water and then attached a hand pump to the nozzle at the base of the rocket. Then, depending on your tolerance, impatience, or desire to break a world record, you began pumping—ten times, twenty times, thirty. At some arbitrary point you made a decision to blast off. That's when you stopped pumping and released the lever that held the rocket to the pump. *Whoosh!* The rocket would climb to the incredible height of five hundred feet! It's the same with relationship change. You pump in incentives for change; you pump, pump, pump until at some point you're able to convince your partner to release the inertia and *whoosh!*

Everyone has a personal go, no-go threshold. For some the degree of confidence necessary to get to a go threshold may be minimal (if you are in a relationship with a relatively secure partner that has had only minor struggle). For others the go threshold may be excessively high (in a relationship where there is significant insecurity, depression, or anxiety along with a major struggle). Regardless of your partner's go threshold, the good news is that if you pump enough confidence, incentive, and optimism into a struggling relationship, all the while building trust, the vast majority of people will get to a point where the risk of releasing their grip on inertia becomes not only possible, but likely. *Whoosh!*

Self-Coaching for Couples

Although I had developed and used my Self-Coaching techniques with my individual patients for years, I didn't realize that these same techniques had found their way into my sessions with couples. It happened inadvertently because I had been thinking of *Self*-Coaching primarily as a tool for individuals, not couples. I had been overlooking the obvious fact that couples are, by definition, two individuals—two individuals combining to form an "Us." As the kids say, "Duh."

I began to realize that as helpful as individual Self-Coaching was, something more was needed to bridge the gap between the "Self component" (each partner's limitations) and the "Us component" (the relationship dynamic) inherent in every relationship. I needed a one-two punch. I already had my first punch in the form of Self-Coaching, which could get me beyond the personality limitations of each partner. What I needed to develop was a second punch that could apply the insights gained from Self-Coaching interactively.

The Catalytic Solution

In high school chemistry I learned that an agent that facilitates or stimulates a chemical interaction is called a catalyst. In an out-of-balance relationship, I observed the same thing. One partner, by conscientiously working on his or her own Self-Coaching evolution, was enough to become a catalyst, stimulating change within the relationship. This observation was the genesis of my Catalytic Self-Coaching program: recognizing that Self-Coaching—which encourages each partner to take personal responsibility for any personal limitations imposed by habits of insecurity—is part of a continuum that starts with individuals and ends with couples. Essentially the difference can be stated as follows: Self-Coaching will enable you to heal, motivate, inspire, educate, and change yourself, while Catalytic Self-Coaching will enable you and your partner to heal, motivate, inspire, educate, and change your relationship.

From the start, it's important to understand that successful Catalytic Self-Coaching depends on a solid and reliable base of *Self*-Coaching. By establishing a solid Self-Coaching foundation, you and your partner will be in a position to launch your catalytic coaching efforts to address all struggle, all friction, and all confusion—often with startling and enduring results. Keep in mind that any approach that focuses solely on the interaction—the *Us*-component—without a strong foundation of individual Self-Coaching is doomed to wind up reverting back to each partner's weakest link (that is, limitations imposed by personal habits of insecurity). Changing the interactive dynamic alone does not change the individual habits of insecurity and control that feed the problems.

These habits will eventually overtake your efforts, leaving you once again repeating old struggles.

If you're convinced that approaching your difficulties from the ground up makes sense, then you're ready to throw the first Self-Coaching punch. However, you still have one significant problem—your reluctant partner may not be ready. With a reluctant partner, the challenge is not unlike my efforts to apply Self-Coaching with a depressed patient. Typically with depression there is a shutting down and withdrawal of energy. The key in working with depression (or for you, working with a partner who has withdrawn energy and enthusiasm) is to initiate a counterforce to the inertia. Initially, in my office practice, this counterforce comes from me. I need to become the legitimate voice of encouragement, capable of generating that energy and enthusiasm. Someone has to *know*—and convey—that psychological friction is unacceptable and that, whatever it takes, success must be demanded. No ifs, ands, or buts! This is what a coach does, and this is what you can do for your reluctant partner.

Because you're dealing with a reluctant partner, by default, you're going to be the one who puts things in motion. Your process begins with your own Self-Coaching as you learn to remove any personal blinders imposed by issues of insecurity and control. Your liberated, nondefensive, expanded perspective will allow you to neutralize resistance in the relationship by unilaterally lessening the friction. It's this shift in the relationship equilibrium that will put you in a position to initiate some Catalytic Self-Coaching.

Okay, time out. I can already hear you asking, "Why do I always have to take the first step?" If you recall from our earlier discussion, you're taking the first step not just because you're the designated catalytic partner, but because you've decided that you have more to gain by making this relationship work than by allowing it to atrophy or, worse, to dissolve. So, take a breath, resist the temptation to feel victimized by your challenge, and instead begin to feel the ripples of empowerment as you recognize that what you're really doing is deciding not to be a victim. You're putting your future in your own hands. How can this not be positive?

From the start it's important for you to be realistic about changing a stagnant or floundering relationship. At first you may feel disappointed if your partner doesn't jump on the bandwagon. Just because you're seeing things more clearly, don't expect the same from your partner. On the other hand, don't be disheartened with resistance either. Try to remind yourself that everyone wants to be happy and no one wants to struggle. Reluctance doesn't happen because someone prefers being stubborn, it happens because the love in your relationship has been inhibited by fear, hopelessness, or frustration. In chemistry, the opposite of a catalyst is an inhibitor.

What Exactly Constitutes a Reluctant Partner?

Before going on, I should point out that the term *reluctant partner* doesn't just include a partner struggling with relationship issues. Sometimes, because of depression or anxiety, a partner is limited in his or her ability to relate meaningfully. Since Self-Coaching originated as a tool to heal anxiety and depression, you will find that whatever the reluctance, the Self-Coaching component of your program is capable of addressing these issues. I therefore use the term *reluctant partner* to encompass any and all hesitations. Whether these are relationship-specific issues (avoidance or aggressive behavior) or personal limitations of your partner (depression, anxiety, and so forth), Catalytic Self-Coaching can help.

Sometimes good intentions, couples counseling, and self-help efforts can all wind up falling short of saving a relationship. Why are some relationships so resistant to healing? One doesn't have to look far for the reason. In any relationship, the potential for any legitimate healing is only as good as its weakest link. If you or your partner suffer from psychological problems such as anxiety, depression, panic, or other control-related limitations such as obsessive concerns, ruminative fears, or habituated insecurity, there's no getting around the fact that if your relationship is going to succeed, you or your partner *must* be healed before your relationship can be healed.

You hold in your hands a proven program that is able not only to address relationship frictions, but to dismantle the deeper, underlying reasons why relationships fail—individual psychological limitations. It is this capacity for personal as well as relationship healing that sets Catalytic

Self-Coaching apart from any other approach. And it is why, from the very beginning, you need to know why it's okay to risk being optimistic.

My claims may sound rather grandiose, but that's because you're probably used to seeing relationship problems and personal limitations as unrelated. They're not. If you recall, I mentioned that control was the bottom line. Once you recognize that struggle—all struggle, personal or relational—has to do with habits of control, you'll begin to understand why this isn't a frivolous claim. As you'll see in upcoming chapters, the solution isn't dependent on years of retrospective analysis or elusive insights; it's this simple notion that your problems—personal or relational—are nothing more than habits. Bad habits of control. And when it comes to habits, you're either feeding them or starving them.

When the Direct Approach Fails

Just as a good coach will get an athlete to overcome fear and hesitation with a good pep talk, you will learn how to inspire your partner to challenge hesitations. Unfortunately, as you're probably well aware, the direct approach doesn't always work. When your partner tunes you out and ignores your pleas for a constructive dialogue, your typical strategies may leave you scratching your head, frustrated and depressed. This is where you'll find that a bit of relationship jujitsu is just the ticket for disarming your partner's resistance. Sometimes, as you'll see in a moment with Karen and Sal, less is definitely more.

Let us assume that you've tried a frontal assault on your relationship problem, only to be met by a stone wall of resistance. You'll find that your Self-Coaching efforts will begin to reduce this resistance by removing any fears that your partner may have that you will do harm—by not loving, by rejecting, by abusing, and so forth. Self-Coaching will teach you to no longer be part of the destructive, reflexive dance that has defined your relationship until now. Once this happens, your partner will begin to experience a shift, a lessening of the friction that has been so chronic. Although this absence of friction may cause a momentary pause in hostilities, it won't necessarily produce any positive changes. But it will provide the fertile soil in which the seeds of change can take root.

As things begin to quiet down, the transition from Self-Coaching to Catalytic Self-Coaching begins. The insights you've gained from your Self-Coaching efforts will make it easier for you to transcend your own former blind spots, while putting you in a position to recognize and understand the *real* problems. It's this awareness that will allow you to initiate the process of getting your partner to join you in your coaching efforts.

Karen and Sal's relationship is a good example of what happens to a struggle when only one partner participates. Remove yourself from your struggle and your partner will respond. As you'll see from this condensed version of their therapy, Karen's Self-Coaching paid off.

Karen and Sal

Karen couldn't convince her husband to join her, so she came to our first session alone. She told me, "Sal's never home to attend to our family. He's in a world of his own. It's as if he doesn't hear me. I feel like I'm invisible. I'm always asking him to help out around the house, to fix the light switch in the kitchen, help with the kids' baths, normal stuff. He's so self-absorbed—he keeps saying it's my problem. That's why he wouldn't come to therapy. I don't know if he's just plain lazy or if he just doesn't care. If only he would help out. I can't help but nag at him."

You might think that Karen's dilemma is rather simple—she's married to a selfish, lazy, uncaring husband. Although this was clearly a part of her problem, it wasn't the whole problem. With some Self-Coaching, Karen was able to recognize that she was, in fact, someone who needed to be in control. At first she was very defensive about admitting that she was an all-the-ducks-in-a-row kind of person. "I don't think there's anything wrong with wanting to get things done around the house or to have a little help. Do you?" "No," I answered, "I don't think there's anything wrong with wanting to be in control, but there is a but. If control is driven by insecurity then it's more of a *have to* be in control than a *want to*." Karen readily conceded that she was rather compulsive about getting things done. If she noticed something that needed attention in the house, it would torment her until it was fixed. For her, it was like a hangnail. This compulsion is why she "nagged" Sal.

Working on her insecurity, Karen was able to recognize that she was liv-ing a black-and-white existence with little room for gray. Everything was in its place or everything was chaos; for Karen there was no in between. As she began to understand that her compulsive need for control was merely a habit of insecurity (more about this in later chapters), which she inadvertently reinforced by demanding control, she was able to see that there was a bigger picture. Sal didn't share her compulsive need for order, nor could he be expected to respond well to her nagging.

Karen began to work on starving her habits of insecurity. Her main task was to begin to be less rigid and inflexible, and to see this issue not as a marital issue but a Karen issue. Her Self-Coaching had a dramatic effect on Sal. At first he was suspicious as he asked, "Why are you being so casual about things? What are you and that doctor up to?" As Sal began to realize that Karen's shift wasn't a flash in the pan, he began to let down his guard. One night he said to her, "You mentioned that Dr. Luciani had offered to see us together. I was thinking that maybe I'd join you this week for your session." Bingo!

As you might expect, Sal saw things very differently from Karen. At our session he informed me, "I travel two or three days a week, and when I come home I'm exhausted. I ignore her because I'm too tired to fight. The last few weeks have been strange. Karen seems calmer. She's not on my case like she was." I asked Sal what effect this had on him. He answered, "Well, at first I thought it was a trap, you know, like she was setting me up for something. But things just kept getting better. I have to admit, it got my attention. I found myself turning off the TV the other night and fixing that light switch she had asked me to fix. I actually wanted to do something for her." As we got into Sal's feelings a bit more deeply, he confessed, "Karen's nagging has always made me feel defensive. If I did what she wanted all the time then she would win and I'd lose. Maybe it was a competitive thing with me, but I gotta tell you, the more she nagged the more I tuned her out."

As you can see, Karen started the ball rolling with her Self-Coaching efforts, which had the effect of disarming Sal and encouraging him to engage in rather than avoid solving the problem. I'm not going to go into the catalytic process that began once Sal became part of our sessions, but suffice it to say that things became not only manageable, they became effortless. The expanded view provided by understanding each other's habits of insecurity was the catalyst for change, both individually as well as for the relationship.

Demonstrating Change

Catalytic Self-Coaching is the way you give your partner a stimulus for wanting to change. Although there are infinite possibilities, the best place to start—since you are the relationship healer—is for you to demonstrate your own Self-Coaching success and enthusiasm. Trust me, there's no better marketing tool than success. Your first job is going to be to challenge your own personal inertia, and once you begin to pick up some momentum, you'll be in a position to spread the wealth.

Looking Ahead

In the next chapter we're going to explore the nuts and bolts of relationship struggle. From this foundation you will begin to lay out your Self-Coaching training program. As you use Self-Coaching to eliminate your relationship-destructive habits, you'll be ready to challenge that problem-avoider partner of yours and begin the process of Catalytic Self-Coaching.

2

Why Your Relationship Isn't the Problem

I'm an amateur paleontologist, a "bone-hound." My wife isn't. She's just a great sport. Together, we trek off to Wyoming's Big Horn Mountains in search of Jurassic dinosaur bones. With the intense heat, fire ants, and occasional rattlesnake, this isn't what you'd call a five-star vacation, which is why I appreciate her willingness to share my interests.

As we trek through the austere surroundings of sage and sandstone, we know from past digs that buried just below our feet lie the bones of Allosaurus, Camarasaurus, Diplodocus, and other Jurassic critters that were buried 150 million years ago. You could walk for your entire life over these Wyoming bone-beds and not know what lies beneath the surface. But the bones, when released from their overburden (the material that lies above them), are beautiful and pristine. (I wish you could see the four-inch Camarasaurus tooth my wife found. The picture I have of her holding the tooth is, as they say, "priceless.")

Your relationship may look to you like a barren, hostile landscape, but that means nothing. Not if you're willing to remove the overburden.

Catalytic Self-Coaching can get you to the bare bones of the love that lies dormant, waiting for you just under the surface.

O Solo Mio

I'm going to assume that you're willing to do some soul-searching. That leaves us with the question of how we include your reluctant partner in the process. Of course, the best way to achieve success would be for both of you to read this book and follow my Catalytic Self-Coaching program and exercises. I can hear you now: "I can't get my partner to talk to me, much less read a book. Can Catalytic Self-Coaching be of any use if I'm the only one reading it?" There's no doubt that two people, motivated and willing to read through my program, will achieve the maximum benefit. But there's more than one way to break through your partner's inertia.

How do I know this? I guess it had a lot to do with my being an only child, an only child who happened to grow up fiercely independent. When I was a kid, since I had limited social resources (in the early 1950s, play dates hadn't been invented yet), I learned to rely on my ingenuity to tackle and solve any problem. Whether it was figuring out how to make an igloo in the snow or building a two-story orange-crate clubhouse, I learned that where there was a will, there was a way.

As an adult, I've built decks, waterfalls, moved boulders weighing hundreds of pounds, and recently figured out how to suspend a 150-pound dinosaur tibia (my paleontology passion) on my wall. It took me days to devise the necessary cable-and-pulley system, but I managed to figure it out. My wife is often amazed at my insistence at doing these projects "on my own."

Of course, I could call a buddy or one of my kids to help out, but that would take the challenge out of the project. To me, half the challenge (and pleasure) is looking at a seemingly impossible problem and then sitting back and figuring out a solution, always with the conviction "There's got to be a way." Okay, what am I getting at? Simply this: every problem, including a difficult relationship struggle, can be solved with understanding, insight, tenacity, and, most important, a willingness to believe that you can initiate the healing process and succeed solo! Eventually you're going to need your partner to join you if your relationship is to succeed, but for now I will challenge you with the following motto: "I'm going to make this relationship succeed, in spite of my partner!" This may sound unbelievable to you now, but I'm going to show you that with you as a catalyst, *you* are all that's necessary to get the ball rolling.

In all fairness, let me say that going it solo is not easy, and certainly not ideal, but it can work. And that's all that's important. Without your partner's help, there's no doubt that you're going to have to sharpen your coaching skills. One way to begin doing this is by setting out to be a great coach. This begins with you and your positive attitude—the conviction that you can win this battle. Then, using the techniques presented in this book, you're going to fortify yourself with insight, understanding, and the courage to let go of any personal restrictions imposed by insecurity. At this point you'll be in an empowered position to begin coaching your partner to join you in reclaiming the love and spontaneity of your relationship.

Don't Miss the Point

When it comes to relationship chaos and struggle, Pogo got it right: "We have met the enemy and he is us." In any relationship, if you struggle and find yourself pointing a finger at your partner proclaiming, "The enemy is you!"—*you*, not your partner, will have missed the point. In like manner, if you insist on seeing your partner as your adversary and the reason for your unhappiness, you're not only missing the point, you're fanning the fires of turmoil. "But," you may protest, "my husband is a monster! He really is, just ask anyone." I'm not trying to pardon anyone, all I'm saying is that in life and in relationships, nothing takes place in a vacuum. As you'll see in a moment, when it comes to destructive, even monstrous relating, there's more to being a monster than behaving like one.

Catalytic Self-Coaching Reflection
Take a tip from Pogo: in a struggling relationship,
the problem is always Us!

Similarly, if you feel the problem is the relationship itself—bad chemistry, bad karma, or bad luck—you're also missing the point. The point is that a relationship is nothing more than a mirror that accurately reflects the best and worst of each partner. Your relationship is only a *reflection* of your problems, not *the* problem. When you look in a mirror, if you don't like the way your hair looks, you don't throw away the mirror, you comb your hair!

"You're saying that my troubled relationship isn't the problem? That doesn't make sense!" Yes, this sounds counterintuitive, but it's a fact. Your relationship difficulties are merely symptoms. The problem is insecurity. Until you understand the role that insecurity plays in life, you will likely perpetuate your problems.

Insecurity: The Source

In the last chapter you learned that feeling threatened, abandoned, neglected, or unloved will precipitate some attempt to gain control over these chaotic feelings. And when attempts to control are either aggressive or avoidant, they become the fuel of discord. Control is extremely damaging to any relationship, but it is only a weed that grows from its root, insecurity. Understanding the source of all controlling behavior will put you in a much better position to handle the friction you experience in your relationship.

My wife and I were at a local shopping mall recently and noticed a mother and her preschool-aged child walking in front of us. The child, seeing something interesting in one of the shops, turned abruptly, stumbled, fell, and bruised his knee. The mother, quick to pick up her wounded son, was greeted with a rather severe punch to the thigh by the now irate tyke. The child, who felt bruised, angry, and having just suffered a humiliating loss of control, did what came naturally to him—he shared the pain! In his little mind it might have gone something like this: "Oh yeah? Well, if I'm going feel this bad, then you're going to suffer right along with me. I'm not going to be unhappy alone!"

As you can see, on some primitive level, this child, feeling out of control, reflexively did something to feel less vulnerable—he delivered a blow to Mom. After all, he wasn't going to be the only one feeling out of control. Misery does seem to love company. When it comes to relationships, whether it's children with mommies or adults with adults, misery (a.k.a. loss of control) has a way infecting and bruising a relationship—sharing the pain.

If you want to get to the source, the real source of your problems, you won't find it by sharing the pain, blaming your partner, or proclaiming your innocence. You will find it only by understanding how insecurity (which triggers attempts to control life) is holding each of you hostage, often producing a nasty tit-for-tat exchange of antagonism. "Wait a second! Did you say insecurity is holding *me* hostage?" Yes, you! And, yes, your partner too. To a greater or lesser extent, you're both unknowing victims of insecurity—insecurity that gets reflected in the negative dynamic of your relationship.

I know this is a difficult concept, especially if you have a reasonably objective and positive view of yourself. But please, don't throw this book at the nearest wall. I want you to understand that insecurity isn't something that happens to someone else. Everyone has insecurity to some extent. Why is this? Because no one grows up in a perfect world, no one has had the luxury of being brought up by perfect parents, and clearly no one escapes illness, loss, frustration, and difficulty in their developmental years. Insecurity is part of being an imperfect human being living in an imperfect world.

What exactly is insecurity? It can be found in any of these common expressions:

- It's the anticipation of vulnerability or helplessness: "I can't help feeling that things are going to get worse."

- It's the false belief that you can't handle life or some aspect of life: "I just can't go on dealing with his coldness, it's driving me crazy!"

- It is based on distortions of reality, not facts: "Look at the way she treats me, I'm just not a lovable person."

- It becomes a habit of thinking and perceiving: "I've been avoiding intimacy for a long time. But why wouldn't I? It just makes me feel vulnerable."

- It minimizes the possibility of accurate self-perception: "I'm such a loser, look at what's happened to my marriage."

- After a while, it feels like a natural part of your personality: "I've always been shy, you married me this way, it's who I am, take it or leave it."

- It becomes worse over time: "I don't understand it, I used to be able to handle criticism."

I'm going to ask you to take a significant leap of faith at this point. Try to understand that if you're embroiled in an ongoing struggling relationship—regardless of the circumstances—it's likely that your own insecurity is a factor perpetuating the chaos. For now, all you need is to keep an open mind. I can't stress enough how important it is for you and your partner to commit to an honest and courageous process of self-scrutiny.

Anita and Larry: Two Peas Outside of the Pod

Larry and Anita, a couple I worked with recently, were both constructive problem solvers who happened to be stuck on opposite sides of the fence, pointing fingers at each other. Although this example doesn't address the issue of motivating a reluctant partner, since both Larry and Anita wanted to find answers, it does show the importance of taking personal responsibility—the need, on the *self* level, for each partner to confront any personal limitations imposed by insecurity. As you'll see, with a bit of Self-Coaching, Larry and Anita stopped blaming each other and became catalytic for each other.

When I first met Anita and Larry, their marital relationship was not only off balance, it was spinning out of control. An incident in which Larry shoved Anita during a fit of rage was traumatic enough to get them into therapy, but it wasn't the escalation of violence that convinced them they needed help. It was the realization of just how ugly their relationship had become.

Even before sitting down, Larry wasted no time letting me know that his needs weren't being met, that he was the victim in this relationship, and that something "damn well has to be done about it!" He went on to filibuster, letting me know how much he was suffering, how fed up he was, and how miserable he was. I asked him to describe what needs he felt weren't being met. He said, "I'm an afterthought in this relationship. We have no intimacy to speak of, and when we do, it's never satisfying. Anita is more concerned about making her friends happy rather than me. When I come home at night, she's always in a bad mood, always sulking, and always on that damn phone. This is not a relationship!"

According to Larry, he didn't have a problem with anger or violence; the problem was Anita's fault for tormenting him, forcing him to lose his temper. Larry was adamant that he was being victimized by Anita's negative attitude. "It's her fault. She makes me lose my temper!" When I asked him to explain how she *made* him lose his temper, he said, "She shuts me out of her life. I try to get her to talk and she either ignores me or walks away . . . that drives me crazy." Pleadingly, he looked at me and continued, "Doc, she's driving me crazy. I don't think I'm asking too much. Do you?" He was hoping that I would agree with him by condemning his wife: "You're right, Larry, Anita is really making it impossible for you to hold your temper. She's ruining your marriage!" That's what Larry was hoping for. It's not what he got.

Anita, as you might expect, had a very different story to tell. She described Larry as a control freak, someone who hovered over her to the point of suffocation:

> I can't go to the bathroom without Larry standing outside the door asking me questions about the phone bill or where I put his magazines. If I'm on the phone, he stands right in front of me and makes a throat-slashing gesture, signaling me to cut off the conversation. If my mother calls, he'll lie and tell her I'm not home.
>
> When I confront him on his behavior he says that I abuse my time with him, so he needs to set limits. He treats me like a child! I'm not allowed to go out with the girls, I'm on a strict spending budget, he even tells me to change my clothes if he doesn't approve! If we visit his family, he's fine, but if we visit my mother or sister, he makes it miserable for me. He's constantly looking at his watch, sighing, and making a fool of himself. He's embarrassed me too many times and I can't stand it anymore.

Then he has the audacity to tell me I'm not passionate enough! I want to scream! He just doesn't get it; a woman needs to feel loved before she feels intimate—all I feel is abused! Can you believe he thinks he's the victim?

So there you have it, Larry the innocent victim of an uncaring wife; Anita the suffocated, controlled wife of a bully. Who's right? Who's wrong?

The 50-50 Proposition

If you were to analyze who's the bigger problem in Larry and Anita's relationship, you might conclude that Larry, the tyrant/bully/control freak, would appear to be contributing considerably more than 50 percent of what's wrong with this relationship. Anita, on the other hand, isn't blameless, but it doesn't take much scrutiny to see that she isn't causing the problem—she's just reacting to Larry's tyranny. Right? As logical as this might seem, it happens not to be true.

The reality is that each partner always accounts for 50 percent of the chemistry of a relationship. No more, no less. How can this be? Larry surely appears to be more responsible for the problem than Anita. How could Anita be equally to blame for this faltering relationship? It just doesn't seem logical.

In order to understand this seeming paradox, think about what happens in human genetics. Every infant comes into the world with a complete genetic blueprint of forty-six chromosomes, twenty-three from Mom and twenty-three from Dad. During conception, the father contributes half of the genetic material and the mother contributes half—no more, no less. Because of the role of dominant and recessive genes, a child may have Mom's eyes, wavy hair, and freckles (in which case Mom's genes for these traits would be dominant), while Dad, whose genes were masked in the presence of Mom's dominant ones, may seem unrelated to the child. Genetically speaking, however, for better or worse, the uniqueness of every child has to do with the 50-50 combination of both dominant and recessive genes from each parent's twenty-three chromosomes.

In a relationship, rather than chromosomes, each partner's personality habits contribute to the makeup of the relationship. Like genes, some of these personality habits may appear dominant—such as Larry's hostility and control—while others appear recessive (Anita's passivity, victimization, and aloofness). The combination and blending of these traits is what accounts for the Us-nature of a relationship.

Portraits

Just as an artist attempts to capture the essence of his subject's personality by painting a portrait, you can capture the essence of your relational struggle with what I call relationship portraits, or Self-Portraits. Throughout this book I'll be using these portraits to illustrate the dynamic of relationships. They represent the simple formula *Self* + *Self* = *Us.* The combination of both partners' Self-Portraits yields a relationship composite—the Us-Portrait. With this graphic composite you can begin to analyze and understand the true nature of your struggle. You will be given complete instructions for sketching your own relationship portrait in chapter 7.

Larry and Anita's situation can be portrayed as follows:

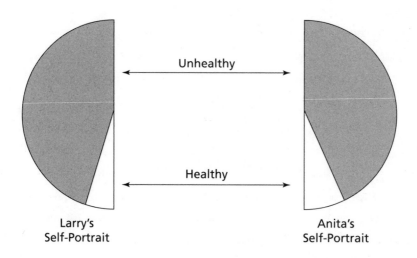

Larry's Self-Portrait illustrates his controlling, bullying tendencies. Clearly his unhealthy personality habits (shaded area) overshadow what is healthy in his personality. But the shaded area of Anita's Self-Portrait has a similar configuration! How can this be? Anita isn't initiating their problems or being abusive, Larry is. What Anita is doing is *allowing*, through her habits of passivity and insecurity, Larry to dominate the relationship. Her insecurity-driven habit of passivity offers no resistance to his behavior. The shaded area in Anita's Self-Portrait reflects what is unhealthy in her—her passive-aggressive avoidance and aloofness. And this has become her contribution to their ongoing problem. Whether passive or aggressive, healthy or unhealthy, right or wrong, the personality and behavior of one partner combines with the personality and behavior of the other to produce the Us-relationship. The diagram below shows Larry and Anita's complete Self + Self = Us Portrait.

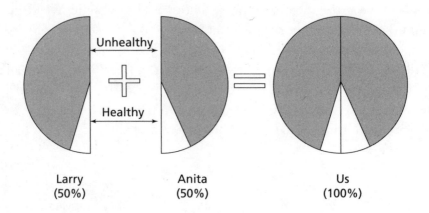

Larry   Anita   Us
(50%)   (50%)   (100%)

What You See Isn't Always What You've Got

Larry's obnoxious, overbearing personality may seem like the reason this couple has problems, but his behavior in the relationship does not occur in a vacuum. It blends and mixes with Anita's behavior and traits. It's the combination of Larry's domineering ways (his 50 percent contribution) with Anita's recessive surrender (her 50 percent contribution) that produces the Us-Portrait, or in Larry and Anita's case, a failing marriage.

What about in your relationship? Have you been guilty of feeling victimized? Do you find yourself pointing a finger of blame at your partner? "He's impossible to live with!" Or, "No way is she going to tell me what to do!" If you're feeling innocent, please take a deep breath, it's time to recalculate. This might not be easy to understand, but burying your head in the sand will not solve your relationship problems. Understanding the 50–50 nature of the Us-Portrait will.

Self-Coaching Challenge

Accept the fact that you are contributing
half of the problem and now it's time for you
to contribute half of the solution.

In a relationship there are no victims. Any relationship where the unhealthy dominates the healthy is a relationship in danger. As depicted in the first figure on page 29, Larry's behavior, although more obviously disturbing than Anita's, was only slightly more influential than Anita's in contributing to the overall relationship struggle. This is important because in any relationship, if you understand the 50–50 nature of the Us-dynamic, you can never be victimized. Larry can assert only a 50 percent influence, no more, no less. Anita feels victimized because she has *allowed* herself to yield to Larry's domination, thus allowing an imbalance to be created in their relationship. Keep in mind that Larry can dominate only if he is allowed to dominate.

Let me fast-forward Larry and Anita's therapy and explain what was needed to rescue their relationship. Larry needed to become aware of his shortsighted expectations and demands, while understanding his inclination to try to dominate and control the relationship. Anita, on the other hand, needed to become empowered. She needed to recapture and redefine her half of the influence and learn to stand up to any inequity. She managed to do this by building a more confident sense of self. This is what Catalytic Self-Coaching taught Larry and Anita, and this is what it will teach you.

You'd be surprised how receptive Larry was to Catalytic Self-Coaching. Once he was able to see himself more clearly and understand that his hostile "reactivity" had everything to do with his reflexive insecurity, he was able to approach Anita in a more reasonable, healthy, and loving manner. He needed to stop seeing Anita as the enemy. In turn, Anita needed to learn to risk dealing with Larry directly, honestly, and confidently. This required overcoming her reflexive feelings of self-doubt and low self-esteem. With small, incremental steps, she was able to build a foundation of trust both in herself and in the relationship. Once empowered, she was able to go nose-to-nose with Larry, who wasn't at all put off by her assertiveness. In fact Larry, who often misinterpreted Anita's ambiguity and passivity as a lack of love, was delighted to know where things stood rather than having to guess.

The figure below illustrates the shift in Larry and Anita's relationship as a result of Catalytic Self-Coaching. Although there still is work to be done (note the remaining dark areas), the difference from the previous figure, the shift from unhealthy to healthy—dark areas to light areas—is unmistakably evident.

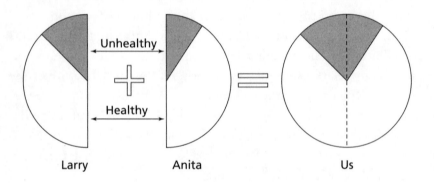

Larry   Anita   Us

Change: Are You Ready to Take the Challenge?

When I first suggested to Larry and Anita that they were in need of a Self-Coaching personality makeover, I was met with understandable skepticism. Anita expressed considerable doubt. "What? You can't change someone's personality!" Larry added, "Changing your personality? Doesn't that take years?" I've found that Larry and Anita's reactions aren't unusual; in fact, I suspect it's the way most people feel about changing who they think they are. It may seem natural to be a worrywart, or a perfectionist, or a pessimist. But just because something feels natural doesn't mean it *is* natural. Or healthy! In one of our early sessions I recall Karen (from chapter 1) telling me, "I know I'm a nag, but it's just who I am. I've always been too critical." I was quick to point out, "No, being a nag isn't who you are, it's what insecurity has turned you into."

If your personality has been shaped or twisted by the influences of insecurity, you've ended up with a distortion of your real self—a distorted *you*. Regardless of what you may believe, the truth is you *can* change your personality, especially if who you are now isn't who you were meant to be. But more than changing your personality, we're talking about *releasing* it from the shackles of distortion imposed by insecurity.

Some of your habits may be long-standing, perhaps even lifelong, but this doesn't change your challenge, the Self-Coaching challenge:

Self-Coaching Challenge
The "you" that lies beneath your habits of
insecurity needs to be released.

Catalytic Self-Coaching is designed to enable first you and then your partner to break the habits of control and insecurity, allowing a genuine capacity for relatedness and love to emerge. And no, it doesn't have to take a long time.

Without insecurity, love really does conquer all. Destructive relating is merely a habit—an awful habit fed by each partner's insecurity. For now, all you need to know is that habits, all habits, are learned—and all habits can be broken. Once you remove the impediment of insecurity, your instinctual and intuitive desire to love and be loved will find expression. After all, the human need for love, companionship, and intimacy is a driving and powerful instinctual force. And yet, as powerful as this instinct is, insecurity can mask it, distort it, or otherwise corrupt it.

With few exceptions, the instinctual desire for relatedness and love doesn't leave a relationship; it only gets buried by insecurity. Catalytic Self-Coaching can work even with a stuck-in-the-mud, reluctant partner, because within every human being there is a primal longing for intimacy. When this instinctual longing is eclipsed by fear or an impending sense of danger, it gets muted—buried. By removing the doubts and fears imposed by insecurity, both you and your partner can again risk the love that resides, intact, within each of you.

Looking Ahead

In the next few chapters we're going to begin shifting our attention away from relationship issues and begin focusing on *you*. You'll learn that your own personal evolution—becoming healthier, less driven by insecurity, control, and defensiveness—will serve as both an example and as the catalyst for engaging your partner. Since every relationship struggle involves two participants, if you remove yourself from the fray, not only will you be altering the destructive relationship dynamic, you will be removing your partner's motivation to resist you. Without reason to resist you, your partner will be in a more receptive mode. This is the catalytic mode.

3

Insecurity and Control
Relationship Baggage

If you're looking for a grand unifying theory of why relationships fail, look no further than insecurity. Bottom line, insecurity creates friction in a relationship. Just as a motor will grind to a halt if there's too much friction on the moving parts, so too will a relationship grind to a halt if the friction of insecurity is allowed to erode your capacity for trouble-free—frictionless—relating. In previous chapters you were introduced to the concepts of insecurity and control; now it's time to tell the whole story.

In life and in relationships, there are essentially two kinds of problems, circumstantial problems and insecurity-driven problems. Circumstantial problems such as physical illness—diabetes, thyroid disorders, cancer, heart disease, as well as any chronic, painful condition—will clearly challenge any relationship, as will other, nonphysical circumstantial challenges such as loss of employment, financial stress, or problems with children or relatives. No one would argue that any of these circumstances will burden and stress a relationship. But it may surprise you to know that it's not circumstances that bring a relationship to its knees—it's how you or your partner's insecurity *interprets* these circumstances.

Catalytic Self-Coaching Heads-Up

Circumstantial problems are usually unavoidable, but insecurity-driven problems are entirely avoidable.

The heads-up featured above is worth elaborating. There's no question that a chronic illness, for example, will influence and challenge the emotional stability of a relationship, but it's not the illness itself—or the loss of employment, or your daughter's rebelliousness, or an unexpected tax audit—that leads to relationship chaos, it's the way each partner reacts to, interprets, and handles the situation. Clearly not everyone responds to adversity in like manner. For some, adversity can be a bad hair day, leading to nasty, cranky behavior. For others, living with even a serious disease like cancer doesn't affect their resolve to embrace life with enthusiasm and verve. Why are some couples, regardless of their circumstances, able to flow through their lives maintaining perspective and offering mutual support and love, while for others, these same circumstances cause deterioration and chaos? The answer has to do with the extent to which insecurity limits and contaminates one or both partners' perceptions.

Emotional Baggage

Difficult life circumstances aren't the only place insecurity will attach itself to; the emotional baggage that each partner brings into the relationship is just as likely to become fertile ground for discord. Insecurity's baggage consists of long-standing habits of defense, protection, and control that wind up distorting the natural personality, turning people into worrywarts, perfectionists, control freaks, avoiders, manipulators, and so on. It's not uncommon for these destructive traits to have been relatively unnoticed during the early years of a relationship. But in time, as the relationship becomes more established, these underlying, default habits of insecurity become more and more pronounced. "If I had known you were such a control freak, I would never have married you!" Or, "What happened to your interest in sex? When we were dating it was never a problem. Was that all an act?"

Catalytic Self-Coaching Heads-Up

To a greater or lesser extent, everyone enters a relationship with "baggage."

My definition of baggage is any past woundedness, trauma, or circumstance that contaminates your present life. It's the emotional baggage (that is, habits of insecurity) that causes us to respond with some form of controlling strategy such as hypersensitivity, emotional aloofness, problems with intimacy, or a pervasive need to actively or passively control others. Controlling strategies are designed to protect us from the vulnerability that insecurity tells us is lurking around every corner. And this is the rub. If you want to get rid of emotional baggage, revive your relationship, breathe life back into your romance, and experience the depth of closeness and attachment, then there's only one choice—you and your partner are going to need to learn to break the destructive habits of insecurity and control.

Relationship Emotional Baggage

Just as personal baggage can follow you through life contaminating your personality, *relationship emotional baggage* can be destructive to your relationship. A common problem occurs when one or both partners use past negative history to support their position in a here-and-now argument. "How can you ask me to forgive you? Do you remember how you used to hurt me when we were first married?" Relationship emotional baggage is often dredged up and used as a weapon to control, sabotage, or otherwise coerce your partner. If you or your partner uses relationship emotional baggage as a weapon, then you're almost certainly going to bog down any constructive attempt for a healing dialogue. Once relationship baggage enters the picture you can count on a defensive brawl. Your best chance for advancing your relationship is keeping it limited to the present. When I insist that couples eliminate historical references, it's amazing how quickly problems get resolved. So if you want to be more efficient in solving problems, instead of perpetuating them, keep in mind: when dealing with here-and-now issues—keep it here and now!

Rube Goldberg Psychology

Rube Goldberg (1883–1970) was a Pulitzer Prize–winning cartoonist, sculptor, and author. Through his various cartoon inventions, he illustrated difficult ways to achieve easy results. His cartoons were, as he said, symbols of man's capacity for exerting maximum effort to accomplish minimal results. Rube believed that there were two ways to do things—the simple way and the hard way—and that a surprisingly large number of people preferred doing things the hard way. For over a hundred years psychology has done a great job at showing a preference for doing things the hard way.

For the average person, psychology is a Rube Goldberg confusion of arcane concepts such as the Oedipus complex, anima/animus, the collective unconscious, prototaxic-parataxic development, and so on. As stimulating and engaging as these concepts may be philosophically, they are almost useless when applied directly to changing your life or your faltering relationship. Fortunately, there is a simpler way.

Ever hear of Occam's razor? It's the principle attributed to the fourteenth-century logician and Franciscan friar William of Occam, which states that when given two equally valid explanations for a phenomenon, one should embrace the less complicated formulation. For some inexplicable reason, human beings seem to feel that the more complicated something is, the more significant, meaningful, or important it is (one reason for Rube Goldberg's success). When, for example, I explain to patients that I treat anxiety and depression as habits, I'm often met with some degree of suspicion—if not resentment. "Clearly you must be mistaken, my depression is much more complicated than that!" Sigmund Freud, the father of psychoanalysis, once alluded to this phenomenon. One day, when asked about the significance of his cigar smoking, Freud replied, "Sometimes a cigar is just a cigar." Even for Freud—whose psychoanalytic theory is anything but simple—not everything needs to be complicated.

Take a Lesson from Aunt Tessie

Catalytic Self-Coaching is not complicated; it reduces all conflict to two elemental concepts: control and insecurity. When it comes to changing your life and your relationship, you don't have to complicate things by digging up the historic *when* or even *why* you began to struggle; you only need to know what you're going to do about it. So let's keep it simple.

My aunt Tessie knew the value of simplicity. Back in the 1950s when color television was the rage, Aunt Tessie decided she would have color on her TV too. Not having the means to purchase a new set, she found a solution. She sent away for a $4.99 plastic laminate that you put over the existing TV screen. The plastic was tinted as follows: blue tint on the upper third of the film, neutral tint on the middle third, and green tint on the lower third. Although we all laughed at the absurdity of this color TV substitute, Aunt Tessie was quite content. According to her, "Sometimes I can see beautiful blue skies and green fields, other times I just ignore the colors." For Aunt Tessie, having a color TV was simple—you just had to be patient for the right scenes to align themselves with the plastic tints. Sometimes all you need are a couple of colors and a little imagination.

When it comes to understanding relationship struggle, you don't have to turn it into a Rube Goldberg challenge. Instead of complicating the problem, let's minimize it. Two words: insecurity and control—your habits of insecurity and control and your partner's habits of insecurity and control. Take a lesson from Aunt Tessie; understanding how insecurity and control distort your life and your relating is all that's necessary to implement change. Why complicate things?

As you progress with your personal Self-Coaching challenge in the next few chapters, you will begin to neutralize your own habits of insecurity, thus eliminating your half of the contribution to your relational struggle. Keep in mind that your partner's defensive persona has depended on your defensive participation—which you are about to remove.

The Struggle Equation

Your partner's defensive persona + your defensive persona
= relationship struggle

Take a look at Rose and Steve, a couple caught up in a defensive, hair-trigger spiral of interacting. While at work, they had the following online, instant-message conversation (my editorial comments have been added in italics):

Rose: This weather's amazing, how about we take a ride to the Berkshires this weekend?

Steve: I'm too tired. I'd rather sit home and chill.

Rose: You're always too tired. [*Feeling resentful, Rose expresses her frustration.*]

Steve: I'm not always tired; you just don't know how to sit still. [*Steve, feeling attacked, fires back—tit for tat.*]

Rose: We never do anything. [*Rose decides to up the ante.*]

Steve: At least I know how to relax. For just one weekend I'd love to be left alone. [*Needing to take control of this conversation, Steve lays out a dangerous, childish challenge.*]

Rose: You'd like that. Fine, from now on I'll leave you alone. I'm going to make plans to visit my sister this weekend. [*Taking the challenge, Rose is now going to teach Steve a lesson.*]

Steve: Oh, now I'm going to be punished. Typical! Baby can't get her way so she pouts. [*Feeling a further loss of control, Steve begins moving toward a more aggressive posture.*]

Rose: No, I'm not pouting and I'm not punishing you, I'm just taking care of myself. Believe me, I'll never ask you to go anywhere again! [*Rose knows about Steve's controlling nature, she's launching a bomb here because she knows this will leave Steve feeling out of control and unsettled.*]

Steve: Fine. Whatever you say. [*Recognizing that he's in trouble, Steve attempts to take control by becoming more obnoxious. This feeble attempt not to care is actually an attempt to gain control by insulating—i.e., if I don't care, you can't hurt me.*]

Rose: You make me sick . . . I have to get back to work. [*Rose, knowing how much Steve hates discord, is leaving this conversation unresolved. She knows Steve hates "loose ends" and will suffer.*]

Steve: Wait a minute! You're not being fair. Why is it that I can never express my opinion in this relationship? [*Feeling vulnerable, insecure, and mildly panicked, Steve, knowing things are spinning out of control, doesn't want to leave this conversation unfinished. He tries to plead his case.*]

Rose: [*Expletive deleted as she signs off her computer. Rose doesn't mind leaving things unfinished; she knows this will gnaw at Steve.*]

As you can see from this exchange, we have a rather primitive, destructive, insecurity-control cycle that's spinning and going nowhere. Well, not nowhere, it's adding one more reason for Rose and Steve to feel out of balance and frustrated with each other.

Let's imagine that that Rose had picked up a copy of this book and did some Self-Coaching homework. Look at how this exchange would be different:

Rose: This weather's amazing, how about we take a ride to the Berkshires this weekend?

Steve: I'm too tired. I'd rather sit home and chill.

Rose: It seems that every time I want to do something you're too tired. Be honest with me, is it because you're tired or is it something else? [*Notice the difference in Rose's response? She's not at all defensive . . . just being curious. Allowing Steve to feel that she can respect his "truth."*]

Steve: No, I told you I'm too tired. Aren't you listening to me? [*Steve is still being ruled by insecurity and defensiveness.*]

Rose: I'm listening. I'm just curious. Would you mind if I asked you one question? [*By asking permission, Rose allows Steve to feel less attacked and more in control.*]

Steve: Whatever. [*Reluctantly, Steve begins to bend.*]

Rose: Maybe I'm wrong, but it seems to me whenever I suggest something, you're too tired. If you were me and wanted to go out, what would you do? How would you approach me? [*Starting out by not being judgmental, Rose gives Steve an opportunity to describe how the world ought to be.*]

Steve: Well, for one thing, I wouldn't spring things on you; I'd give you a heads-up. [*Not bad! Steve is actually giving Rose some useful, constructive, and reasonable data.*]

Rose: Okay, that's helpful. Sometimes things are just spur-of-the-moment with me, but I can try to give you some advance notice. Do you really think it might help? [*Nondefensive Rose is able to admit the relevance of Steve's request, but she also wants him to know that she's a different person with different preferences and sometimes this will show. By asking if he thinks this might help, she's allowing Steve to support his suggestion.*]

Steve: Yeah, it might help. [*One small step for Rose, one large step for the relationship.*]

Rose: Great, let's see if it makes a difference. [*Here's a subtle challenge, i.e., "Okay, you're suggesting that I give you advance notice, I'm willing to do it, let's see if your suggestion helps." Since this was, in fact, Steve's suggestion, he's much more likely to make it happen.*]

Way to go, Rose! Maybe this doesn't seem like a major breakthrough, but from this scenario you can see that Rose has taken a defensive Steve and actually has him engaged in some legitimate problem-solving. His admission, "Yeah, it might help," shows us a Steve who has put his guard down and has become more accessible. And it's this accessibility that we're after in your relationship.

Beware the Child-Reflex

How many times have you and your partner wound up like Rose and Steve, squabbling like two children. "I'll show you!" Or, "If you do that, you'll be sorry!" This all too familiar childlike clashing isn't unusual;

in fact, when it comes to relationship conflict, it's almost universal. In upcoming chapters I'm going to be discussing your Child-Reflex, but for now it's important to recognize that when challenged in a relationship, things get primitive—childlike primitive. You wind up with whining, sniping, tantruming, and pouting. If you're shaking your head and saying, "Not *my* relationship," try tape-recording one of your arguments. The proof, as they say, is in the pudding.

But let's take a closer look at Rose and Steve's hypothetical, Self-Coaching exchange. How exactly did this happen? It happened because Rose took away Steve's need to protect himself by resorting to a Child-Reflex of control. It took a bit of warming up on Steve's part, but he eventually put his guard down and admitted that "Yeah, it might help." You've probably experienced this point many times in an argument; it's the point where everything goes from being congested, negative, and contentious, to being released. Any stressor, emotional or physical, when released leaves us with what I call the "Ahh" experience." One wife told me that she often felt like she was being whipped. She went on to say that one good thing about being whipped was, "It feels so good when it stops!" In a relationship struggle, when the whipping of tension, angst, frustration, and pain suddenly stops and things slide back to normal, that's when you experience the "Ahh" of frictionless relating.

Relationship Reflection
Eliminating the Child-Reflexes in your relationship will produce a well-deserved "Ahh" experience.

Take an inventory. You don't have claws like a tiger, an exoskeleton of armor like a lobster, or wings like a sparrow to carry you away from a wide-eyed cat; truth is, you're rather ill-equipped when it comes to handling dangerous situations. We have bodies that bleed, hurt, and otherwise become easily damaged. In a similar manner, we also have egos that can bleed, hurt, and otherwise become damaged. Humans are vulnerable creatures. From your first skinned knee to the first loss you felt growing up, vulnerability is part of everyone's life. Someone told me the other day that when people are traumatized, the most frequently uttered word is "Mom!" I don't know if this is true, but it sounds right to me.

Vulnerability makes us feel childlike, alone, frightened, with a primal need of protection.

Most people confuse vulnerability with insecurity. The difference is simple but crucial. For starters, vulnerability is a fact of life, insecurity isn't. Protecting yourself from vulnerability makes sense: that's why you buckle your seat belt, take vitamins, and learn to say no. The problem with insecurity isn't the seat belt, the vitamin, or the assertiveness, it's the worrisome anticipation of a car accident, illness, or being victimized by others. It's anticipating what can go wrong in life and then worrying about it. As with most things psychological, there's always room for some confusion.

Insecurity, by its very nature, has the tendency to make you feel vulnerable when you're safe and oftentimes to exaggerate vulnerability to the point of absurdity. A hypochondriac may feel convinced that a pulled muscle is the onset of terminal cancer, the pessimist may interpret his wife's aloofness as an indication that she's having an affair, and the worrywart may be tempted not to sign a permission slip allowing her daughter to go on a field trip because she remembers reading about a child abduction in the papers recently. Insecurity not only can exploit vulnerability, it can create it as well. The key, which you will be reading about in upcoming chapters, is learning to separate facts from fictions. Once you begin to understand that feelings are not facts, you'll be in a position to differentiate between real vulnerability and insecurity's projections of vulnerability.

When it comes to insecurity, the operative word here is *feeling* out of control. Descartes got it right with his now famous perception, "Cogito, ergo sum"—I think, therefore I am. What we think, what we believe, is what we become. Often unnoticed, insecurity will mesmerize you with defensiveness, doubts, fears, and negatives while taking over your life and your relationship, leaving you, along with your partner, its unwitting victims. There can be no solace or true optimism for an insecure person; they've been convinced there is no ultimate safety, not with all their vulnerabilities.

In a relationship, insecurity and the exaggerated perception of vulnerability lie at the bottom of all struggle. Whether it's one partner's attempt to dictate and bully the other, another partner's hesitancy about letting go to intimacy, or the insecurity and panic over strained finances, insecurity can take any problem and amplify it. When insecurity is steering, the result becomes two people protecting themselves from the perception of harm that might be perpetrated by the other. Take a look at Alice and Wally.

Alice is a successful, self-made, controlling, rather arrogant black-and-white kind of thinker. Wally is just the opposite. He lacks confidence, has never been able to hold a job for more than a year, is often depressed, and struggles with various compulsions. Listening to Alice, you can't help but think of Wally as nothing more than an anchor, holding her back from her true potential:

> Wally doesn't get it. In order for us to live where we live, to afford a nanny, and do the things we do, I have to work. I can't help it that I have to travel. He's always telling me that I should be home with the family, that I put my career before him. If he could hold a job maybe things would be different. And why would I want to be home anyway? He just mopes around, whining and complaining. Tell you the truth, I don't listen to him anymore, in one ear out the other. I refuse to allow Wally to bring me down. I can't help it if he doesn't like being a Mr. Mom. That's not my choice.

Wally didn't disagree with Alice's facts, but he did disagree with her perception of him:

> Alice thinks I'm a loser. Sure, I've had a string of bad luck. But that doesn't make me a loser. It's easy to criticize someone when your bucket is filled. Maybe she's right, I'm a little depressed. Who wouldn't be? But she doesn't help. She's never there when I need her, she's impatient with my struggle, and mostly she treats my efforts to pull myself out of this rut as trivial—she's got more important things to worry about.
>
> Do I sulk? Do I whine? Maybe, but isn't a marriage supposed to offer comfort and support? I learned a long time ago that if I want comfort, Alice is the last person I go to. She'll be the first to criticize me or my efforts. Nothing I ever do is important enough

for her. Do you know how humiliated I feel? Lately we both seem to be avoiding each other. I've been sleeping on the couch for the last month, and the truth is, I don't think either one of us would want to share a bed at this point. I know that Alice is disgusted with me.

The dialogue continued:

Alice: No, I'm not disgusted with you, I'm embarrassed. Do you know what it's like when someone asks, "What's your husband do?" What do I say, "Nothing"? Look, I told you a long time ago that if you had any love for me you'd find a job and stick with it. If you're not man enough to do that, then why should I coddle you?

Wally: I'm not asking you to coddle me! I'm asking you to care, to support me, and not put me down. It's not my fault I can't find a job . . . Forget it, I need to stop looking to you for anything.

Alice: Please, do me a favor, don't look for a job, look for a life! I think it's time that you consider moving out of the house.

Ouch! If anything, this exchange demonstrates the spiraling destructiveness involved in protecting yourself from perceived vulnerability. For Wally, Alice's "embarrassment" was hitting too close to home. Wally is already embarrassed, wounded, feeling powerless and depressed. He's getting swallowed up in a self-defeating implosion of depression and self-pity. He may not be admitting it, but Wally's looking to be rescued. Alice, for her part, is not about to let Wally's ineffectiveness jeopardize her need for control. Her controlling solution is painfully simple: insulate herself by pulling away and asking him to leave. Clearly, the capacity for working together has been sabotaged as this couple begins to create barricades of protection. It's all about the feelings of vulnerability generated by insecurity and control, the two reasons why couples wind up with self-perpetuating chaos.

Why do couples resort to defensive strategies that invariably wind up making matters worse? Obviously, when caught in such a struggle, you're not aware that you've become part of the problem. As far as you're concerned, you're part of the solution, the pitiful solution of protecting yourself from being hurt. Looking at Wally and Alice, we can see that neither one can understand or appreciate the other's struggle. Alice treats Wally's stagnation and depression like a hot stove, reflexively pulling away, trying not to get burnt. Wally can't understand how Alice's black-and-white need to feel in control causes her to flee both him and the relationship. It may feel like a lack of love to both Alice and Wally, but this isn't the case, it's because neither one can tolerate feeling out of control.

It's been my experience that human beings are survival machines. As I mentioned in chapter 1, we abhor being out of control. When confronted with a loss of control, we instinctually react by trying to regain control and balance in all things—including an unbalanced, out-of-control relationship. Wanting to control real-life circumstances by balancing a budget, taking vitamins, or putting on sunscreen isn't a bad thing, but when it comes to relationships, it's a terrible thing. The goal is never to control a relationship, it's to allow it to breathe and move toward a more natural and spontaneous expression. This can't happen when insecurity is threatening you. Nor can it happen when you're defending yourself by trying to control your partner.

Keep in mind that attempts to control a relationship aren't always obvious. Take, for example, one of the most common yet overlooked controlling strategies—complaining. Complaining is what you do in a relationship when you're feeling powerless to do anything else. If you're feeling out of control, defeated, frustrated, or helpless, complaining can become a feeble, desperate strategy to control your partner. But since this strategy rarely accomplishes anything constructive, there's a tendency for complaining itself to become a chronic problem within the relationship.

Nick and Mary were a young couple I worked with who couldn't help but point a complaining finger at each other. In our first counseling session, Nick wanted to make it perfectly clear that he was a victim of his wife's complaining:

> Mary is a complainer. All she does is complain—about everything! She complains about our apartment, the car we drive, the fact that I've gained weight, everything! She drives me crazy. She knows our situation and that I need to stay with my company for another year before we can get out of the city, but does she work with me? Does she accept that we have a limited budget? *No!* All she does

is complain. She hates Manhattan, she hates my work hours, she complains about not being able to go on vacation.

I can't quit my job. I don't decide how much money I make. It's not my fault! I can't stand it. To be honest, I think she just likes to complain. She's been that way since I met her. It's not fair that she makes my life so miserable.

It was obvious to me that Nick had just spent a good deal of time complaining about Mary's "complaining." Mary had the following to add:

Sure I complain, who wouldn't? He makes all the decisions, he treats me like I'm his child—complaining that I spend too much, that whatever I do just isn't good enough. In Nick's eyes I never do anything right, and believe me, he's the first to whine and moan about it! He complains because I don't agree with everything he says. I don't know why I waste my breath; he really doesn't listen to me when I talk. As far as Nick is concerned, in his mind he already knows how I feel, what I think, and why I'm wrong. It's disrespectful. It hurts . . . Yeah, I complain because I don't know what else to do.

Both Nick and Mary were quick to assume the role of victim, pointing fingers, complaining about the way they were mistreated, and yet neither had a clue that they were both engaged in a destructive pattern of control based on mutual feelings of powerlessness. Chronic complaining was their last resort to control the situation by pointing out each other's faults. But as you can see from this scenario, complaining, focusing only on what's wrong with the relationship, offers nothing constructive, it only adds friction and more resentment.

Sure, everyone complains now and then. But when complaining becomes a defense against legitimate relating, it becomes chronic, polarizing each partner's defensive position. You can guess what my first homework assignment was for Nick and Mary—for one week, they were not allowed to criticize, critique, or judge each other. Instead of trying to change, berate, or attack each other, they were to make every attempt to respect each other's differences. The results were amazing. At first disoriented by not being able to point fingers, they found themselves talking about differences without feeling threatened or hopeless. As Mary put it, "We certainly don't agree on everything, but now we seem to be able to talk about our differences. It was as if the clouds parted and everything became clear! He doesn't hate me anymore for disagreeing, and I've found that I can respect his point of view. I'm not saying I accept it, at least not yet, but I do respect it. I think we're both seeing that it's the respect that's going to work for us. That's really something new for us."

No More Confusion

Confused with what's going on in your relationship? Can't explain why your partner's so hostile, withdrawn, cranky, or defiant? Look no further than control. Here's a Catalytic Self-Coaching promise: understand the concept of insecurity and control and you will always—100 percent of the time—have an answer to why you (yes, we're being honest here) or your partner do appalling things to each other. I know this sounds like a rather grandiose promise, but I can only tell you that I've been trying to prove it wrong for more than a decade. Whether I'm working with an individual or a couple, whenever I see destructive, shabby, self-defeating, or relationship-defeating behavior, I ask myself three Catalytic Self-Coaching questions:

1. **Why is she/he feeling out of control?** What are the circumstances that are creating or evoking this insecurity/loss of control?

2. **How is she/he feeling out of control?** What type of controlling behavior is evident, such as avoidance, manipulation, rigidity, dishonesty, disinterest, hostility, and so on?

3. **How is this behavior an attempt to establish control?** Avoidance is an attempt to gain control by retreating from danger; hostility an attempt to gain control by pushing away a perceived threat, threatening person, and so on. (You will be learning more about the various strategies of control in the next chapter.)

Understanding the implications of insecurity and control is like having psychological X-ray vision. You can take any struggle and, by asking the three Catalytic Self-Coaching questions, recognize that the answer isn't doing battle with your partner, it's reducing the insecurity that promotes the battle (that is, the defensive need to control). This is why you're the designated problem solver—the catalyst, because it's you who will initially understand what's *really* going on and what it takes to stop fueling the motor of relationship insecurity and defense.

Sounds like a lot to ask of you? Not really, especially when you begin to recognize that your partner's not trying to hurt you, he or she is only trying to control their vulnerability. Understand this and you will avoid the trap of taking relationship struggle personally. I can't begin to tell you the benefits of not getting personally entangled in a defensive dance when you're trying to make sense of chaos. When your partner is constantly picking out your negative qualities, or criticizing you for almost everything you do, I know not taking things personally may sound like a tall order, but trust me, *it's not personal.* Your partner is only reflexively trying to reduce vulnerability. By learning to reduce this vulnerability, you will be taking a catalytic leap forward.

Catalytic Self-Coaching Heads-Up

When dealing with struggle, remember your mantra is "Don't take it personally."

4

Self-Coaching

Eliminating Your Contribution to the Problem

In this chapter I'm going to ask you to switch gears and forget about your partner and your relationship for the time being. (I bet you can use the break.) Previously, I emphasized how every relationship struggle reflects each partner's patterns of insecurity. Whether one partner is too active, the other too passive; one too aggressive, the other too docile; one overly involved, the other detached—any way you mix it up, it's going to be bad for the relationship. In order for you, as the catalytic partner, to eliminate your contribution to the problem, you're going to have to get beyond your own personal limitations, whatever they are.

Since I hold each partner mutually responsible for the relationship struggle, it's up to you to create a relationship "vacuum" by removing your 50 percent contribution. This may seem like a daunting task, especially if you've struggled with your own issues in the past, been to counseling, or have conceded that you can't change who you are. For now, I'm going to ask that you suspend any apprehensions. Once you realize how simple Self-Coaching can make the task of personal empowerment and improvement, not only will you have the tools to revitalize your own life, but you will be in the best possible position to coach your partner forward, toward a more liberated and spontaneous capacity for genuine intimacy and relatedness.

Self-Coaching's Simple Answers to Complex Problems

For the past three decades I've made it my life's work to show people that change, real and legitimate change, is not only possible, it's almost a certainty if you follow a few simple Self-Coaching practices. For starters, Self-Coaching isn't overly concerned with your history and therefore will not require any extensive excavation of your past. Whether your potty training was too strict or too lenient isn't as important as that same "potty behavior" that gets expressed today as defiance, control, or stubbornness.

Just because a traumatic incident may have occurred when you were three or four doesn't mean it's locked away in the depths of your repressed unconscious waiting for your discovery to set you free from its ill effects. There's no question that the painful circumstances of your early life affect who you are today, but from a Self-Coaching perspective, digging into your past in order to recognize the epicenter of your current problems does nothing—absolutely nothing! When it comes to liberating yourself from the habits of insecurity (which include anxiety, depression, panic, and so on) that exist today—the historical truth shall *not* set you free! Sure, it will illuminate the "why" you do what you do—which is always helpful—but it will not change the patterned reflexes that continue to feed the insecurity. And if insecurity is fed, then insecurity will continue to wreak havoc in your life!

It helps to think of a cigarette smoker. Do you think it really matters *why* that smoker took his first cigarette? Of course not! It only matters that he figures out what he can do to quit smoking today. The smoker needs to ask, "What am I going to do to stop my nicotine habit?" You need to ask what you're going to do—today—to stop the here-and-now patterns of insecurity that are fueling not only your personal struggles, but your relationship frustrations as well. Learning to take the necessary action to break the habits of insecurity that contaminate your life is the essential goal of Self-Coaching. Insight alone will do nothing to stop a bad habit; action, on the other hand, will!

How Do You Stack Up?

In earlier chapters you learned about the shaping influence of insecurity on your personality. Since insecurity is an inescapable component of life, everyone's personality, to a greater or lesser extent, reflects the patterns of insecurity that have slowly been accumulating since childhood. Think of your "here and now" personality as a stack of coins. Any habit of insecurity (a.k.a. Child-Reflexes) would be like inserting a bent coin into the stack. The resulting tilt of the stack will thus reflect the number and extent of its bent coins. For some people the tilt may be minimal, while for others—well, let's just say it might look a bit like the Leaning Tower of Pisa! The more your personality veers away from its true and spontaneous center, the more your life is contaminated by the unchecked effects of insecurity.

Self-Coaching is a way of removing the bent coins of insecurity by giving you the tools necessary to correct your faulty view of reality. This "corrected view" happens when you learn to replace antiquated Child-Reflexes (bent coins) and faulty perceptions with truth. What's the truth? That's who you naturally are and what you become when the overlay of insecurity is removed.

Risking

When it comes to understanding your personality, the whole is definitely greater than the sum of its parts. No single experience is responsible for who you are today; it is the combined synergistic effect of all your experiences that winds up producing the person you see before you in the mirror. From these accumulated, trial-and-error experiences you've had growing up, you've come up with strategies to protect yourself from what your insecurity perceives to be harmful. At first the strategies may be primitive and unformed—like sulking, crying, lying, and so on—but in time a kind of Darwinian evolution takes place. Those strategies that offer the most control over feelings of insecurity and vulnerability will endure and become your go-to patterns of defense, while those that don't work become extinct.

For you to realistically challenge these patterns, you're going to have to build a reservoir of self-trust in order to risk vulnerability. Although it may feel risky to abandon your defenses and trust your more spontaneous, reactive nature to handle life, it is not risky at all. In fact, you are much more capable of handling life when you mobilize all of your instinctual, intuitive potential rather than just the limited, defensive view of the ego. Still, it will no doubt take a leap of faith to convince you to shed your defenses and risk trusting that you don't have to anticipate, avoid, snarl, bully, or otherwise manipulate life in order to be safe. All you need to do is trust that in safe situations, doing nothing is in fact doing something. Trusting that you can handle life without resorting to controlling defensiveness is the ultimate Self-Coaching goal. I call this Reactive Living.

Reactive Living is learning to step out of the shackles of insecurity, coming out of the overthinking, defensive, protective box of fear and learning to risk being exactly who you are. When I first introduce the concept of Reactive Living to someone I'm working with, it's not uncommon for me to hear, "If I were to be reactive, I would have thrown a dish at him!" The key is to realize that *before* Reactive Living can be successfully employed, you must first neutralize the contaminating effects of insecurity (which we will do in this and the next chapter). At that point you can begin to let go and experience the effortless life potential that will ensure your success as a person and as a partner. So let's begin at the beginning, dismantling and neutralizing insecurity. Then we shall proceed to a format for Reactive Living.

Self-Coaching Basics

Self-Coaching is a form of therapy based on sound and proven psychological techniques, and most importantly, it is also a motivational plan for personal empowerment designed to challenge the status quo dictated by faulty perceptions of insecurity. Whatever you struggle with, whether anxiety, depression, panic, fear, anger, or just passivity, Self-Coaching will simplify the confusing science of psychology into a simple, commonsense approach that can be broken down into three easy steps.

Before getting into the specific steps, let me first cut to the chase and give you the punch line. When it comes to your personal liberation, it all comes down to whether you're feeding insecurity or starving it. That's it! All habits, if they are to persist, must be fed. Cut off the food supply and they die. All habits! Now that you know that insecurity is nothing more than a bad habit, it's time to look more closely at what you're doing that feeds and sustains it (in chapter 8, you will learn to starve insecurity using a three-step technique called Self-Talk).

Since insecurity is the Rosetta Stone of my Self-Coaching method, let's begin our hands-on work with an insecurity self-quiz. It's important for you to assess your general level of insecurity as we begin your catalytic process. There's no need to fudge your answers, we're only after a baseline at this point. Later in the program you can come back to this quiz to see your relative degree of improvement. We'll eventually encourage your partner to take the quiz, but for now, do not offer it. Our job in this chapter is a *You*-makeover. We'll get to your partner after we've eliminated or neutralized any contaminating, defensive tendencies you may possess as a result of your habit of insecurity.

Insecurity Self-Quiz

Please read the following questions carefully, but don't overthink your responses. The quiz is not meant to be a precise assessment of your personality; it's only intended as a helpful guide to predicting your general level of insecurity. Circle your responses as being mostly true (T), sometimes true (S), or mostly false (F) as they generally pertain to your life. Answer every question even if you have to guess. Scoring is at the end of the test.

T S F   Socially I tend to be shy, tense, or uneasy.

T S F   I'd rather stay home than go to a party.

T S F   I don't feel smart enough.

T S F   I worry about not having enough money.

T S F   I tend to be more of a pessimist than an optimist.

T S F   When I look in a mirror, I always focus on my flaws.

T S F   I'm usually too cautious.

T S F   If people knew the real me, they would think differently.

T S F   In relationships, I have a tendency to become too attached.

T S F   Trusting others is too risky.

T S F   If someone's too quiet, I might think he or she is angry at me.

T S F   Getting too close to others can be dangerous.

T S F   I worry too much.

T S F   I have lots of fears.

T S F   I feel vulnerable when my feelings show.

T S F   In relationships, I can be hostile and defensive.

T S F   I often wonder what people *really* think of me.

T S F   In relationships, I have a tendency to become too aloof.

T S F   I often feel upset about my looks.

T S F   I tend to be a yes person and have a hard time saying no.

T S F   I'm too sensitive.

T S F   I worry about getting sick.

T S F   I often feel guilty.

T S F   I can't stand the way I look in pictures.

T S F   I'm not an emotionally strong person.

T S F   In relationships, I find it hard to be totally honest.

T S F Intimacy scares me.

T S F I never completely trust my partner.

T S F I'm very impatient.

T S F I often start my thoughts with "what if?"

T S F I have trouble getting things done on time.

T S F I worry about my health.

T S F I generally feel like I'm on edge.

T S F I'm often unhappy.

T S F I have too much doubt.

T S F I know I'm insecure.

T S F I dread things going wrong.

T S F I have to have things done my way.

T S F I have a hard time relaxing.

T S F In life, you can never be safe enough.

T S F I exaggerate problems.

T S F I often compare myself to others.

T S F I fear growing older.

T S F I have phobias (such as closed spaces, bridges, open spaces, social encounters, etc.).

T S F I often feel like a child.

T S F I have a lot of regrets.

T S F I often feel like a victim.

T S F I have a hard time trusting others.

T S F In life, it's better to be safe than sorry.

T S F I think too much.

Score each mostly true response (T) one point, each sometimes true response (S) one-half point, and each mostly false response (F) zero points. Tally up all your points.

A score of 1 to 20 indicates a mild degree of insecurity. You'll be using this program more for personality expansion rather than for repair. Your relative stability along with low levels of insecurity ensure that you have considerable potential to be an effective catalytic partner.

A score of 20.5 to 35 indicates a moderate level of insecurity. Insecurity is probably undermining your capacity for effective relating and successful living. With some Self-Talk tweaking, you can expect this program to empower you to make significant adjustments that will make a big catalytic difference in your relationship.

If you scored above 35.5 you may be struggling with substantial interference due to insecurity. Since your self-worth and confidence have been eroded by insecurity, you'll find your Self-Coaching training invaluable as you begin to restructure your thoughts and perceptions. Through your Self-Talk efforts you can expect to recognize a heretofore unknown capacity for effectiveness and confidence.

Insecurity and Control

Now armed with a baseline understanding of your insecurity, you're in a better position to assess the weeds of control that grow from the root of insecurity. Remember, an insecure person will always gravitate toward a life of control in order to feel less vulnerable. Unfortunately, these attempts to control life, and thereby your relationships, create friction. Why? Because control is oppressive—no one likes feeling controlled, bullied, or manipulated. If someone tries to hold your head underwater, what do you do? Answer: anything to prevent drowning. You instinctually begin to flail about, thrashing, fighting, whatever it takes to get that next breath. It's no different in a relationship when you think you're drowning. When someone tries to control us, we typically resort to desperate countermeasures, attempting to keep our head above the waters of conflict.

Since in this chapter we're focusing on your own insecurity and control (which we are going to be challenging and removing from the relationship dynamic), let's take a look at how you became part of the problem rather than part of the solution.

Breaking Your Control Patterns

Controlling life requires effort, maintenance, and vigilance—it's truly an exhausting way to live. So why do we do it? By eliminating or at least minimizing vulnerability, we become convinced that we can control fate. Controlling life may sound appealing, especially if you're feeling insecure and unsafe, but the reality is that such control is a myth, and the more you try, the more hooked you become into compulsively seeking to avoid rather than legitimately handle life's challenges.

When the need for control becomes too important, we wind up susceptible to certain traps. I call these control-traps. Control-traps are defensive, insecurity-driven thinking or attitude habits. They are insecurity's attempt to gain control over whatever threatens us. It's easy to get hooked into a treadmill-like belief that your ultimate salvation depends on having just a little more control—and more—and more. These traps can quickly become the underpinnings of friction in any relationship, but if you're going to become more catalytic, you must free yourself from insecurity's illusions of control. The following are some of the most common control-traps:

The Holier-Than-Thou Trap

"Let me handle it, you'll just mess things up." "You don't know what you're doing." "Don't worry, I don't expect you to understand my needs." Having a condescending attitude is a way of minimizing your partner. An arrogant posture allows you to feel superior, and feeling superior makes you feel more in control. If, for example, you see your partner as being incompetent or less intelligent, you're automatically raising your status with this comparison. "Poor thing isn't as quick as I am at figuring out the bill."

A holier-than-thou attitude allows you to dismiss what challenges you. "So I forgot to make that call. Big deal! Unlike you, I have a lot on my plate." As you'll see in chapter 5, those who exhibit Elephant, Peacock, and Raccoon traits are particularly fond of using condescension to control a relationship. It's a smug, arrogant attitude that is both obnoxious and quite toxic to any real feeling of balance or potential relatedness. One reason why the holier-than-thou partner needs to feel superior is because in a balanced relationship, he/she would not be the one in control.

Sarcasm is a variation of the holier-than-thou trap. "Don't mind my complaints, everyone knows you are a perfect person with no flaws." Or, "No, you're wrong. I think you should go to Atlantic City this weekend with the boys. We can always celebrate our anniversary *next* year!" Sarcasm bites, smarts, stings, and insults. It's a form of passive-aggressive condescension bathed in arrogance. Yuck!

A healthier alternative is to recognize that the issues that come up in a relationship are rarely about who's right and who's wrong (although it may feel this way); it really has to do with *perceptions* of right and wrong. One spouse may feel that cheating on your taxes is a moral outrage, while the other partner may feel it's a God-given right. Perceptions are about individual views, not necessarily about facts. It helps to embrace each other's differences rather than the condescending partner insisting, "You're wrong, I'm right."

The Should-Thinking Trap

"You should treat me better." "I should lose twenty pounds." "We should go out more." Should statements, although they may be rooted in factual reality, are actually criticisms. It's like wagging a finger and becoming the parent. A healthy alternative is to replace should-thinking with more positive assertions. By saying, "I should lose weight," you're disapproving of yourself and more than likely to produce a negative drag on any serious ambitions. By contrast, a more positive assertion—"I'm going to join the gym and quit eating junk food"—has the opposite effect. It mobilizes energy rather than suppressing it.

Should statements, when leveled at your partner, are a form of complaining that quickly become translated into nagging, whining, and so on. Rather than "You *should* help with the shopping," a less controlling, more assertive statement would be, "I need help with the shopping." In all fairness, you may not get the help you need at this point, but as you progress through this program and begin to work more catalytically together, fairness will not only become a possibility in your relationship, it will become the basis for it.

The Worrying/What-Iffing Trap

"What if I ejaculate too quickly?" "What if I don't get the job?" "What if we can't have a baby?" Worrying (and its common expression of what-iffing) is an attempt to control life. The rationale is: "If I can figure out what's going to go wrong before it goes wrong, then I can prepare and brace and—maybe—protect myself from chaos." The problem is that worry only begets worry. It really doesn't prepare you. What prepares you for handling life is trust. Self-trust. With sufficient self-trust you're willing to take the leap of faith necessary to trust your intuitive capacity for handling life as it unfolds in the moment, rather than wasting your energy by allowing yourself to treat the fictions of insecurity as if they're facts.

Take a leap of faith and ask yourself, "What are the facts?" When you have the facts in front of you, then ask what you can do about them. It's important to keep in mind that insecurity with its attempt to control outcomes by worrying just takes a difficult situation and makes it feel impossible! A healthier alternative is to realize that worrying undermines your self-confidence by insisting you can be safe (that is, in control) only if you can anticipate what's ahead. Self-Coaching teaches you to be safe not by worrying and what-iffing, but by courageously trusting your ability to handle life.

The Tunnel Vision Trap

"I'm just married to a cranky old man." "Life is only heartache." "I can't do anything right." Insecurity is notorious for narrowing our perceptions. Tunnel vision prevents you from seeing the bigger picture, with possible alternatives and solutions, and limits you to one pessimistic aspect or component of the difficulty, thus allowing you to feel vindicated for quitting or giving up. If you have no positive expectations either for yourself or your partner, then you're not going to be disappointed. And if you're not disappointed, then you're not going to feel out of control. This is a thinking trap designed to protect you not only from getting disappointed, but also from having to take responsibility. "Why should I keep trying, our relationship died years ago?" The healthy alternative is to recognize that life is rarely limited to one point of view, one option, or one solution.

The Mind-Reading Trap

"I know she doesn't love me." "He does that because he doesn't care about my feelings." "She thinks I'm a loser." Mind reading is an attempt to know what you can't know—someone else's thoughts. When there's struggle and chaos, it's tempting to feel in control by interpreting what we think is going on. This isn't necessarily a problem until we treat our interpretations as if they are factual. The guy, for example, who has convinced himself that his partner doesn't love him may be unaware that his partner's withdrawal and moodiness isn't about him—it may be the partner's stressful situation at work. When you consider how easy it is to misinterpret your own thoughts, you begin to understand what a folly it is to believe you know someone else's.

The *Have-to* Trap

"We have to have more sex." "We have to go on vacation." "I have no choice, I have to call my mother every day." *Have-tos* are similar to *shoulds*. Whereas should-thinking is a backhanded attempt to move you toward change ("We should go to church more often"), have-to thinking does this in a much more compulsive way by attempting to eliminate choice altogether ("I have to go to church!"). With have-to thinking you've convinced yourself that you have no choice other than to capitulate to your goals. It offers the illusion of control by attempting to eliminate ambiguity. Since I have no choice, there's no more struggle with indecisiveness, everything is now settled—case closed, in control! This is the predominant process in all compulsivity—spending, cleaning, working, even sex. What's the healthy alternative? Work to replace the *have-tos* in your life with *want-tos*.

The Black-and-White Thinking Trap

"I'll never be happy." "He will never be considerate of my feelings." Black-and-white thinking is impulsive thinking. When you're feeling frustrated, it's easy to become impatient. Something is either all good or all bad, positive or negative, always or never. Black-and-white thinking offers the illusion of control because, like have-to thinking mentioned above, it eliminates ambiguity. Let's face it; if you're insecure, you're much more inclined to want to feel sure and in control than to feel lost in a world of gray possibilities.

The healthy alternative is to learn to tolerate some ambiguity in your life, to recognize that an impulsive solution, if wrong, only creates more problems. What's important is to insist that you *can* live with some uncertainty if in fact the ultimate correct solution depends on the process of sifting and sorting through the facts. The black-and-white thinker is saying, "I just want this to be done, finished, I can't live with the stress of not knowing." The secure person takes a deep breath and says, "I may not want to live with this stress, but I do want to make the best possible conclusion. I will be more patient."

The Name-Calling Trap

"You're stupid." "You're such a wimp." "I'm too tall/short and skinny/fat." Name-calling is nothing more than a ruse. If you beat yourself or your partner up, then you can give up, quit, or walk away from any confrontation. You're creating excuses for you or your relationship's shortcomings, and you might as well just give up. Similar to black-and-white thinking, you become much too eager to settle an argument because insecurity has you convinced you can't tolerate living with it.

As with black-and-white thinking, you need to understand the impulsive habit involved in this behavior. The healthy alternative is to get tough and tell yourself that name-calling is *not* allowed. You're just not going to permit it! Keep in mind that when the name-calling is aimed at your partner, then you're only building resentment-equity in your relationship.

Ted and Celeste and the Saga of the Raspberry Kitchen

The aim of this chapter has been threefold: first, to acquaint you with *your* habits of insecurity; second, to lay a foundation of understanding that will prepare you for your Self-Talk work that will be introduced in chapter 8; and third, to sensitize you to how easy and reflexive control-traps can become. I've selected a transcript from a session I had with Ted and Celeste. From this rather blatant example of insecurity gone wild, you can begin to understand how insecurity and control are your real problems. Not your partner.

I had been working with Ted and Celeste for a few months. Ted, a thirty-nine-year-old salesman, was a consummate narcissistic bully who was prone to loud, sometimes frightening tantrums along with his many angry outbursts. His demands were often irrational and childlike, with impossibly high standards for his wife to follow. Celeste, a manager at a bank, a mild-mannered woman in her early thirties, was prone to avoidance, feelings of intimidation, and withdrawal. Less frequently, she was also prone to roller-coaster behavior including hysterical sobbing one moment, defensive snapping the next.

The following is a snapshot from a session we had following a debacle over what color to paint the kitchen. (Brace yourself.) I've inserted my comments in italics to give you an idea how I, as the psychologist, try to pick out the control-traps and reflexive patterns that typically fly fast and furious in a relationship clash.

> Ted: Celeste decided we needed to paint the kitchen. I had no problem with this and encouraged her to go look at some paint samples. Two hours later she comes back with a gallon of raspberry red paint! Not only did she go against me [*Defensive insecurity: She's against me!*] and not bring home samples, but she *knows* I hate trendy colors. [*Control-trap: mind reading. Assuming your partner "knows" something may or may not be accurate. Also: black-and-white thinking. Verbs like "hate" that express extreme views are usually a tip-off of black-and-white thinking.*] The point is she didn't care what I wanted. [*Control-trap: mind reading. Ted can't know that Celeste didn't "care."*] She did exactly what she wanted and I wasn't going to stand for it. [*No self-respecting tyrant would!*] I refused to let her paint. [*Aggressive attempt to control: "I refused to let her . . ." I'm in charge here!*] (Glaring at Celeste) Go ahead, tell him what you did. [*Ordering Celeste: "tell him" is an attempt to control the situation by bullying.*]

> Celeste: Typically I would have just cried and tried to bring the paint back. [*Martyr behavior 101*] Ted is such a bully. I honestly

thought he told me to pick out paint, not bring home samples. If he was so adamant about what color to use, he should have gone with me. [*Control-trap: should-thinking delivered with an attempt to justify or defend.*] I started to pry open the lid. I thought if I showed him the beautiful color, maybe, just maybe, he'd change his mind. Am I stupid or what? [*Control-trap: name-calling. Although sounding a bit tongue-in-cheek here, it's still a self-admonishment.*] Ted, in twelve years of marriage, has *never* changed his mind about anything. [*Control-trap: black-and-white/tunnel thinking.*] He's always right! He's such a baby. [*Control-trap: name-calling.*] He always has to have his way. [*Adverbs such as "always," "never," etc. are tip-offs to black-and-white thinking.*] Anyway, I'm beginning to pry off the lid and he comes over, grabs the can out of my hands, and starts pushing the lid back down [*"grabs the can out of my hands . . ." Physical aggression is always a violent attempt to control.*], yelling that he doesn't care what f***ing color it is, it's going back to the store. [*Ted's yelling and cursing is aggressive and verbally abusive. This is an attempt to control through intimidation.*] Well, needless to say, the can went flying with the half-sealed lid coming ajar. Paint splattered everywhere. Ted was seething. He took the almost empty can and threw it. [*Blatant aggressive control through intimidation.*] Paint splattered everywhere . . . it was a disaster. I got so upset, I ran out and called my sister to pick me up. [*Defensive avoidance? Possibly, but under the circumstances this is a justified response. Bottom line: with any potential for abuse, it's always safety first.*] I stayed out all night to teach Ted a lesson. I came home the next morning. [*Since Celeste's motive here was to "teach Ted a lesson" by staying out all night, this would be labeled passive-aggressive behavior.*]

Ted (*interrupting*): See, that's what I mean! She stays out all night to punish me. [*Control-trap: mind reading. Although Ted may be correct in his assumption, mind reading is a destructive form of communication. Notice how Ted is trying to position himself to become the innocent victim of this brouhaha.*] The paint falling was an accident and I got upset. [*"What's a poor, innocent guy to do?" In this case, being a victim of circumstances is a rationalization, i.e., a good excuse,*] *but not the real reason.*] (Looking at me) Wouldn't you get upset if a gallon of paint fell on your floor? [*Control-trap: tunnel vision, "I had no other choice."*] She does this to me all the time, she knows how sensitive I am, why does she just abuse my needs? [*Ted's the only one not tiring of his martyr violin solo.*] I had no idea where she went that night, and to tell you the truth it just made me madder. When she came home, I was fit to be tied. Sure, I confronted her; I mean how dare she stay out all night? [*Narcissistic translation: "How dare she disrespect the supreme ruler!"*] I'm her husband, for God's sake! [*Husband/supreme ruler*] Who does she think she is? [*Narcissistic self-importance: "Nobody disobeys me!"*] From now on, I'll have to protect myself [*Control-trap: have-to thinking*], and believe me, she's not going to like it! [*Control through intimidation: "Hey, you hurt me—I don't get angry, I get even!"*]

As you can see from this transcript, insecurity, reflexive patterns, and control-traps work in unison to turn any bad situation into an impossible one. Mishaps, miscues, and spilled paint happen in every relationship. As unsettling as these conflicts can be, they're not the root of what's corrosive. The root is the way insecurity traps us into reacting to our problems.

Moving On

In the next chapter we're going to describe in much greater detail the five most common reflexive patterns that underlie most relationship struggles. Armed with these powerful insights, you will begin not only to handle your problems more effectively, but as we've discussed previously, you will also be creating that vacuum . . . a vacuum that your partner will find very unsettling. And this is a good thing. Without anyone to battle, there's no incentive to go on fighting.

From Ted and Celeste's transcript above you can see where Celeste's insecurity fueled the fires of battle. If we were to remove Celeste's insecurity from the picture, Ted would have been left playing his violin to deaf ears (not to mention his chest-thumping displays of violence). Without an audience, bullies begin to become very unsettled. As you'll see in chapter 12, this is exactly what catalytic coaching is all about—creating a vacuum in the relationship dynamic in order to cause change.

5

Are You a Tiger, Turtle, Elephant, Raccoon, or Peacock?

Learning Your Reflexive Personality Style

In the last chapter I made you a promise that if you understood the concept of insecurity and control, you would—100 percent of the time—be able to understand the "why" you and your partner are struggling. In this chapter I would like to give you the necessary foundation that will allow you to see through your struggles with a clarity that will astonish you. For the first time you will be able to peer deep into the heart of your relationship problems and find yourself no longer stumbling around in the dark. Enough promises, let's roll up our sleeves and get down to work.

Bicycle and Relationship Mechanics

My wife's a kindergarten teacher who long ago pointed out that I'm a visual learner. I've always felt that a good visual is, as they say, worth a thousand words. So, in an effort to conserve words, let me portray the dynamics of your relationship by asking you to visualize a bicycle. Just as every relationship is composed of two people, every bicycle has two wheels. With both bicycles and relationships, if you have a problem with one or both wheels, it's pretty hard to keep pedaling.

The unique quality of a bicycle's wheel is determined by the configuration of its spokes and hub. Any biking enthusiast will tell you that when it comes to speed and efficiency on the road, less is more—it's all about weight. The most efficient wheel, therefore, would be the lightest wheel. If you were to needlessly increase the size and therefore the weight of the hub, you would be adding to the effort required to pedal. The same goes for a relationship. If we allow the hub of each wheel to represent insecurity, then the bigger the core of insecurity (yours or your partner's), the more weight, and therefore the more effort (struggle) required to keep things rolling.

If the hub represents insecurity, then each "spoke" represents a specific pattern or habit of control. As you recall from the previous chapters, human beings abhor being out of control. It's a protective instinct that has served us for millions of years. The problem isn't wanting to be in control of our lives when there is danger; the problem is when insecurity perceives danger in safe places—like your relationship. When, for example, your partner perceives that he or she is unloved (because you forgot the anniversary flowers), they might resort to a typical controlling "spoke strategy" of withdrawal designed to create a turtlelike shell of protection.

Adding more and more spokes to an oversized hub will add more unnecessary weight and drag to your ride. In this chapter I hope to convince you that by understanding the hub-spoke (insecurity-control) qualities of your relationship, you will be able to get at the source of the drag that's been put on it. Catalytic Self-Coaching isn't about learning to live with mismatched wheels; it's a matter of replacing oversized, weighty wheels with more efficient racing ones.

Reflexive Patterns

You can see from the bicycle imagery example that I'm truly a visual person. I honestly can't help it—it's the way I think and express myself. I do, however, partially blame my fondness for visuals on my wife. As

I mentioned earlier, she's a kindergarten teacher who understands the value of simplicity. So, in the spirit of creating helpful visuals rather than bland, abstract descriptions, I'd like to now acquaint you with a few "animals" that may have infiltrated your relationship. These are Tigers, Turtles, Elephants, Raccoons, and Peacocks. You'll find this little menagerie very helpful in analyzing the reflexive dynamics of struggle.

Let's face it, schizotypal, histrionic, or narcissistic personality patterns are not nearly as apparent or understandable as the images of a withdrawn Turtle, a manipulative, snarling Raccoon, or an overbearing bully of an Elephant. You may not be as fond of visuals as I am, but it's not important what we call these patterns, only that you begin to recognize them. Feel free to stick with my visuals or to substitute any image or description that works for you. What's important is that you have a working understanding of the five general reflexive patterns in order to begin the necessary catalytic work of defusing them before any further erosion of your relationship can take place.

Reflexive Relating

You're probably familiar with the knee-jerk reflex: a physician taps your kneecap with a rubber mallet; your lower leg jerks involuntarily. The same thing happens in relationships, only instead of tap-jerk, we have a perceived threat, followed by a controlling response. The operative word here is *perceived*. Because of insecurity, we begin to see danger in safe places. For example, the hypersensitive partner may respond to any criticism—however benign—with a reflexive counterattack. "You don't like my shirt, why don't you take a look in the mirror at your hair?" *Tap-jerk*. An insecure husband's wife mentioning that they should stop and ask for directions might bring about a reflexive bark. "Shut your mouth! I know what I'm doing!" *Tap-jerk*.

Reflexive controlling habits are so automatic that they're often overlooked in the heat of battle. What's of particular importance for the catalytic partner is the realization that not only can these patterns be made more conscious and recognizable, they can also be anticipated. Being able to anticipate the tap-jerk nuisances of your relationship puts you in a position where you can avoid your own contribution of reflexive responding. This is key to understanding your role as a catalytic partner. By not getting caught up in these knee-jerk patterns, you can interrupt the cycle of reflexive relating. At this point you become a legitimate part of the solution.

Take a look at the following list of the five most common reflexive, controlling strategies (along with their associated animal counterpart) and see how many you can recognize either in your personality or your partner's. Although these designations are offered as discrete categories, you will often notice considerable overlap. The categories are only meant to give you a broad anticipation of the typical patterns that you might expect to encounter in your day-to-day struggles. You'll find that being able to predict these patterns—in yourself and in your partner—is critical when trying to neutralize defensiveness. Use these designations to help alert you not only to the everyday reflexive patterns that exist in your relationship, but also to the specific reflexive behaviors that occur less frequently as isolated eruptions.

Tigers: Those Who Control through Aggression

Tigers fight by using their claws, teeth, and strength to overpower their prey. In order to survive, Tigers must be aggressive. Tigers are also stealthy. They're able to pounce on an unwary adversary without warning. When a partner resorts to Tiger-like aggression or hostility to control a relationship, on some level he or she is feeling desperate. And when Tiger-types feel they are trying to survive some form of perceived threat, it's a no-holds-barred world where hostility and even abusiveness (verbal or physical) is used as a controlling strategy to threaten and, at times, hurt the partner who is perceived as a threat.

A Tiger defense is a primitive form of protection that clearly is unconcerned with the consequences—all that matters is taking control of a situation and annihilating anyone who poses a threat. This is a big problem with Tigers because they're so easily threatened. If, for example, you were to put on a few pounds, your Tiger partner might take this as a personal insult and challenge. After all, you're not conforming to the Tiger's preconceived notion of how you *should* look—and this could feel threatening to a Tiger. In which case you might get a biting, sarcastic comment designed to both control and punish: "Go ahead, have another piece of cake. It really doesn't bother me. I just try not to look at you."

Unfortunately, when unchecked, Tigers often wind up in divorce court or being issued restraining orders. Taken to the extreme, Tiger qualities can end in violence.

Take a look at the following list to determine whether you or your partner have Tiger tendencies or a potential for Tiger tendencies:

- Often exploitative—taking advantage of a person or situation
- Often arrogant—as a defense to hide low self-esteem
- Often impulsive or explosive
- Often irritable
- Often lacking remorse
- Often lacking empathy
- Often sarcastic—to make points or punish
- Generally aggressive—as a defense against basic feelings of inferiority
- Self-important—as a defense against low self-esteem
- Generally defensive
- Generally possessing inadequate self-control

Turtles: Those Who Passively Control through Avoidance

Turtles have one defense against danger, withdrawal into their shells. Once in their shell, they become impervious to attacks. Human Turtles have shells called withdrawal, passivity, apathy, avoidance, and so on. Where a Tiger reflex controls with aggression and hostility—a fight-response—a Turtle strategy of avoidance may be seen as a flight-response. Retreating from or avoiding perceived harm is one way to avoid further damage, hurt, or vulnerability. By pulling away into a protective shell, we're attempting to protect ourselves by creating a barrier between us and that which threatens us. Unfortunately, turtles and people can't stay hidden indefinitely.

Take a look at the following list to determine whether you or your partner have any Turtle reflexes:

- Withdrawal from conflict or intensity
- Often suspicious
- Preoccupied with doubts about loyalty or trust
- Hypersensitive to criticism or rejection
- Emotionally inhibited
- Reluctant to take risks
- Feeling inferior
- Fearful or rigid in intimate relationships, especially sexual expression
- Prone to worry and rumination
- Reluctant to make decisions
- Unable to express disagreement
- Lacking self-confidence
- Possessing low self-esteem
- Overly conscientious
- Prone to depressed or anxious mood

Elephants: Those Who Control through Bullying

Elephants aren't fleet of foot and have neither claws nor quills, but they have mass. Elephants control adversaries by throwing their weight around. Elephant-types feel vulnerable unless they are in charge and steering the situation. They are used to bullying, harassing, dictating, and intimidating. Elephants are similar to Tigers, with one distinct and important difference—where Tiger-types are aggressive and attacking, Elephants don't necessarily want to hurt you, just to dominate you. For example, they want to decide where you eat, who drives the car, where you go on vacations, and so on. Elephants also like to throw their intellectual weight around, insisting that they are always right and you are always wrong. They never take responsibility for their shortcomings and are always quick to rationalize and explain their faults away. Elephants, by nature of their power, are always willing to escalate a problem to any level in order to intimidate and get you to back off. Unfortunately, Elephants reap what they sow—angry, avoidant, unhappy partners.

Take a look at the following list to determine whether you or your partner have any Elephant tendencies. Remember to keep in mind that, unlike Tigers, Elephants only want to dominate you—not hurt you (at least not intentionally):

- Easily irritated—quick-tempered
- Lacking remorse
- Lacking desire for closeness or nonsexual intimacy
- Stubborn
- Often irresponsible
- Prone to lying, rationalizing, or denying
- Often impulsive
- Displaying a know-it-all attitude
- Lacking empathy
- Usually exploitative, looking to take advantage of a situation
- Displaying grandiose self-importance
- Displaying an arrogant attitude

Raccoons: Those Who Manipulate

Anyone who has ever wondered how a raccoon managed to pry the lid off a garbage can will attest to the raccoon's ingenuity, dexterity, and determination. In the wild, raccoons are masters at manipulating their environment. In the realm of relationships, human Raccoons use manipulation to gain control. Whether control is achieved through martyrlike, woe-is-me behavior, guilt, or emotional tactics, Raccoons know how to get what they want from their partners. Raccoon-types live by one set of rules—theirs!

Raccoons are scavengers and not likely to engage in attacks, but don't corner them. Their sharp teeth and claws can inflict serious damage. And if you've ever tried to get a raccoon out of an attic or garage, you know just how nasty they can be. In relationships, a Raccoon defense is characterized by a profound insecurity, low self-esteem, and a lack of self-confidence that expresses itself as either manipulation or retaliation. While some Raccoons are prone to being perpetual manipulators, others are just plain nasty. Others, depending on circumstances, vacillate back and forth between these extremes.

Although Raccoon snarling can become quite aggressive, it's a less destructive form of aggressiveness than Tiger aggressiveness (all snarl and a lot of hissing). Where a Raccoon might let you have it with a hissing "Can't you hear, I said leave me alone!" a Tiger might impale you with, "Are you deaf? Or just deaf and stupid?"

Take a look at the following list to determine whether you or your partner have any Raccoon tendencies:

- Using manipulation through guilt, intellectual cleverness, or stubbornness, rather than assertiveness
- Nasty, bite-your-head-off snarling
- Indecisive, depending on others to make decisions
- Unable to express disagreement constructively—highly defensive
- Hard time being honest
- Lacking self-confidence
- When in conflict, either excessively remorseful or excessively insensitive
- When upset, usually preoccupied with details, lists, or organizing
- Prone to woe-is-me whining or feeling persecuted
- Often feeling like a victim
- Prone to depressed or anxious mood
- Untrusting, never feeling safe enough
- Often excessively emotional or dramatic
- Seeking approval

Peacocks: Those Who Love Themselves

When you think of a peacock you usually think of its fancy display of iridescent feathers displayed like a fan for all to see. Human Peacocks also like to be noticed, but more importantly they are the ones who are most impressed with their plumage. Peacocks control by creating an egocentric world of self-adoration that allows them to become less dependent on others (thereby less vulnerable) for their sense of safety and control. Let's face it, if I can feel totally in love with myself, why do I need to depend on others?

Although Peacocks can initially come across as great lovers and romantics, this is nothing more than a display of their feathers; in time Peacocks invariably seem to lose interest in a relationship—this is their unconscious defense against the vulnerability inherent with legitimate intimacy. It's this defensive disinterest combined with the Peacock's appetite for being adored and admired that can lead to infidelity. On the other hand, Peacocks are definitely capable of legitimate love and commitment in a relationship, but they must first be willing to stop using their plumage as a defense against true intimacy.

Take a look at the following list to determine whether you or your partner have any Peacock tendencies:

- Grandiose and self-important
- Requiring excessive admiration
- Liking being the star
- Lacking empathy and patience for others
- Displaying an arrogant attitude
- Usually opportunistic, seeking to take advantage
- Possessing inflated self-image or self-worth
- Seeing others as inferior
- Typically forming shallow relationships
- Preoccupied with self, not a good listener, egocentric
- Liking being the center of attention
- Typically becoming bored when the focus is on someone else

- Craving for material things—clothes, cars, wealth, etc.
- Unable to make a true commitment
- Not desiring close relationships

Catalytic Self-Coaching Heads-Up

As with all the reflexive strategies, it's not uncommon to see overlap. Often there's a thin line separating Elephant dominance from Tiger aggression, Raccoon manipulation from Turtle withdrawal, or Peacock arrogance from Elephant conceit. Your aim is to use the designations laid out here only as a general guideline to help you identify any and all destructive, insecurity-driven behavior.

The important thing to understand is that regardless of what we call it, all insecurity-driven behavior has the same root—insecurity. And that's what we're going after in the chapters ahead.

The Importance of Control

Now that you're familiar with my menagerie, we're going to emphasize *why* these patterns exist and why they're so resistant to change. But first, note that it's not uncommon for a person to employ more than one strategy of control. For example, a partner who resorts to emotional abuse (Tiger-type) can at times easily slip into a dominant, Elephant-like type of bullying. "If I can't pick the restaurant, then I'm not going!" The same partner, given the right circumstances, may also resort to drinking too much or excessive TV watching, all in an attempt to avoid communicating (Turtle-type). What's important is for you to begin to recognize your partner's typical *patterns*. Why? Because patterns are predictable. By not being caught off guard, you'll stand a much better chance of not becoming involved in your usual tit-for-tat struggles. At first you may find it confusing, but in time you will see that there are always discrete clusters of behaviors that are indeed predictable—if not inevitable—outcomes of insecurity. *Tap-jerk.*

At this point, let me introduce you to Roz and Frank. Their rather turbulent marriage will illuminate this critical concept of reflexive relating.

Roz and Frank: Twenty-Eight Years of Struggle

Roz, a fifty-year-old artist and mother, only seemed to be tuned in to her husband Frank's negativity, which she felt she understood chapter and verse. But what she didn't know was that it was insecurity that drove his negativity, and that she and her husband had long ago entered into a destructive dance of reflexive relating.

It was the summer of 1977 when Roz met Frank at a New York City nightclub. If it wasn't for her friend's engagement celebration, Roz would never have agreed to leave her apartment in the Bronx for that celebratory drink. Like so many other New Yorkers that summer, she was worried about a serial killer on the loose known as the Son of Sam.

Roz didn't recall why, sitting at the bar with her girlfriend, she was attracted to the stocky, rather short guy sitting next to her, but when he struck up a conversation and told her that he was attending the police academy, she felt an inexplicable sense of safety and security—something she had been lacking all that summer.

Roz and Frank dated for about a year and then were married. Frank was all that Roz was looking for—strong, confident, a man in control—a man you could feel safe with. He graduated from the academy and became one of New York's finest—at least that's how he felt about himself.

Roz always knew about Frank's controlling ways—after all, this is what she was initially attracted to. But in those early years when she was dealing with her own insecurities, Frank's take-charge attitude only seemed like a tonic. Over time, however, his strength slowly began to morph into something abrasive and ugly as Roz began to feel emotionally pushed around by him.

> Shortly after we were married, Frank started telling me how to live my life. He told me who I could hang out with, who I could call . . . and God forbid I didn't want to hang out with his buddies on

the force. When we'd party with his friends things would quickly get out of hand; too much drinking, smoking, and if you ask me, too much vulgarity.

When the twins were born—as you can imagine—I was totally absorbed. Frank was fine at first, but then he began giving me grief about not spending enough time with him, accusing me of neglecting his needs and thinking only of the twins. That was the point in our marriage where Frank became . . . ugly . . . nasty. Since then, his habit is to always find fault in everything I do or say. He constantly criticizes me and embarrasses me in front of others. To be honest, I don't know why I've put up with it this long.

My girlfriends tell me that Frank is just being a jerk—that doesn't help. I'm finally beginning to see just how selfish Frank is. For Frank, intimacy isn't about intimacy, it's about sexual gratification—his gratification! He's let me know more than once that a man needs intimacy and if he wasn't going to get it at home, I couldn't blame him if he looked somewhere else! Maybe he's right, but I honestly have no desire. Maybe if we had a decent relationship.

We've been married twenty-eight years and if you were to ask me if Frank has ever had an affair, I wouldn't be able to tell you. He could be going out and cheating, I just don't know, he can be very destructive. I guess it all hit me one morning when I went to the computer and found that he never logged off of his AOL account. I clicked the recent history tab and what I saw brought everything I've been feeling into focus. Most of the sites he had recently visited were porn sites, but some were for singles . . . dating services! As soon as Frank walked in the door that night, I told him I was going to make an appointment for marital counseling. He just snickered and did what he always does when I try to get him to talk—he heads straight for the refrigerator to get a beer.

I made the counseling appointment and decided not to tell Frank until the morning of the appointment. Big mistake. He went ballistic! "You're kidding, right? I don't need counseling, maybe you do. I have no intentions of some kumbaya shrink telling me his view of right and wrong." Not wanting to cancel the appointment, I decided to come alone.

Roz went on to tell me about Frank. He was the youngest of three brothers and was always picked on and humiliated by his rather sadistic oldest brother. His father died when he was young and the family went to live with his grandmother in a run-down basement of a two-family house in New Jersey. In elementary school, Frank was noticeably smaller and stockier than everyone in his grade, which fetched him the nickname "Fire Hydrant"—"Hydrant" for short. Frank was so tormented by these taunts that he, more than once, superficially cut his arms and legs with a razor.

In Frank's eyes, everyone else was better off. He particularly resented the kids who were dropped off at school by their parents. These were the kids with clean, pressed clothes—that fit! In a world of privileged kids who seemed to have everything handed to them, Frank felt he was a have-not. In order to insulate himself from the pain and insecurity that he felt, he did the only thing that seemed to make a difference—he began to create a tough-guy persona. He remembers thinking, "If you can't beat 'em, beat 'em." Frank was on his way to becoming the class bully.

Every morning, rain or shine, Frank was up at the crack of dawn delivering newspapers in the neighborhood. He managed to save every penny until he could afford a set of weights. He built a bench in the garage and began in earnest to build up his muscles. Within a year he had a formidable build, one that served him well in his frequent fights at school.

By the time he was in high school, Frank had become a bit more confident with the newfound respect his classmates showed him. He went out for the football team and found a channel for his hotheaded rage. He became a star linebacker on the team and earned some league honors for his accomplishments. This was a turning point for Frank. Now he was respected and revered for his strength and intimidating powers. By his senior year, he actually began to feel pretty good about himself. For all intents and purposes, Frank's deep-seated reflex of insecurity was dormant. Years later it would reemerge in his marriage to Roz.

Roz's Predicament

By understanding Frank's reflex of insecurity, you are now in a better position to appreciate Roz's catalytic challenge. From his history you can see where Frank may have managed to sidestep his insecurity, but sidestepping his problem didn't make it go away—clearly not in his marriage. Frank was "Mr. Innocent" in his own mind. He would be the first to tell you that since he had no problems with other relationships or at work on the police force (even though he was reprimanded twice for excessive use of force), it was obvious to him that Roz's complaints were nothing more than her own incessant nagging.

Frank was living in a self-made, defensive bubble. He saw no point in questioning his need to drink excessively (drinking excessively is a form of Turtle escape) or to put Roz down and humiliate her (this is a form of Elephant domination). He was just having a good time, and as for Roz, well, she was just too damn sensitive. Frank was used to excusing himself and rationalizing his behavior away. (This is an Elephant tendency to intellectually dominate; that is, Elephants always excuse themselves, turn the tables on you, or tell you that you don't know what you're talking about.) All in all, Frank was quite pleased with himself—especially when he was in uniform. He would often boast to Roz how he would get someone he pulled over for a traffic violation to squirm or beg for his "mercy" (this is both Peacock grandiosity and Elephant dominance). According to Frank, *he* had no problems.

Through our talks, Roz began to understand and appreciate that the impetus for Frank's abominable behavior was his fragile ego. Where she once felt that he was driven by power, now she knew the truth—it wasn't power, it was weakness and insecurity. This new perspective opened Roz's eyes as she began to see many examples where Frank would need to escape, deflect, or deny anything or anyone that started to get too close to his pocket of insecurity. This was where Roz's Catalytic Self-Coaching began—with an awareness of Frank's knee-jerk reflexiveness.

Roz's insights enabled her to take a significant step forward and to stop challenging Frank's insecurity. Armed with understanding and insight, she was in a much better position to extricate herself from the cycle of reflexive relating that she too had become a part of. But in order for her to fully break out of the reflexive cycle, she needed to proceed with one more insight—an awareness of her own controlling patterns. She needed to open her eyes and check out her own "animals."

Roz's Catalytic Solution

For starters, Roz had to get in touch with her worrisome, avoidant (Turtle) habits of control, and simultaneously to stop comparing Frank to other men she knew: "Why can't you be like Dan? He's so nice to Alice. He helps around the house, he's a real gentleman—he knows how to treat a woman." Ouch! (This is a snarling, manipulative Raccoon tendency with a slight hint of Tiger aggression, that is, wanting to hurt.) What really helped Roz tame her own "animals" was the realization that Frank feared true intimacy. Keep in mind that ever since those early days delivering newspapers in the freezing cold, Frank was determined to rise above his insecurities. He had long ago pushed aside his doubts and fears and now needed to stay one step removed from them. Roz needed to understand the paradoxical situation that Frank's lack of true intimacy (not his tunnel-visioned view of sex = intimacy) was an expression of fear. "What if someone gets to see the real me? The fearful have-not who isn't as good as others?" Frank had been unconsciously steering his marriage in such a way as to minimize the opportunity for Roz to "find him out."

From these details, you can see that one of Roz's most important catalytic efforts was to remove her Raccoon habit of challenging or snarling at Frank. Once she understood Frank's insecurity-driven reflexes, she was in a position to see the solution. You may be wondering why or how Roz would just let go of her insecurities and give up her defensiveness. Although this may sound like a tall order, it doesn't need to be. Not once you understand—really understand—that your partner's shabby behavior isn't personal. It's not about hurting, humiliating, bullying, or threatening you—it's about your partner desperately clinging to habits of defense. Why? Because the ego, when insecure and feeling threatened, does what comes naturally: self-preservation, or strategies designed to control that which we fear.

Bottom line, the catalytic partner's goal is to reduce the perception of danger and threat so that the problem partner's fragile ego can be encouraged to abandon its defensive posture. I can't stress enough how important it is for the catalytic partner to remove any and all behavior that is perceived as threatening to the fragile-egoed partner. Do this and you will be creating the necessary vacuum where neutrality can be established, followed by constructive healing.

Resolution

Roz, armed with a newfound awareness of the bigger picture, began to work to encourage (rather than discourage) Frank to see himself more clearly in the here and now, rather than allowing his past to distort his present. (Want a great definition of neurosis? It's a contamination of the present with the past.) As Roz diligently used her Self-Coaching insights to defuse her own insecurities and reflexive behavior, the vacuum she created (she was no longer part of the problem) was clearly catalytic in getting Frank to agree to join us in counseling. By this time he was ready to put his guard down and become a man—a real man, not a facsimile based on an adolescent, macho interpretation.

Once in counseling, Frank needed to learn to stop identifying with his "Fire Hydrant" past and to recognize that his "animals" were attempts to compensate for his fragile ego. His job was to learn to see himself and his relationship based on here-and-now issues and realities. This required both effort and awareness, but it wasn't as difficult as you might think—not once his defensive bubble was removed. All Frank needed to keep motivated was to ask himself, "What's the truth?" And now, with corrected vision, he was in a position to choose truth over old, outdated perceptions. Where distortions of the truth (fictions) were once dictating, now the objective reality was becoming obvious. As is the case with all struggle, personal or relational, the truth shall set you free!

No longer having to protect himself from Roz, Frank began to find that underneath his Elephant need to dominate and bully, there was a sensitive, caring person. Since he didn't need to impress Roz with his aggressive Elephant-Tiger control over the relationship, he felt free to explore different aspects of himself (although I must admit, when Roz mentioned that Frank tried to hide his tears while they were watching a sad movie together, Frank, which wasn't at all his style, blushed and actually began shuffling his feet). This, the cop with the attitude, the bully who left his classmates quaking in their boots, this was Frank's ultimate victory. Victory over his habit of insecurity—Frank no longer feared being honest about who he was.

Frank and Roz and You

With Frank and Roz as an example, you may now understand the two essential components of Catalytic Self-Coaching mentioned in the introduction of this chapter—insecurity and control. It's insecurity that underwrites reflexive relating by attempting to protect us from perceived harm. Reflexive relating sooner or later becomes toxic to effective relating. Roz and Frank had a 50-50 problem where Frank's underlying Elephant-Tiger-Peacock habits of insecurity contributed 50 percent and Roz's inadvertent Turtle-Raccoon reflexives contributed the other 50 percent. By subtracting her 50 percent of the problem, Roz was able to create a relationship vacuum, which was the catalytic instigation for Frank to abandon his need for unwarranted protection. Underneath all the reflexive defensiveness was a natural and spontaneous capacity for legitimate relating and loving.

P.S.

Remember when I mentioned that Roz discovered Frank was visiting dating sites on his computer? Turns out that he would visit these sites not with cheating on his mind, but to see whether he was still competitive. Since he ultimately felt he was going to be abandoned by Roz, he was trying to figure out where he would stand if he were single. It was all a matter of his trying to see if he was going to be okay. He was just trying to feel more in control.

6

Assessing Your Reflexive Personality Patterns

If you're honest with yourself, you probably already have a relatively accurate appraisal of your shortcomings. After all, don't forget you're the problem-solving partner. Unfortunately, when it comes to maximizing your Self-Talk efforts, you're going to need more than a "relative" appraisal. To be truly effective, you're going to need an objective understanding of exactly what you have to work on.

The quizzes that follow are designed to help you gain a much-needed working awareness of your destructive menagerie of habits. By using the personality data from the self-quizzes in this chapter, you will have no trouble in upcoming chapters generating a Self-Portrait that will express these reflexive, controlling patterns in an easy-to-understand diagram. Once armed with this information, you'll be in the best possible position to begin to neutralize your negative contributions to the relationship struggle, which in turn will allow you to maximize your catalytic effect.

The Truth Shall Set You Free

When you take the series of quizzes that follow, try to be as honest with yourself as possible. If you want to be truly catalytic, you must know what you're dealing with. Any self-deception at this point will only hinder your efforts later when you approach your partner. And don't be overly concerned with your current scores. They're only used to establish your baseline, from which you will be able to mark your progress as you follow your Self-Coaching training. You'll be testing yourself again at a later date to compare and record your progress.

One final caution: please understand that these quizzes are not meant to be a precise assessment of your personality; they're only meant to be used as tools to alert you to any destructive tendencies that may exist—tools, nonetheless, that you will find invaluable when it comes to creating your Self-Portrait. In the next chapter you will learn how to use your scores to produce your Self-Portrait.

Self-Quizzes

The following five quizzes represent the various reflexive patterns that may have infiltrated your behavior. Take each of them. Following each quiz you will find a simple scoring method. Keep your quiz scores handy as you read the upcoming chapters. (Note: since later in this program you may be offering these same quizzes to your partner, I suggest that you don't mark your answers directly in this book. You wouldn't want your partner to be influenced by your answers.)

Turtle Self-Quiz

Please read the following questions carefully, but don't overthink your responses. Circle your responses as being mostly true (T), sometimes true (S), or mostly false (F) as they generally pertain to your life, especially how they pertain to your relationship with your partner. As with all the quizzes in this book, the following is meant to be a general reference guide and not a validated scientific instrument. Answer every question even if you have to guess. The scoring is at the end of the quiz.

T S F I go out of my way to avoid confrontations.

T S F I prefer solitude.

T S F I don't care about socializing.

T S F I don't take criticism well.

T S F I generally feel uncertain or doubtful.

T S F I tend to be overemotional or hypersensitive.

T S F I never feel completely safe.

T S F I have a hard time telling my partner my true feelings.

T S F I often feel inferior to others.

T S F I worry too much.

T S F I find it difficult to trust my partner.

T S F I tend to be suspicious of other people's motives.

T S F I don't like to take risks.

T S F I usually have a hard time making decisions.

T S F I don't like commitments.

T S F I usually struggle at parties.

T S F If I drink, I usually become more outgoing.

T S F I watch too much TV (computer, reading, etc.).

T S F Relationships have always been a problem for me.

T S F I often feel guilty.

Score each mostly true response (T) one point, each sometimes true response (S) one-half point, and each mostly false response (F) zero points. Add up your points.

Your score: _____

Tiger Self-Quiz

Please read the following questions carefully, but don't overthink your responses. Circle your responses as being mostly true (T), sometimes true (S), or mostly false (F) as they generally pertain to your life, especially how they pertain to your relationship with your partner. Answer every question even if you have to guess. The scoring is at the end of the quiz.

T   S   F   I often feel attacked.

T   S   F   When threatened, I can do or say things I later regret.

T   S   F   I'm often irritable.

T   S   F   I tend to be too sarcastic.

T   S   F   My feelings often leap from dislike to hate.

T   S   F   I'm too competitive.

T   S   F   I'm easily angered.

T   S   F   I've gotten "physical" with my partner at least once.

T   S   F   I often regret my behavior.

T   S   F   In general, I'm not a trusting person.

T   S   F   I usually have to get even.

T   S   F   I can be very hurtful.

T   S   F   I'm often suspicious.

T   S   F   I'm too negative.

T   S   F   My anger has gotten me in trouble in the past.

T   S   F   I have a quick temper.

T   S   F   I've been told I yell too much.

T   S   F   I can be threatening.

T   S   F   When I'm upset, I don't consider consequences.

T   S   F   I have poor impulse control.

Score each mostly true response (T) one point, each sometimes true response (S) one-half point, and each mostly false response (F) zero points. Add up your points.

Your score: _____

Elephant Self-Quiz

Please read the following questions carefully, but don't overthink your responses. Circle your responses as being mostly true (T), sometimes true (S), or mostly false (F) as they generally pertain to your life, especially how they pertain to your relationship with your partner. Answer every question even if you have to guess. The scoring is at the end of the quiz.

T   S   F   I'm often very stubborn.

T   S   F   I like to be in charge.

T   S   F   I can usually prevail in an argument with my partner.

T   S   F   In an argument, I usually don't back down.

T   S   F   I tend to be black and white with my opinions.

T   S   F   I'm an opportunist who will do whatever it takes to win.

T   S   F   I tend to lie or twist the truth to get my way.

T   S   F   I get irritated very easily.

T   S   F   When I'm right, I'm right—no regrets.

T   S   F   I'm not very affectionate.

T   S   F   I've been told I'm arrogant.

T   S   F   I'm not very sensitive to my partner's feelings.

T   S   F   I've been accused of being irresponsible.

T   S   F   My needs come first.

T   S   F   I have a hard time if someone else tells me what to do.

T   S   F   No one bullies me.

T   S   F   If I'm not getting my way, I can be very intimidating.

T   S   F   I have a hard time admitting that I'm wrong.

T   S   F   I have a hard time *feeling* that I'm wrong.

T   S   F   I'm often irresponsible.

Score each mostly true response (T) one point, each sometimes true response (S) one-half point, and each mostly false response (F) zero points. Add up your points.

Your score: _____

Raccoon Self-Quiz

Please read the following questions carefully, but don't overthink your responses. Circle your responses as being mostly true (T), sometimes true (S), or mostly false (F) as they generally pertain to your life, especially how they pertain to your relationship with your partner. Answer every question even if you have to guess. The scoring is at the end of the quiz.

T   S   F   I have a hard time making decisions.

T   S   F   I have low self-confidence.

T   S   F   I absolutely hate conflict.

T   S   F   I sometimes feel depressed.

T   S   F   I've been accused of being a martyr.

T   S   F   I need a lot of approval.

T   S   F   I can't help being suspicious of my partner.

T   S   F   I often feel like a victim.

T   S   F   In an argument, I usually avoid disagreeing—I prefer fleeing to fighting.

T   S   F   I often feel anxious or overly stressed.

T   S   F   I'm too emotional.

T   S   F   I know I'm too insecure.

T   S   F   I usually get my way by manipulating: whining, pouting, or complaining.

T   S   F   I can flip from cringing to snarling.

T   S   F   I often use guilt in order to get my way with my partner.

T   S   F   When frustrated, I'm prone to being nasty.

T   S   F   I'm often not honest.

T   S   F   I have compulsive tendencies.

T   S   F   I have lots of fears.

T   S   F   My emotions can be excessive—especially if I feel cornered.

Score each mostly true response (T) one point, each sometimes true response (S) one-half point, and each mostly false response (F) zero points. Add up your points.

Your score: _____

Peacock Self-Quiz

Please read the following questions carefully, but don't overthink your responses. Circle your responses as being mostly true (T), sometimes true (S), or mostly false (F) as they generally pertain to your life, especially how they pertain to your relationship with your partner. Answer every question even if you have to guess. The scoring is at the end of the quiz.

T S F My partner has accused me of thinking too highly of myself.

T S F I need to be admired, applauded, or recognized for what I do.

T S F I like being the center of attention.

T S F I'm not a good listener.

T S F Many people like me, but I don't have many close friends.

T S F I usually find ways to win.

T S F I think I'm better than most people.

T S F My clothes are very important.

T S F I care a lot/too much what others think.

T S F I try to impress others.

T S F I like to flirt.

T S F I try not to depend on anyone.

T S F I'm impatient when I don't get my way.

T S F What goes on in my day seems more important than what goes on in my partner's day.

T S F I don't need people.

T   S   F   My looks are important.

T   S   F   I'm not afraid to take advantage of others.

T   S   F   I often feel that I'm better than others.

T   S   F   I wouldn't mind having an affair.

T   S   F   I'm not a giver.

Score each mostly true response (T) one point, each sometimes true response (S) one-half point, and each mostly false response (F) zero points. Add up your points.

Your score: _____

Moving On

Now that you have the raw data from your quizzes, it's time to begin some actual sketching. Sharpen up your number two pencils and get ready to start creating some visuals that are going to become crucial in your catalytic quest for further self-understanding and relationship clarity.

You may be tempted to look beyond your quiz scores and speculate about your partner's reflexive patterns. There's nothing wrong with that, but since we'll be doing this more formally in the chapters to follow, for now I suggest you keep your Self-Coaching efforts disciplined and focused on you as you proceed in the next chapter to learn to sketch your Self-Portrait. Having an accurate Self-Portrait in hand is a necessary prelude to the important Self-Talk work that begins in chapter 8.

7

Sketching Your
Self-Portrait

In chapter 5 you were introduced to five reflexive patterns of relating:

- Tigers: those who use aggression and hostility as a form of control.
- Turtles: those who control through avoidance and passivity.
- Elephants: those who bully or intimidate as a form of control.
- Raccoons: those who feel powerless and resort to manipulation, whining, or "snarling" as a form of control.
- Peacocks: those who control by becoming selfish, egocentric, and self-absorbed.

Now it's time to assess the extent to which these patterns contaminate your own personality. Before moving on to the Self-Talk training in chapter 8, it's time to do a bit of sketching. In this chapter I'm going to give you the tools to both assess and sketch your Self-Portrait. We'll be getting to your partner's patterns later.

It's important for you to understand that any reflexive patterns you may possess, as destructive as they may appear in your everyday life, are not life sentences. They have absolutely nothing to do with mental illness, genetic limitations, or character flaws; in fact, they're nothing more than *habits*—habits of insecurity that have infiltrated your life, your personality, and your relationship. And like all habits, they were learned, they can be broken, and they can be eliminated.

Self-Talk will be your tool for breaking these habits, but before you can effectively begin any Self-Talk training, you must first have a thorough awareness of any destructive patterns that may be tripping you up. In order to overcome personal limitations, and later to catalytically put an end to relationship struggle, only one motto will suffice: "Know thine enemy." Now it's time to see how to use the information derived from the preceding self-quizzes to sketch your Self-Portrait. In the diagram below, you will notice a half circle with numbers ranging from zero to 100. Each self-quiz represents a fifth of your total Self-Portrait with a maximum score of 20 points.

Self-Portrait Template

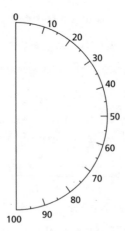

Let's say you had the following scores: Turtle score 8.5; Tiger score 3; Elephant score 10; Raccoon score 10.5; Peacock score 13. The example on the top of the next page would be your Self-Portrait.

Self-Portrait Example

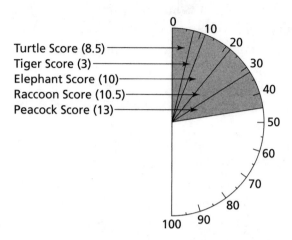

Turtle Score (8.5)
Tiger Score (3)
Elephant Score (10)
Raccoon Score (10.5)
Peacock Score (13)

On the half circle below, fill in each of your five scores. The area that contains your five scores is considered the relationship-unhealthy (RU) component of your personality. The area that remains after you've sketched your scores is the relationship-healthy component of your personality (RH).

Your Self-Portrait

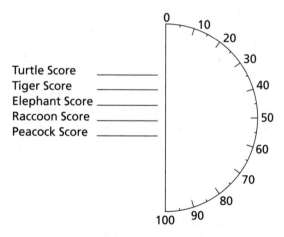

Turtle Score _____
Tiger Score _____
Elephant Score _____
Raccoon Score _____
Peacock Score _____

The scores from your quizzes are designed to show your reflexive patterns of insecurity and how these impact your relationship. Please note that your "healthy" component (RH) is not meant to be a measure of your *personal* mental health, but rather an estimation of your *relationship*-healthy potential. Your catalytic goal will be to use your Self-Talk training to decrease your unhealthy profile, while increasing your healthy profile.

Your Reflexive Pattern Ratio

Before concluding this chapter, there's one more piece of data we can use to help you understand your Self-Portrait—the Reflexive Pattern Ratio. If you're like me, just mentioning a ratio is enough to turn you off, but trust me, it's not complicated. Using the chart below, all you need to do is look up your relationship-healthy score and you'll see your ratio next to it. (For anyone inclined to do the math, the equation looks like this: Reflexive Pattern Ratio = RH/RU).

Using the data from the figure on the top of page 95 as an example, we begin by simply adding up the five quiz scores: Turtle 8.5 + Tiger 3 + Elephant 10 + Raccoon 10.5 + Peacock 13 = 45. The resulting score of 45 is the relationship-unhealthy score (RU). Since the half circle is 100 ticks, the remaining relationship-healthy score (RH) is 55 (that is, 100 − 45 = 55). Referring to the following table, you'll see that an RH score of 55 yields a ratio of 1.2. As you'll see from the discussion on pages 99–100, this score indicates moderate interference from reflexive patterns. Once you have your Reflexive Pattern Ratio, find the description that applies to your ratio on pages 98–101.

RH Score	Ratio Score		RH Score	Ratio Score
1	.01		11	.12
2	.02		12	.13
3	.03		13	.14
4	.04		14	.16
5	.05		15	.17
6	.06		16	.19
7	.07		17	.20
8	.08		18	.21
9	.09		19	.23
10	.11		20	.25

RH Score	Ratio Score	RH Score	Ratio Score
21	.26	56	1.2
22	.28	57	1.3
23	.29	58	1.3
24	.31	59	1.4
25	.33	60	1.5
26	.35	61	1.5
27	.36	62	1.6
28	.38	63	1.7
29	.40	64	1.7
30	.42	65	1.8
31	.44	66	1.9
32	.47	67	2.0
33	.49	68	2.1
34	.51	69	2.2
35	.53	70	2.3
36	.56	71	2.4
37	.58	72	2.5
38	.61	73	2.7
39	.63	74	2.8
40	.66	75	3.0
41	.69	76	3.1
42	.72	77	3.3
43	.75	78	3.5
44	.78	79	3.7
45	.81	80	4.0
46	.85	81	4.2
47	.88	82	4.5
48	.92	83	4.8
49	.96	84	5.2
50	1.0	85	5.6
51	1.0	86	6.1
52	1.0	87	6.6
53	1.1	88	7.3
54	1.1	89	8.0
55	1.2	90	9.0

(Continued)

RH Score	Ratio Score		RH Score	Ratio Score
91	10		96	24
92	11		97	32
93	13		98	49
94	15		99	99
95	19			

Ratio below .29: Extreme Interference from Reflexive Patterns

You need to understand that your excessive need to control, which is reflected in your reflexive patterns, is a major obstacle in your plans for relationship success. Your Self-Talk efforts, which are going to be a critical component to any catalytic success, are your first priority. It's imperative that you review your quiz results and become more familiar with your defensive tendencies. This familiarity is your first step in becoming more aware of your behavior. These efforts will serve you as you progress with your Self-Coaching/Self-Talk training. Since your score is in this range, you should plan on retaking the five quizzes in chapter 6 weekly in conjunction with your ongoing, daily Self-Talk efforts. Always compare your most recent quiz scores with your original scores. This is the best way to give yourself feedback while simultaneously assessing your Self-Coaching/Self-Talk progress. On the quizzes where you scored the highest, spend some time reflecting on your responses. Don't be critical—just more aware. For now, it's important that you stay encouraged and motivated. Increasing your awareness is the first step.

Ratio between .29 and .51: Significant Interference from Reflexive Patterns

Your significant need for control (reflexive patterns) is an obstacle in your plans for relationship success. Your Self-Talk efforts are going to be a necessary component to any catalytic success. Since your score is in this range, you should plan on retaking the five quizzes in chapter 6 weekly in conjunction with your ongoing, daily Self-Talk efforts. Always compare your most recent quiz scores with your original scores. This is the best way to give yourself feedback while simultaneously assessing your Self-Talk progress. You might want to review your quiz scores to help develop more awareness of your defensive, reflexive tendencies. Awareness is critical. Before there can be adequate change, you're going to need to increase your capacity for seeing defensive, insecurity-driven behavior while it's happening. Soon, with your Self-Coaching training, you'll be using this awareness to promote positive change.

Ratio between .53 and .85: Strong Interference from Reflexive Patterns

Your need for control (reflexive patterns), although not excessive, is still capable of producing ongoing obstacles to your plans for relationship success. Your Self-Talk efforts will be a necessary component to any catalytic success. Along with your Self-Talk training, make sure you begin to develop a capacity for catching any reflexive, insecurity-driven behavior. Once you catch yourself—stop! The awareness required to accomplish this won't be easy, but with practice you will improve. Since your score is in this range, you should plan on retaking the five quizzes in chapter 6 every two weeks in conjunction with your ongoing, daily Self-Talk efforts. Always compare your most recent quiz scores with your original scores as this is the best way to assess your Self-Talk progress. It's a good idea to review your quiz scores to help develop more awareness of your defensive, reflexive tendencies. The quicker you learn to stop yourself from falling prey to insecurity-driven patterns, the quicker you will progress.

Ratio between .88 and 1.3: Moderate Interference from Reflexive Patterns

Your moderate need for control (reflexive patterns), although not excessive, is still capable of producing occasional problems with your plans for relationship success. Your Self-Talk efforts will enhance your constructive approach to your relationship, thus contributing to your eventual catalytic success. Although there is still moderate interference, you definitely have the capacity for improvement. With a little patience, you should show rapid improvement. After reviewing your quiz results, begin insisting on more appropriate, less defensive behavior. You'll need to work at this, but if you stay patient and persistent, you'll see significant results. Since your score is in this range, you should plan on retaking the five quizzes in chapter 6 once a month in conjunction with your ongoing, daily Self-Talk efforts. Always compare your most recent quiz scores with your original scores as this is the best way to assess your Self-Talk progress. Although it's going to take some practice, you definitely have the capacity for interrupting or stopping reflexive behavior—work at it!

Ratio between 1.4 and 2.3: Mild Interference from Reflexive Patterns

Your mild need for control (reflexive patterns) is probably not a major obstacle to your plans for relationship success. Your Self-Talk efforts will be a way to fine-tune your already positive approach to your relationship, thus assuring your eventual catalytic success. Since your score is in this range, you should plan on retaking the five quizzes in chapter 6 once a month in conjunction with your ongoing, daily Self-Talk efforts. Along with your Self-Talk training you should review your quiz results to increase your awareness of any reflexive patterns. You should have no trouble catching yourself and putting a stop to any defensive behavior. This doesn't mean you won't have to practice, just be aware that with your mild interference, there should be no excuses—just do it! Always compare your most recent quiz scores with your original scores as this is the best way to assess your Self-Talk progress

Ratio of 2.4 or Higher: Minimal Interference from Reflexive Patterns

Your minimal need for control (reflexive patterns) is probably not going to interfere with your plans for relationship success. Your Self-Talk efforts will be a way to enhance your already positive and secure approach to your relationship, thus assuring your eventual catalytic success. Since your score is in this range, you should retake the five quizzes in chapter 6 after one month to verify your solid profile. Comparing your retest scores with your original scores is the best way to assess your Self-Talk progress.

For you, it's important to realize that your Catalytic Self-Coaching efforts need to become a way of life that ensures not only successful relating, but ongoing positive growth.

Getting Ready for Self-Talk

What you've accomplished in this chapter is an essential prerequisite to the Self-Talk steps that follow in the next chapter. Having a vivid understanding of your reflexive patterns will allow you to focus your attention and efforts where they're needed—on eliminating control and insecurity from your life and then from your relationship. Keep in mind that having a Self-Portrait to refer to is an indispensable tool in keeping you focused and tuned in to those areas of your personality that require your special attention.

8

Self-Talk, Step 1

Separate Facts from Fictions

I developed my technique of Self-Talk to help my patients, as well as the many visitors to my Web site, who kept asking what they could do on their own—independent of a private therapist or personal coach—to get beyond the habits of insecurity and control that were ruling and ruining their lives. When I introduced Self-Talk in my first Self-Coaching book, I designed the technique specifically to break the habits of insecurity that led to anxiety and depression. Since then, Self-Talk has gone through a significant evolution both in dealing with specific psychological problems and becoming an indispensable tool for achieving overall mental health.

For this book, I've further refined Self-Talk not only to reflect your need for personal growth and liberation from insecurity, but also as a tool to be used in your catalytic relating. You'll find Self-Talk to be a powerful technique that can change the course of your life and your relationship, no matter what the problem is. Sound far-fetched? Not if you understand that all psychological struggle is based on nothing more than a repetition of old habits and perceptions fueled by insecurity. Once you learn what you're doing that feeds these habits—and what you can do to starve them—you will be in a position to guarantee your success.

Catalytic Self-Coaching Reflection
No habit can persist if it's not fed.

Origins

In my earlier writings, I expressed how I was no stranger to anxiety, worry, rumination, and an assortment of other "controlling" life habits. My personal struggle was a major reason why I wound up in psychology. Unfortunately, my education didn't give me answers, just more questions. After years of study, exploration, training analysis, and frustration, I realized that I wasn't feeling much better than when I started! In some ways I was worse. I was still a chronic worrier, my fears were as entrenched as ever, and I plodded through life feeling discouraged and somewhat hopeless. How could this be? After all, I had spent over a decade in therapy exploring my childhood, my mother's controlling ways, my father's explosive temper, my anxiety, perfectionism, chronic fears, and so on—I *did* understand my past, but I was still quite miserable! Either I was a hopeless case or . . . what? It never occurred to me that maybe my therapy and my approach to understanding my problems was in fact the problem—until a rather serendipitous intervention from my training analyst set me free.

On that fateful day, my therapist inadvertently slipped during one of our sessions. As usual, I had been whining about how stuck I felt and how terrible my struggle was; in his understandable frustration with me as a patient, he blurted out two sarcastic words that changed my life forever: "Yes, dear." That was it! Those two words were about to send my world into a tailspin. As I drove home from the city that day, I was fuming. "How dare he treat me like a child!" "I'll show him!" That's when it hit me: *he was absolutely right!* I *was* acting like a child. Week after week, I was showing up and going over the same laundry list of can'ts, shoulds, have-tos, and what-ifs. I was literally asking him to tell me what to do, to guide me, and yes, to *save* me . . . from me!

On the heels of this revelation came perhaps the single most important word that has ever crept into my mind—*responsibility.* I realized that if I was going to stop struggling, if I—without my therapist—was going to change, really change, I was going to have to take personal *responsibility* for my life. For years, I had inadvertently handed over responsibility for change to my therapist. Why? Because I, like so many others over the past hundred years, had become indoctrinated with the belief that psychological struggle has to do with arcane, unconscious forces that are beyond the reach of mere mortals to decipher—at least not without the trained guidance of a psychologist.

So I realized I had a choice: I was either going to spend another ten years scratching my head, or I was going to take responsibility for my problems. I opted to take responsibility—but how? Since my traditional efforts had failed, I was left with one conclusion—break tradition and head out in a totally new direction. After all, I was trained in psychology. Right? What was stopping me from doing some exploring? As I saw it, I had nothing to lose. Absolutely nothing.

Coaching versus Therapy

In the decade following my training analysis, my trial-and-error efforts at taking responsibility for my mental health began to pay off. I was honestly beginning to change! At first I couldn't put my finger on exactly what I was doing, or why, but I was acutely aware of one thing—I was taking responsibility for my life, especially my thoughts.

Slowly, more instinctively at first, I was beginning to see psychological struggle in a whole new light. As I began moving away from traditional approaches that included dream interpretation, free association, and endless historical dissection, I quite naturally found myself trading in my old attitude of passivity for a more active and energetic relationship with my patients. I realized that in order to get my patients to assume responsibility for their problems I was going to have to (1) offer a new, simplified understanding of psychological struggle, (2) overcome the inertia perpetrated by insecurity, and (3) devise and implement a simplified plan for dismantling the patterns of thinking that support habits of insecurity.

Let's review these three points.

1. A Simplified Understanding

First, the simplified understanding of psychological struggle was, as I discussed earlier in this book, the idea that the root cause of psychological suffering is not mental illness or genetic anomalies. The cause is insecurity—insecurity and the habits of control that result from trying to protect ourselves from the learned vulnerability of our past. As you might suspect, many people balk at the simplicity of my ideas. Last year I gave a lecture at New York's 92nd Street Y discussing my Self-Coaching philosophy. Afterward a psychotherapist trained in Freudian psychoanalysis came up to me and told me that she totally understood what I said and felt excited by it, but unfortunately in order for her to truly embrace my methods, she would have to abandon all her years of training. I knew where she was coming from; it's hard to shift gears and give up old routines and beliefs—hard but not impossible.

2. Overcoming Inertia

The second point, overcoming inertia and convincing my patients that they could change, was pivotal in forcing me to take that final step away from my traditional psychological roots. I remember working with a young man who had been struggling with anxiety and panic attacks. I heard myself telling him, "You keep looking to me to make your anxiety go away. I can't do that for you. And as long as you're waiting for me to 'heal' you, you're avoiding the responsibility necessary for you to change. Stop thinking of me as your psychologist . . . Think of me as your . . . coach!" This session happened ten years before I ever heard the term *coaching* used for anything other than athletics, yet the metaphor had a dramatic and immediate result, both for my patient and for me.

Coaching! This was the concept I had been looking for. No longer was I analyzing, interpreting, or being responsible for my patients' struggles—I was *coaching* them to take responsibility for their destructive habits and to believe and trust in themselves and in life. Now I had a concept for my approach. My patients immediately connected with this idea, confirming what I suspected: Self-Coaching was just a better, friendlier, more effective concept for producing results than traditional therapy. As they say, the proof was in the pudding.

Ask yourself, what comes to mind when you think of therapy? Sage advice from a doctor? Dream analysis? Murky, unconscious interpretations? Okay, now what comes to mind when you think of the word *coaching*? Someone standing on the sidelines, prompting, encouraging, and rallying his athletes? Someone who provides a winning strategy or game plan? Or how about someone who picks you up when you're down and infuses you with motivation to prevail? In my opinion, combining coaching with therapy is what's needed if psychology is ever going to evolve from its century-old malaise.

3. A Simplified Plan Called Self-Talk

The third element in helping my patients and readers was to furnish them with a simplified plan for dismantling the patterns of thinking that support the habits of insecurity. That plan is called Self-Talk.

As my new philosophy began to crystallize, I began to understand just how wily our thoughts can be when we feel victimized by life. "I can't do that!" "Yes, but what if I fail?" Without ever really noticing these thoughts, we inadvertently wind up feeding our habit of insecurity. One major reason why we're such easy marks for insecurity is because we've become identified with these habits—it feels totally natural for a perfectionist to struggle with loose ends or for the worrier to ask "what if?" It feels natural, not because it *is* natural, but because we are creatures of habit and in time what gets repeated often enough begins to overshadow and overwhelm our true personality lying beneath it.

If you're intent on breaking a habit of insecurity, then, be prepared for a struggle, just as with any other habit you've faced in the past. Habits, by their very nature, are resistant to change. Ask any nail biter or cigarette smoker. Mark Twain once quipped, "Quitting smoking is easy. I've done it a thousand times." And with any habit, there's a point where the habit, not you, begins to call the shots. Yet in spite of their insidious nature, all habits are learned and all habits can be broken. All habits!

It all boils down to whether your habit gets fed or whether it gets starved. In order to starve a habit you need to cut off its food supply. Food supply? With smoking it's nicotine, with obesity it's sugar and starch, and with insecurity it's cutting out defensiveness, doubts, fears, and negatives. These are the insecurity-driven thoughts that keep your habit of insecurity well nourished.

Self-Talk is my three-step plan for interrupting the food supply to these habits, thereby liberating you from the patterns of control that have crept into your life. If you do nothing, your habit will own you. As you probably know from previous attempts to change, doing something without proper direction or true understanding will only frustrate you. But doing something that includes a proven strategy for conquering these needless destructive patterns will not only give you the relief you've longed for, it will also be your foundation for becoming a true catalyst for your partner.

Separating Facts from Fictions

The first step in learning Self-Talk is to separate facts from fictions. With a little practice, you'll find this a relatively straightforward task. You can begin practicing Step 1 the next time you find yourself upset, struggling, anxious, or depressed, simply by asking yourself the following question: "Is what I'm feeling (or reacting to) a fact or a fiction?" If, for example, you're feeling stress over an actual tax audit, then you can acknowledge that your stress is circumstantially driven and is indeed a fact. If, on the other hand, you're feeling anxious because you fear you *may* be audited this year, this is a fiction. It's a fiction because you're peering into the future and predicting something that may or may not happen—I call this *time-traveling*. Fictions are based on projections of insecurity (that is, things that may go awry in life, the what-ifs), not actual and factual life circumstances. I quote Mark Twain once again, who got it right when he wrote, "I am an old man and have known a great many troubles, but most of them never happened."

For most people, habits of insecurity, like most habits, become reflexive over time. It's not unusual for any habit that gets repeated enough to feel natural. Saying this differently, over a long enough period of time, we become identified with our habits. "I'm just a worrier." "I've always been a perfectionist." When your insecurity makes you an overthinker, worrier, or ruminator, you inadvertently wind up with the habit of treating fictions as facts—a habit that can easily go unnoticed. Unnoticed doesn't mean you're not affected. Just ask anyone who suffers from panic attacks how devastating groundless thoughts can be, especially when such fictitious thoughts are being treated as realities.

Starting right now, let's begin your training by looking more closely at any feeling that's driven by insecurity. You may recall from past chapters that insecurity typically expresses itself in the form of doubts, fears, or negatives. Keep a keen eye open for any of the usual suspects and be willing to challenge yourself: "There's no hope for this relationship." Fact or fiction? "After what happened, I'll never feel excitement for my partner again." Fact or fiction?

Perhaps the single most important point I can make is that *feelings are not facts*. Sure, a feeling that your partner is hopeless or that you'll never feel excitement again might *feel* like a fact, but it's not. Why? Because you can't know the future, and as improbable as a hopeless partner changing may seem, or however unlikely it seems that you will ever find excitement, you can't rule it out—stranger things have happened! No one has a crystal ball, and yet insecurity acts as if you were Nostradamus, treating your predictions and anticipations as factual revelations.

Insecurity isn't limited to gazing into the future, asking "what if?" Sometimes insecurity will simply wind up misinterpreting the available facts—misinterpreting according to insecurity's view of the world. Let me tell you about Jill and how her insecurity took a few facts and turned them into fictions—fictions that drove her and her husband, Mike, into therapy.

Jill happens to be a very jealous Raccoon who thought her worst nightmare had come true. She had a handful of facts that mistakenly led her to conclude that Mike was having an affair. It all started one morning when Jill was cleaning her husband's desk. As was her jealous habit, she would often rifle through his things, "just to be sure." She came across a crumpled note that had missed the wastebasket. Scribbled on the note was a cryptic message: "Call Lisa *today* re: date for dancing—Jill's not around next week!" Jill felt a chill as she suddenly began to connect the dots: Mike had recently lost fifteen pounds; he had joined a gym, and lately seemed to have a lot more late-night meetings. And now she had this note! One thing she knew for sure: Mike, who always complained of having two left feet, never, ever danced with her! And now he was planning a meeting with someone named Lisa to go dancing!

Jill recalls feeling her legs buckle as she began to feel a wave of nausea and anxiety. "The bastard! How could he do this to me?" Her mind began spinning out of control. "How could I have been so stupid . . . What if he's getting ready to leave me? I can't manage on my own . . . "

Jill spent the next twenty-four hours ruminating, vacillating between anger, depression, anxiety, and confusion. Finally she couldn't take it any longer. She called her husband, who had just left for work, and told him to turn around and come home. "We have to talk." When Mike walked in the door, Jill was in a snarling Raccoon frame of mind—she blurted out, "You pathetic coward! I knew it! I knew it! Who is this slut Lisa?" Flummoxed, Mike was frozen. "How did you know about Lisa?" Jill was gasping for breath, almost collapsing as her worst fears were unfolding—"He admits it!"

After a long pause, Mike, now red-faced, fired back, "For our anniversary this year I wanted to do something special. I booked a cruise for us this summer and made an appointment at the dance studio for us to learn a few dance steps before the vacation—with our new dance instructor, Lisa! I had to cancel our *surprise* first lesson because the other night you told me you were going out of town to visit your mother this weekend."

This story, which was recounted for me in therapy, was the impetus for Jill and Mike to come into counseling. You might think that after her misinterpretation, Jill would be a bit less willing to leap to conclusions. According to Mike, just the opposite happened. "Jill does this to me all the time. She is constantly suspicious and insisting that I'm not being forthright. I'm tired of being called a liar. Since the Lisa episode, Jill has been on a mission to prove there's something wrong with our marriage. It doesn't make sense." It didn't make sense to Mike until he began to understand that Jill's profound sense of insecurity—which she fed by treating her doubts (fictions) as if they were facts—compelled her to look for reasons why she couldn't trust her husband, why she couldn't feel safe.

As a postscript to this story, Mike had joined the gym and lost fifteen pounds because his annual physical indicated that his blood pressure was too high. Rather than start on medication, he chose to try some lifestyle changes. Unfortunately, he also chose not to burden Jill with this news. As for his late-night meetings, well, they were just late-night meetings, coincidences. Coincidences can easily become the fuel of neurosis!

Don't Be Fooled

Why are we, like Jill, so likely to treat feelings and insecurity-driven thoughts as if they are facts? What exactly can be done when insecurity mugs you? For starters, you can begin simply by asking, "Am I reacting to facts or fictions?" Just asking this question will reorient you. Rather than automatically leaping, you're at least insisting on some conscious scrutiny. And most times, just this consideration is enough to derail potential problems—not always (that's why we have two more Self-Talk steps), but often. Unless you learn to differentiate between the facts of your life and the distortions perpetrated by insecurity, like Jill, you will never progress beyond your own confusions—nor will your relationship.

> *Catalytic Self-Coaching Reflection*
> Unless and until you can verify something,
> treat it as a fiction.

In the previous example, how about we cut Jill a bit of slack? Based on the coincidence of events, she certainly had cause to be concerned. But if you recall from earlier chapters, concern deals with facts, worry with projections of negativity. What were the facts for Jill's jealousy? Fact: there was an unexplained note about a person named Lisa. Fact: her husband's behavior had changed (losing weight, buying clothes, meetings). The fictions were: he was having an affair with a woman named Lisa. Fiction: losing weight, buying clothes, and so on were an indication that he was interested in another woman. I'm not saying that Jill didn't have reason to be concerned. Let's face it, even a very secure person would have been thrown off balance by that note. But had Jill been able to recognize that it wasn't the so-called facts that upset her, it was her *interpretation* of those facts, she might have been able to avoid her meltdown—or at least temper it by insisting that she was going to hear Mike's explanation first.

Catalytic Self-Coaching Reflection
Without verifiable facts, remain neutral.

In all fairness, let me present the other side of the coin. Sometimes feelings (and fictions)—especially when not driven by insecurity—can become verified as facts. Had Lisa actually been someone Mike was having an affair with, then Jill's feelings would have been elevated to fact status. But until and unless you can confirm a tentative fact (or feeling) as an actual fact, you must remain neutral and treat it as a fiction. I know how hard this can be, especially when insecurity is throwing horrific thoughts into your mind and you lack sufficient self-trust to know the difference. Just keep in mind that you have much more to gain by waiting for facts than by risking the damage of half-baked fictions. No innocent person likes to be accused wrongly.

Mike and Jill's story shows you how insecurity can project itself into a relationship. But insecurity is opportunistic, and it can just as easily become a personal nightmare. Everyone at one time or another has had crazy, silly, embarrassing thoughts. While a more secure person will pay little or no attention to these inane fictions as they flit by, an insecure person latches on to them. When this happens, these absurd fictions become hooks for insecurity to snag itself on. I've worked with patients who have gone to stealthy measures to "prove" infidelity—everything from E-ZPass and cell phone records to phone tapping, video surveillance, and private detectives. In a broken relationship, these measures could be explained, but in a relationship that's not broken and only eroded by distrust, they become time bombs. Without a sufficient amount of self-trust, the resulting confusion over what is factual and what is fiction can be very disorienting.

Here are a few of insecurity's wily thoughts that I've encountered over the years. Each of these fictions was initially felt to be a fact, yet every one was debunked in the course of therapy:

A perfectly happy husband, for no apparent reason, had the following thought/fiction: "Maybe I don't love my wife!"

Fact: Every time this husband began to feel too comfortable and safe, he would invariably encounter an intrusive, insecurity-driven thought. "Maybe I don't love my wife! How can I be sure that I do? Maybe I'm fooling myself?" This happens when insecurity convinces you that you need to be looking over your shoulder in order to stay safe. Without adequate self-trust even thoughts without any factual basis are treated as potential realities . . . just in case! As for him feeling that he didn't love his wife, well, this was the just his apprehension du jour.

An unbelievably loving, instinctual mother had the following upsetting thought/fiction: "How do I really know that I won't hurt my child?"

Fact: More than anything in the world this mom wanted to be a great mother, but she had so little self-trust, she could only believe that she would be the "worst" mother. Her history was replete with projections of negativity and failure. Insecurity will always look for your Achilles' heel in order to throw you off balance. FYI: she did turn out to be a *great* mom.

A perfectly healthy, athletic woman, following an annual physical, had the following thought/fiction: "How do I know I don't have cancer? Doctors miss things all the time."

Fact: This woman's health was verified by the many doctors and tests she had, so her fear had nothing to do with her physical health. This fiction was reflecting her deep-seated insecurity that had her convinced, "Since I can't trust life, how can I trust that my body won't fail me?"

A perfectly reasonable, responsible man of fifty had the following scary thought/fiction: "How do I know I won't jump off that balcony?"

Fact: This man was not suicidal or even depressed; he was suffering from an insecurity hook. He didn't want to hurt himself, far from it; he took great care of himself, jogged every day, and took his health very seriously. He *knew* this was a fiction from the start, but he just couldn't take the risk to let go of the thoughts. He said, "What if I'm wrong?"

A businesswoman who has traveled without incident for the past ten years had the following intimidating thought/fiction: "What if I panic on my flight this weekend?"

Fact: Ten years of effortless flying had little bearing on this woman's projection of insecurity, which had an almost hypnotic effect— once the suggestion of panic was implanted, insecurity began to feed this fiction as if it were now a fact. Once insecurity is able to hook you, then any possibility, however remote or unlikely, begins to feel like a probability. If insecurity can make you feel off balance, it owns you.

A loving, devoted husband in a solid fifteen-year marriage had the following thought: "How do I know I don't want to hurt my wife?"

Fact: This husband adored his wife. His fiction tormented him because he believed that he was capable of destroying the most important thing in his life. Without self-trust, you have a reflexive tendency to anticipate that you will inevitably screw things up.

You may think some of the thoughts listed here are frightening or perhaps just bizarre. If you knew more of the case histories of the people involved, you'd find out that these weren't horrific facts, mostly they were just plain silly fictions. This is exactly what insecurity can do when it feeds a fiction. In each of these examples, there was absolutely nothing to support any of these fictions—nothing other than insecurity. I'm not saying there aren't unbalanced people with severe mental problems, but in order to separate truth from fiction, you need to look at the whole person and the objective data from someone's life. Only then can you begin to appreciate just how crafty insecurity can be when it tries to get your attention.

I should mention that in the cases mentioned above, every one of these people was able to tell me, "I know these thoughts are crazy, I know it's just my insecurity, but . . ." It's the "but" that gets you by injecting just enough doubt to convince you that maybe, just maybe, you might really be in danger. For an insecure person, all it takes is insecurity's big toe to get in the door. Once the door of rationality is ajar, then it's only a matter of time before you become overwhelmed with defensiveness, doubts, fears, and negatives.

As I mentioned earlier, sometimes it's difficult to differentiate between facts and fictions, especially if insecurity has you scared and off balance.

The key is to begin to recognize how insecurity manages to turn the tables. You'll find that in most cases, if you're honest, you really can tell the difference. You might be afraid to believe the truth, but for now just knowing the difference between fact and fiction is all that's required in Step 1. In the next chapter you'll learn how to use the insights from Step 1 to stop listening to insecurity-driven fictions.

Wrapping Up

Insecurity (which is another word for lack of self-trust) is able to take rational, healthy people and convince them—often without any provocation—of the most absurd things. If your trust muscle has atrophied, you're probably prone to "fictionalizing" your life, which is why Self-Talk is so important. The ultimate goal of Self-Coaching is for you to build your own trust muscle and then, catalytically, your partner's. Now that you have the first step, use it whenever and as often as you can.

Training Suggestion
Get into the habit of listing your fact-fiction struggles.

It's a good idea to keep a written record of the struggles you go through while attempting to separate facts from fictions. Thinking something, writing something down, and reading something are all processed by different parts of your brain. By keeping a log of your fact-fiction struggles you will be offering yourself a multidimensional opportunity to recognize the habits and susceptibilities that trip you up.

Starting today, keep track of your efforts to separate facts from fictions. Factual clarity is essential if you're eventually going to take the leap of faith required to trust yourself.

9

Self-Talk, Step 2
Stop Listening to What Hurts You

In the last chapter you learned to tell the difference between facts and fictions. As important as this distinction is, insight alone isn't always enough when it comes to breaking through some of insecurity's more deep-rooted habits. In this chapter we're going to use the insight and awareness you gained in Step 1 to put a stop to insecurity-driven thinking.

Prelude

I'm sure you've heard the one where the patient goes to the doctor and says, "Doc, my arm hurts whenever I move it like this. What should I do?" The doctor replies, "Stop moving it like that." Although questionable advice for an ailing arm, it happens to be great advice for insecurity-driven thinking—*stop thinking like that!* And this is exactly the goal of Step 2—to stop listening to the fictions thrown at you by insecurity, distortions that seem to have a nefarious life of their own.

When I explain to new patients that they need to learn to stop listening to insecurity's defensiveness, doubts, fears, and negatives, I'm usually met with blank stares—especially from those who are prone to overthinking, chronic worrying, ruminating, or obsessing. "I can't control what goes through my mind. You can't just stop yourself from worrying . . . can you?" Habits of insecurity become so reflexive, you're often unaware of their influence on your thinking or on your behavior. As you recall from chapter 5, a *perceived* threat is enough to initiate a reflexive Turtle, Tiger, Elephant, Peacock, or Raccoon response—all examples of controlling strategies that become so automatic, they're often overlooked.

When you feel vulnerable, insecurity kicks into high gear and begins to fill your mind with defensive rumblings. You become a passive observer sitting on the sidelines as these unsettling thoughts flow unimpeded though your mind. "I just can't stop worrying about my surgery." "I'll never be comfortable with sex." "She can't get away with that, I'll show her!" These thoughts seem to have a mind of their own, popping into your head and then having their way with your emotions and your behavior. Just ask your partner.

Invariably, whenever I discuss the concept of stopping listening, I always bring up Grandma Luciani's favorite expression: "You can't stop a bird from flying into your hair, but you don't have to help it build a nest." Translation: you may not be able to stop a thought from popping into your mind—at least not at first—but you don't have to start building a nest by adding a second thought, a third thought, and so on. The fact that certain thoughts do just seem to erupt is why we have the erroneous impression that what goes through our minds is out of our hands. Since we're talking about Grandma's birds, let me add one more helpful avian adage: "One sparrow doesn't make a summer." Translation: one errant thought will not hurt you. Not if you learn to hit the brakes and prevent that thought from running rampant.

Determination

The problem isn't that we can't say no to our thoughts. We do it all the time. Let's see, so far today, I've actively said *no* to a piece of apple pie lying on the kitchen counter—and didn't eat it; *no* to a second cup of coffee—but did have it; and *no* to my desire to go for a jog instead of paying bills—I paid the bills and then went for the jog.

Most adults have had some experience with dieting. If you're one of these people, you're probably familiar with the yo-yo phenomenon: some days you're "good" and you watch what you eat, and some days you're "bad" and you fall off the wagon. As you can see, sometimes we say no and mean it, other times we say no and don't. What's the difference? The difference is our intention. The dictionary defines *intention* as a determination to act in a certain way. What you intend to do and what you actually do depends on your determination. Determination is essential if you're going to say no to insecurity's fictions. Say no, and mean it! Let's explore this critically important concept.

Determination = focused energy

A life of struggle, whether it comes from low self-esteem, lack of confidence, anxious or worrisome fears, hopelessness, or just plain ineffectiveness, can wind up leaving you feeling victimized and powerless. Let's face it, if you're continually frustrated or blocked from reaching your goals in life, you'll eventually quit trying altogether. This capitulation isn't a reaction to your life circumstances; it's a capitulation to insecurity that's telling you, "I can't." I'm reminded of something the comedian George Carlin said: "If you try to fail and succeed, which have you done?" My answer to this humorous question would be, you've succeeded at failing. This to me is the sine qua non of insecurity—with insecurity, you're better off staying safe than risking that you "can" and winding up being sorry. You're succeeding at failing.

Self-Coaching Reflection
Determination depends on legitimate hope along with
realistic expectations.

If you're going to liberate yourself from insecurity's grip, you *have to* have legitimate hope along with realistic expectations. (This is the one time I'll use the term *have to*.) And if you have these two ingredients, you'll find that a determined attitude *is* something you can sustain. After all, if I know—*really* know in my bones—that I'm going to prevail, I gotta tell you, I can be determined to succeed. But on the other hand, if I'm not sure, if I have the slightest doubt or if I sense that my goals are unrealistic, then all bets are off as my determination begins to fade.

If you're like most people and your life has been compromised by habits of insecurity and control, no doubt you've also struggled with hopelessness. If so, you'll find that Self-Coaching can give you what you've been looking for—legitimate hope with realistic expectations. Your Self-Talk training will convince you of this by demonstrating that (1) human beings are creatures of habit, (2) an insecurity-driven life is a habit, and (3) all habits can be broken.

A Few Words about
Anxiety and Depression

As a psychologist, I see hopelessness all the time in patients who arrive at my office filled with doubt and fear, especially those suffering from anxiety or depression. "I wake up shaking every morning, I can't control my thoughts . . . something's very wrong . . . I must have a mental illness." Since anxiety and depression are so prevalent today, and so often an element in relationship struggle, I feel I should make specific reference to these problems.

Remember what I said earlier about the destructive influence traditional psychology has had on our thinking and perceptions. I feel that most people are too quick to define a debilitating psychological struggle as a mental illness. What we call something is very important. Words shape the way we think and feel. Mark Twain (I confess, I'm a Mark Twain devotee) put it best: "The difference between the right word and the almost right word is like the difference between lightning and the lightning bug." To me, when we call mental illness an *illness*, it isn't "almost" the right word; it's the wrong word! When I think of an illness or a disease, I think of something you catch, a sickness that infiltrates your body leaving you its victim. You catch a cold or the flu. You don't catch or contract anxiety, depression, panic, or other forms of psychological struggle. You generate it.

Why is this important? Because with a cold, flu, or tetanus, you're nothing more than a passive victim of some outside nefarious biological agent. And by definition, a victim is someone who is helpless, powerless. If you think of psychological struggle as an illness, then you must be a victim!

So I changed the language. Rather than using the terms *illness* or *disease*, I've proposed the rather heretical notion that psychological struggle needs to be seen as a habit. A habit that *you* generate. In no way am I minimizing the fact that anxiety and depression are real problems with both psychological and biological underpinnings. But it's important to understand that anxiety and depression are self-generated conditions brought about by ongoing patterns of stress. I'm talking about the stress perpetrated by insecurity's attempt to control life with defensiveness, doubt, fear, and negatives. Over time these thoughts have a corrosive, depleting effect on us, both emotionally and chemically—which is why medication often works in the treatment of these conditions.

Bottom line, if you treat anxiety and depression as habits, then the course of treatment becomes straightforward and personal as you ask yourself, "What am *I* doing that feeds these problems and what am *I* doing to starve them?" Self-Talk is especially important if you or your partner is struggling with anxiety or depression. (For a more detailed explanation of a Self-Coaching approach to treat anxiety and depression, I refer you to my earlier work *Self-Coaching: The Powerful Program to Beat Anxiety and Depression*.)

Stop Listening

Step 2 requires that you take your life back from the grip of insecurity by learning to say no to caustic thinking. Unlike Step 1, which is more contemplative, Step 2 is an *action* step—stopping thoughts instigated by insecurity. Sometimes, you'll find that with just a bit of awareness and effort, this can be accomplished with nothing more than a firm act of will—an emphatic decision to stop contributing thoughts that fuel insecurity. "Stop feeling so insecure! It's not me she's mad at; she's just having a bad day." But, more often than not, when you're caught in a rapidly spiraling onslaught of insecurity-driven thinking, your will can wind up quickly wilting: "Why didn't he call me at lunchtime? Maybe he really doesn't care. He can't even take five minutes out of his precious lunch to call me. Maybe I did something to get him mad? I was tired this morning . . . I should have been more upbeat . . . Why am I getting so upset over this?"

The next time you have an intrusive, defensive, or upsetting thought, you begin by first orienting yourself—that is, determining whether what's roiling about in your mind is a fact or a fiction. Armed with this awareness, you next dig your heels in and recognize the need to stop the avalanche of reflexive, insecure thinking. Here are a few digging-your-heels-in techniques.

Pulling the Rip Cord

You know about my fondness for visuals and their usefulness in dealing with psychological issues. Let me offer a few examples that I've used successfully with my patients, but I encourage you to be creative. The best visual is the one that works for you. As you read though my suggestions, feel free to embellish, tweak, or modify my images to best fit your needs and personality.

Let's say you're feeling stressed about inadvertently running your credit card bill up for the month. You begin to hammer yourself. "I don't know what's wrong with me. I promised my husband I wouldn't spend this month. Maybe I can't control my spending? Maybe I have an addiction to spending? This is terrible. I feel like such a loser . . ."

There are two ways to respond to this harangue. The first would be to do nothing and allow insecurity to run wild. "I'm not fit to be in this relationship. I'm a failure. I can't go home. I'm so embarrassed, so humiliated." As any worrywart will tell you, the only thing that worrisome, foreboding thoughts accomplish is more worry, more stress, and more anxiety.

The second option is to simply *stop* listening! I can hear you now: easier said than done. Like anything else, once you get the hang of it, with a little practice you'll find that stopping the flow of insecurity-driven thoughts can be as easy as reaching for a "rip cord" and pulling! Let me explain.

Imagine falling out of a plane and not realizing you have a parachute strapped to your back. You can guess how irrational and frantic your thinking would become as you plummet to what will be your inevitable annihilation. This disorienting "free fall" panic is exactly what insecurity needs to flourish—that is, the less rational you are, the more panicked and stressed you are, the more the habit of insecurity gets reinforced. (Habits, if they are to persist, rely on you to reinforce them.)

What's the alternative? The alternative is to recognize that you do indeed possess a parachute! Your parachute is your innate capacity for empowerment, determination, and intention—your capacity to stop free-falling with thoughts of insecurity. All you need to do is grasp the rip cord and pull! With a *swoosh*, your parachute will open, and in that instant your free fall stops as you gently and safely float to earth (rationality and solace).

Anytime you find your thoughts free-falling, I want you to visualize yourself grabbing for that rip cord and yanking! Pulling the rip cord is your mental trigger to interrupt the flow of insecurity-driven thinking, thereby *stopping* your free fall: "These thoughts are not facts! I know I'm not a failure! I refuse to beat myself up any longer."

What does pulling the rip cord represent? It's your way of engaging your will and demanding to put a stop to needless, destructive fictions. This process of stopping free-falling thoughts may seem vaguely familiar to you. I'm sure that in your own way, you've probably tried various ways to pull the rip cord on wayward thoughts. You may even have succeeded at times. What we're trying to do now is formalize the process by giving you a go-to image that you can use every time you're challenged by insecurity, an image that you can rely on to interrupt your habit of free-fall thinking.

If free-falling doesn't appeal to you, here's an alternative. In my previous writing I used the image of insecurity-thinking being like a runaway train. Imagine yourself reaching for the dangling red emergency brake . . . and yank! The train comes to a screeching halt as you stop the runaway train of thoughts that were just cascading through your head.

Regardless of the visual that you employ, remember that you're only trying to establish a new reflex of empowerment and determination, one that enables you to take charge and not be victimized by insecurity. A reflexive action that takes your life back from needless, destructive habits.

You're probably familiar with Nike's now famous slogan, "Just do it!" This is the attitude that's needed for Step 2—just do it! No thinking, no contemplating—just do it! Whether you reach for the emergency brake or the rip cord, or simply say *no*, there's no longer a need for rehashing, ruminating, dwelling, obsessing, or figuring out—only for action. Face it, Nike's slogan wouldn't have had much appeal if it read, "Just think about doing it."

I realize that taking action while trying to stand up against the tidal wave of insecurity requires a powerful incentive. This is why I prefer the term *coaching* to therapy or analysis. Rather than going back and asking what happened to you in your childhood, just forget the past! Forget the interpretations and explanations and realize that if you're going to extricate yourself from the habits that are ruling and ruining your life there's something you can do about it—right now. Go ahead, pull the rip cord, grab the brake, or just *stop* listening. Enough is enough!

Changing Channels

For some, free-falling from a plane or being caught on a runaway train may be a bit too . . . stimulating. For those who would like a more mundane visual to put a stop to reflexive insecurity thinking, let me suggest *changing channels*. Imagine that you're riding in your car, listening to the radio. The announcer interrupts with a news bulletin about a heightened terrorism alert for the holiday season. You find yourself beginning to tense. As you continue listening, you notice that your mood is becoming increasingly more anxious. Finally, you can't take it anymore. You reach over and hit another button on the radio and immediately your car is filled with Mozart's Serenade for Winds. You begin to relax.

Each radio channel represents a possible variation of your own thinking—the number of channels you set up on your radio is entirely up to you. You might, for example, find that one of your channels is the Panic

Channel, where you begin to feel totally out of control as your thoughts run rampant. Obviously, when you tune in to this channel you're going to want to make a change. Another channel might be called your Distraction Channel, where you can contemplate doing something that pulls you away from thoughts—it might be making a phone call, listening to music, or going for a jog. A third channel might be a Fact-Finding Channel, where you tune in to scrutinize your thoughts, looking to further separate facts from fictions.

You can decide to change channels in your mind the same way you decide to change an annoying radio station in your car. You simply do it! Here are a few more examples that will help you set up your own channels:

- **Change the Doom-and-Gloom Channel to the Affirmation Channel.** The Doom-and-Gloom Channel is the depression channel. It's oppressive, pessimistic, negative, and geared toward one thing: getting you to give up and retreat from life. By switching to the Affirmation Channel you recognize that whenever you allow yourself to become swallowed up by negative thoughts, you're ignoring the positives in your life. The Affirmation Channel insists that you recognize the complete picture, which includes the positive thoughts. Whether it's your next vacation, your weekend plans, your son's baseball game, or the dinner you've planned for you and your partner, don't let the Doom-and-Gloom Channel fool you—positives are only a choice away.

- **Change the Anxiety Channel to the Here-and-Now Channel.** Anxiety is always looking into the future, anticipating chaos. By switching to the Here-and-Now Channel, you pull yourself away from living in the future and begin asking yourself what's going on in the moment. Force yourself to come out from your congested head and, as they say, smell the roses—notice the weather, the scenery, feel the sun, the breeze. If you're with someone, pay more attention to what's going on and what's being said. If you're working, connect yourself more with the task at hand. The Here-and-Now Channel is all about moving your focus from internal ruminations to external reality.

■ **Change the Worry Channel to the Concern Channel.** The worry channel, similar to the Anxiety Channel, looks into the future and projects negatives—things that may never happen. The Worry Channel's most popular program is the "what if?" show ("What if I can't make enough money?" "What if I get sick?") The Concern Channel is where you can look at the real issues (rather than the fictions of worry) that are of legitimate concern. The Concern Channel will tell you about learning to deal only with the significant, legitimate problems that are on your plate today—not what may be on your plate tomorrow.

■ **Change the Insecurity Channel to the Trust Channel.** The Insecurity Channel is a combination, mixed-bag station where panic, worry, fear, doubt, defensiveness, and negativity broadcast 24/7 from its 50,000-watt transmitter located at your core of distrust. Without trust you may find yourself listening to the Insecurity Channel more often than you realize. You tune in because you want to figure out how to control life, and as you've learned, controlling life appeals to you when you're feeling vulnerable. By switching to the Trust Channel you'll allow yourself to be inspired to take the leap of faith necessary to risk trusting your instincts, your intuitions, and your gut reactions to life. Rather than trying to control life, let the Trust Channel teach you to let life unfold, giving you the opportunity to handle (rather than control) in real time any challenges that may arise.

Training Suggestion #1

Using the examples here as a guide, create a log of the various "channels" that you find yourself listening to throughout the day. Every time you identify a destructive channel, jot a brief description of it on a piece of paper, then see if you can come up with a station that presents the opposing point of view. At first you'll probably find that most of your channels are insecurity-based. This is why it's important to write each down and ask what the counterprogramming needs to be. You can sketch out a radio and label each button with your choices.

Now, armed with your choice of stations, you don't have to be victimized by any thought (channel) that upsets you. You simply reach over and change the channel. Don't like what you're hearing? Change the channel. Once you get the hang of it, you'll see just how simple this can be.

Training Suggestion #2

Before moving on to the next chapter and the final Self-Talk step, try to look for opportunities to practice Steps 1 and 2. Get in the habit of not only increasing your awareness (fact versus fiction) of every struggle, but also get used to taking action and putting a stop to destructive, insecure thinking. You may, for example, find yourself worrying about silly things like not wanting to phone your mother-in-law, or forgetting to pay the phone bill. Whatever the issue, these are useful opportunities for you to flex your muscles and put a stop to any defensiveness, fear, doubt, or negativity. Getting used to stopping the ruminations of insecurity is the goal of this exercise. Once you begin to recognize that you have the choice and the power to override anything destructive in your thinking, you'll be well on your way to liberating yourself from insecurity's hypnotic suggestion that you can't.

10

Self-Talk, Step 3
Let Go of What Hurts You

Y ou're about to find out that the culmination of your Self-Talk efforts has ultimately nothing to do with "talking," but everything to do with letting go and, well, doing nothing! This may sound a bit crazy, especially if you're an overthinker. But if you'll permit me to take this one step further, you're about to find out that when it comes to taking your life back from the grip of insecurity, less is definitely more. Okay, enough with the oxymorons. Step 3 will show you that letting go isn't at all contradictory; in fact, it happens to be the logical conclusion of working with Steps 1 and 2.

Spinning Your Wheels

By now, you should be well aware that everything that's psychologically destructive comes from a form of mental congestion caused by too much worrying, anticipating, fretting, anguishing, or just plain overthinking.

You know from experience that getting mired down with insecurity-driven thinking can be an unpleasant way to spend an afternoon (or morning, or evening). Imagine for a moment that you're in the midst of some serious worrying as you try to brace yourself for your mother-in-law's upcoming weeklong visit.

Out of the blue you get a phone call from an old roommate you haven't been in touch with in years. As you and she ramble on about old sorority days and crazy dates, you find that your pre–phone call anxiety has . . . vanished! You're feeling elated, upbeat, and altogether jubilant! How can this be? Your mother-in-law is still en route to your house. Circumstantially, nothing's changed. The answer isn't complicated, not once you learn to stop spinning your wheels. Let me explain.

When I was very young, one of my favorite toys was a small tin "spark wheel." (Hey, there weren't any video games when I was growing up!) Perhaps you've seen one. It consists of a small, flat wheel attached to a kind of plunger—like a metallic lollipop. By pushing the plunger up and down you cause the wheel to spin, rubbing against a few pieces of flint, causing sparks to shoot out in all directions. My point is that you can only make sparks on a spark wheel while you actively press and release the plunger. As soon as you stop, the wheel quits spinning and the sparks are no longer produced. In the example above, just prior to that call from your old roommate, you were actively generating sparks of mother-in-law thoughts—not on a metallic wheel, but from your insecurity-driven wheels of doubt, fear, and negativity.

The key word here is *generating.* It doesn't matter whether you're experiencing anxiety or depression, worry or trepidation, Turtle reacting or Tiger reacting, the bottom line is that these are all sparks of insecurity generated by you! Step 3 will help you understand exactly what you're doing to generate the friction that causes the sparks. Take a look at Liz, a thirty-year-old lawyer who was doing her best to stop being a worrywart. Her efforts were an example of how, when it comes to breaking the habits of insecurity, good intentions don't necessarily lead to good results. Here's what she said at our first meeting:

> I guess I've been a worrier all my life. My mother died when I was two and I didn't get to see much of my father, who worked all the time. My grandmother tried, but she was a nervous wreck. She was

a hypochondriac, always complaining and worrying about getting sick. I was pretty much on my own, without much comfort or security. I think I've picked up a lot of my grandmother's traits. I'm always worrying about getting sick, especially about getting cancer. I watch what I eat, I'm paranoid about the air we breathe, the chemicals that are put in our food, and lately, ever since my friend was rear-ended at a stop sign and wound up crippled with a few herniated discs, I've been afraid to drive.

My fears have become anxieties. I even think I had a panic attack recently when I read that using plastic in the microwave allows toxic chemicals to drip into your food. I've been using plastic wrap in the microwave for years! I have to be honest, I feel there's cancer somewhere in my body right now and it's just a matter of time before I get really sick.

I knew I had to get a grip on my fears so I began to read as much as possible about anxiety and self-help. The more I read, the more confused I felt. I've done everything. I've been to counseling, tried medication, nothing helps. I spend hours every day writing in my journal, I'm constantly trying to figure all this out, and yet it just seems like all I'm doing is driving myself crazy. What am I doing wrong?

Liz was clearly trying to do her best to feel better, but as you can see, all her efforts only wound up making matters worse as she became more and more congested with worry, trepidation, and anxiety. This brings us to the Self-Coaching oxymoron that I mentioned at the beginning of this chapter: less is more. For Liz, when it came to spinning thoughts, her unfortunate motto was: more (worrying) is never enough. Liz's excessive worrying was her feeble attempt to gain some level of control by at least preparing herself for the worst. Whenever an underlying fiction of insecurity is able to go unchallenged, it has the power to take over your life.

You might be scratching your head, thinking, "But wasn't Liz challenging her insecurities? Isn't that a good thing?" Well, yes and no. Yes, she did challenge the many symptoms of her insecurity, which would have been okay if she kept her focus on here-and-now issues rather than looking into the future and projecting negatives ("I'm going to get cancer . . ."). And no, it wasn't a good thing because Liz never got to challenge the faulty premise from which her reflexive symptoms emanated—the long-standing historical belief/fiction that she couldn't trust her life to feel safe.

Self-Coaching Reflection
The ability to risk trusting yourself and life is the final cure
for all psychological friction.

As you can see from Liz's attempts to feel more secure, she only wound up spinning her wheels faster and faster. In counseling, she had no problem understanding what she was doing. She readily acknowledged that she was her own worst enemy. Liz's "sparking" was obvious, allowing her to readily distinguish facts from fictions and implement strategies to stop her runaway train of thoughts. Where she did encounter some difficulty, however, was when she got to Step 3—letting go. Later in this chapter, I'll discuss Liz's challenge to take that final leap of faith and risk—for the first time—trusting her life. For now, let me say a few more things about generating insecurity.

The Subtlety of Insecurity

Unlike Liz's situation, sometimes we generate insecurity in less obvious, more subtle ways. I find that it's not uncommon for someone who's been doing very well with their Self-Coaching to ask me why they still encounter pockets of friction after seemingly breaking their habit of insecurity. Upon questioning them, I usually find some variation of this theme: "Now that I'm doing so well, I can't help wondering if my anxiety will come back." Or, "I keep wondering how long these good feelings will last." Sounds innocent, no? Clearly these statements aren't as bad as Liz assuming she had cancer, but they nevertheless represent a subtle form of generating insecurity.

By wondering if anxiety will come back or how long the good feelings will last, you're actually looking over your shoulder and expressing doubt. ("Maybe I'm kidding myself that this can last." "How do I know it won't come back?") If you had adequate trust, you'd be willing to risk believing that you're safe and that whatever comes your way, you'll handle it!

Self-Coaching Reflection
Believing and trusting that you can handle
life eliminates doubt.

If you truly believe that you'll handle what unfolds in your life, then you don't have to be on guard duty, scanning the horizon for danger. Step 3 is about letting go, but a more complete description would be: letting go and becoming reactive to life. Along with taking the plunge and just letting go of insecurity-driven thinking, you're about to be introduced to a concept called Reactive Living, which will convince you how you can take that final leap toward self-trust.

Letting Go

Whereas the first two Self-Talk steps are thinking steps, Step 3 is the opposite of thinking and figuring, letting go of thoughts. We've all had head colds. You know if you dwell on your symptoms, you feel miserable. Yet a simple distraction can get you to almost forget you're sick. By learning to stop focusing on doubts, fears, and negatives, you can begin to become less agonized—less congested. You're only wedded to these thoughts in the first place because of your lack of trust—you're trying too hard to control life. Learning to let go begins by challenging your belief that controlling life somehow helps you sidestep vulnerability.

Self-Coaching Reflection
Controlling life rather than trusting life is never the answer;
it's always the problem.

In the last chapter you learned that if you're just a passive observer of your thoughts, insecurity can and will have its way with you. Once you stop the destructive avalanche of insecurity-driven thoughts with Steps 1 and 2, it's time to recognize that stepping out of your head and into the world is the absolute best way to demonstrate a willingness to risk trusting. If, for example, I'm willing to stop beating myself up for snapping at my wife, then why go on brooding about it and constantly bringing it up in my mind? Typical answer: "I brood, I worry, and I ruminate because this is my habit—my habit of insecurity."

Since I've declared that I'm *willing* to stop brooding, then one way to implement my resolve is to stop feeding my habit. I do this by coming out of my congested head and connecting with my external world. I might, for example, notice the snow falling outside the window, or perhaps respond to my daughter's instant message on my computer, or I might simply decide to phone a friend. It doesn't matter what part of my external world I choose to embrace, the key is shifting the focus from internal "spinning" to external living. I call this Reactive Living. But before I explain this crucial component of Self-Coaching, I'll offer you a few visuals to assist you as you practice letting go.

Balloons and Soccer Balls

Imagine yourself holding a bunch of balloons. Each balloon may represent a particular doubt, fear, or negative thought. See yourself releasing one of the balloons. Watch it slowly rise toward the sky . . . slowly shrinking, shrinking, until it vanishes. If you prefer something a bit more aggressive, imagine that you're on a soccer field and there are soccer balls rolling out in front of you. Each ball represents an insecurity-driven thought. See yourself going over to a soccer ball and *whack!* Kick it off your field. Worry, *whack!* Fear, *whack!*

My award for most creative (albeit somewhat coarse) visual goes to a man I was seeing who described his attempts at letting go of noxious thoughts as follows: "I'm seeing my worry-thoughts floating in a toilet bowl. I press the lever and flush . . . all the thoughts begin to circle the drain and *whoosh*, are gone!" From that point on, "circling the drain" was my patient's way of letting go of (flushing) any insecurity.

As with all the visuals presented in this book, they are meant to be used as tools to encourage you to break through your entrenched habits of insecurity. You may find that visuals, step-by-step techniques, and Self-Coaching reflections and training tips all seem tedious to you at first. But keep in mind that you're up against a long-standing, imprinted system of distorted thinking and believing. Once you begin to actually gain some momentum breaking these habits, you'll find that you become less reliant on the specific techniques mentioned in this book. But for now, don't be tempted to abandon them too quickly.

Alternate Nostril Breathing: A Letting-Go Technique

I've learned a lot from my yoga practice and especially from meditation. Meditation essentially teaches you that you have a choice to step out of the ever-flowing stream of consciousness reverie and focus your attention on an alternative experience—breathing. I distinctly remember my first attempt. My instructor offered the simple instruction to "clear your mind." This didn't sound like such a difficult request—until I tried. I started out fine, watching my breath . . . in . . . and out . . . in . . . and out. Within seconds I was thinking about the gas I had to get for my car, the phone calls I had to make, and my dog Lulu's veterinary appointment later that day . . .

Oh yeah, I was supposed to be watching my breath! The only other instruction I had was not to cling to any stray thoughts, to let them blow in like leaves and then to effortlessly let them blow out—always coming back to my breathing. It took practice, but I did get better at it. The key was to keep coming back to the breathing. In time you begin to learn to quiet the mind, and then your focus on your breathing can occur for longer and longer periods of time without interruptions.

To let go, you must recognize that you can choose to step apart from insecurity-driven thinking. Instead of focusing on your breath, you can focus on any aspect of your external life. But like meditation, it's going to be hard at first to stay detached from your long-standing habit of overthinking. With practice and patience you'll realize that (1) absolutely nothing bad happens when you stop spinning insecurity-driven thoughts, (2) your ability to stay detached will become easier with time, (3) you'll begin to feel 100 percent better, and (4) you'll be building your trust muscle, which is the goal of Self-Coaching.

To help you grasp this concept of detaching and letting go, I offer you a technique I leaned in my yoga class called alternate nostril breathing. This simple technique will give you a clear idea of the benefits of meditation and will also allow you to step apart from any thought that needs to be abandoned. Here's all you need to do:

Simply sit up straight, press the right nostril shut with the right thumb, and inhale for a count of three seconds through the open left nostril. Next, squeezing both nostrils shut with the thumb and index finger, hold the breath for three seconds, then release the thumb holding the right nostril and exhale through the right nostril for a count of six. Repeat the same process in reverse—inhale for three seconds through the right nostril, hold three seconds, exhale six seconds through the left nostril. Continue until you are relaxed and free from intrusive, reflexive thoughts.

The meditational effects of this technique are profound, but for our purposes of stopping and letting go of reflexive thinking, it's almost foolproof. Since it requires concentration, precise counting of breaths, switching nostrils at the proper moment, and, most important of all, breathing evenly, with no jerks or pauses, it's almost impossible to stay involved in reflexive thinking. A simple technique such as this can begin to teach you in a very direct, hands-on (pun intended) way that letting go and liberating yourself from insecurity's reflexive living is as simple as three-three-six. By finding out that you can willfully step away from the negative effects of reflexive thinking, you will begin to understand the ultimate truth that anxiety and depression are choices.

Reactive Living

Reactive Living is learning to live your life reactively rather than proactively. I realize that *proactive* usually has a positive connotation, and sometimes this is true, especially when life's demands require some forethought and planning. For example, it's a great idea to be proactive if your partner is feeling stuck and looking for stimulation. You could proactively find some local fairs, concerts, or bed-and-breakfasts to visit. Being proactive when dealing with the facts of your life is fine and sometimes downright constructive. But when insecurity attempts to control life by being proactive about the fictions of your life, it's anything but fine—and it's definitely destructive.

For the insecure person, proactive behavior is synonymous with anticipatory projections (fictions) of doubt, fear, and negativity—all of which may never happen! The opposite of proactive living is Reactive Living, and this is the final component of Self-Talk. Learn Reactive Living and you will never be victimized by insecurity again.

Caution. Before proceeding, there is one caveat. It is essential that before attempting Reactive Living, you have successfully completed the following Self-Coaching training:

1. Using the scores from your self-quizzes, you've established your Self-Portrait and have a reasonable understanding and awareness of the role that insecurity and control play in your life.

2. You have developed the ability to separate the facts from the fictions in your life (Self-Talk, Step 1).

3. You have a reasonable capacity for stopping insecurity-driven thinking (Self-Talk, Step 2).

4. You have learned to let go of insecurity-driven thinking and have embraced a willingness to risk self-trust (Self-Talk, Step 3).

The reason I pose these cautions is because without sufficient awareness of insecurity's capacity to distort your perceptions, you could find your efforts at Reactive Living to be hit-or-miss, leaving you vulnerable to frustration and confusion. If, for example, you're still susceptible to Elephant defensiveness, you might feel that raising your voice and intimidating your partner is being reactive. Although yes, this is reactive in a literal sense, it's clearly not the kind of reactivity we're after with Reactive Living.

The bottom line is, you don't want to trust insecurity's attempts to control your life, which is why I've offered the above cautions, but you do want to risk trusting who and what you are once you've liberated yourself from insecurity. And once you have a more grounded and stable self-perception, you'll find that risking trust and living reactively will not only motivate you (success is very encouraging), but will vastly improve the quality and depth of your life experiences, allowing you to become an effective catalyst for your relationship.

Reactive Living Explained

The simplest way of explaining Reactive Living is to ask you to imagine driving your car. When you head out on the roads, I'm sure you're not thinking, "What if a squirrel runs out in front of my car, what will I do?" Quite the contrary, you more than likely drive along, window down, enjoying the breeze, the view, and the music on the radio. If a squirrel happens to run out in front of your car, what happens? Instinctively, you hit the brake, grab the wheel, and veer off to the side. You didn't have to prepare for this, you just reacted.

In order to become more reactive to life, you're going to have to risk coming out of your habituated, congested way of thinking and trust that you can handle life as it unfolds. You have six million–plus years of evolutionary hardwiring to back you up on this. You have countless personal examples of handling, surviving, and getting beyond problems. Let's face it, you're nothing less than a survival machine! The simple fact is you can handle your life. The simple fiction is that you feel powerless to do so. The only reason you feel powerless is because insecurity has mucked up your instincts by insisting on controlling life rather than simply living it.

The Intellect versus the Gut

Controlling life depends exclusively on your intellect to protect you from *perceived* threats. Yet your intellect, as formidable as it is, pales in comparison to the full array of mental talent that you possess. It helps to imagine the controlling, intellectual part of your psyche as a small island in the middle of a vast ocean of instinctive, intuitive potential. When you live reactively, you trust all of yourself—not just your intellect—to handle life spontaneously, as it unfolds. Living reactively by definition is living in the moment, not by time-traveling into the future or looking back over your shoulder into your past.

In order to begin living reactively you need to exercise your trust muscle. As with most exercise programs, you start with small, incremental steps and challenge yourself as your capacity grows. You can begin to get some trust-exercise by risking nonconsequential decisions. You can, for example, start off by listening to your gut about what movie to see, what dessert to have, or what book to read. Rather than go through a lot of intellectual calculating, see if you can just go with the first impulse that grabs you. At first you may wind up regretting your choices, which is why we start out with inconsequential decisions. But remember that with an atrophied trust muscle, you can't expect proficiency right away. In time you will develop a much better connection with your intuitive ability and it will work alongside your intellect as a much more reliable resource for handling life.

Getting Back to Liz

Now that you've been introduced to all the steps of Self-Talk, it's time to revisit Liz. If you recall, Liz was a consummate worrywart, worrying incessantly about getting cancer, having accidents, and driving herself crazy with introspection. Here are excerpts from her journal. You'll find them not only self-explanatory, but very instructive. My comments are in brackets:

> Monday, January 2—Left Dr. Joe's office feeling pumped up, like I could really do this. I still feel like I can . . . well, kind of, but doubts are already beginning to creep into the picture. We talked about separating facts from fictions. I've known all along that my fears aren't facts, but I never let myself *really* know. Okay, so now I know, let's see how I do. [*I've found that when someone's swimming with doubts, fears, or negatives, if you pin them down and ask them directly whether their feelings are facts or fictions, they'll tell you, "I know my fears are foolish, I just can't ignore them." Insecurity's voice, when left unchecked and unchallenged, will dominate your perceptions—even to the point of absurdity. But, using Self-Talk, not only can these perceptions be challenged, you absolutely can learn to ignore them! Separating the facts in your life from the fictions is the first step in liberating yourself from insecurity.*]

> Tuesday, January 3—Not a bad day. I actually caught myself quite a few times thinking of cancer and each time I made myself go through the drill asking, "Is what I'm feeling a fact or a fiction?" Of

course, I couldn't lie, my feelings were fictions. Just admitting this has made a subtle difference. Can't describe what's different . . . just a feeling like maybe there's hope.

Monday, January 16—Facts, fictions! Man, I can't believe how I never saw this before. [*Habits of insecurity have a way of distracting you from the truth.*] Almost all of my thoughts are fictions! I still find myself getting upset, but at least I know I'm battling, as Dr. Joe says, a bogeyman and not a reality. [*If you tell yourself there are bogeymen—there will be bogeymen! As you would tell any child, "Open the closet door and see for yourself"—no bogeyman! Open the door to your fictions, see the truth, and stop running!*] In therapy we talked about how I used to have many fears when I was a child . . . burglars, getting kidnapped, that kind of thing. Funny how I can see now that those were silly fictions, yet I can't see my fears today as clearly. [*With practice, Liz will have no trouble seeing clearly.*] I'm staying encouraged.

Wednesday, January 25—We discussed Step 2 today, stopping the thoughts. I heard what Dr. Joe said, but it's not sinking in. I've tried to stop these thoughts for years, I just can't do it! [*Believing that you "can't" say no to reflexive thinking reflects a lack of awareness, understanding, and self-trust. I always point out that we say no to our thoughts all the time, i.e., "I'm not going to have that ice cream." "No, I'm not going to stay in bed any longer." The problem is that we become passive victims of our thought process. With awareness and determination, you begin to recognize the simple truth—"I can."*]

Thursday, January 26—I was going to call Dr. Joe today and tell him I can't do this, but decided to try one of his visuals. I've never been one for that kind of thing, but what the heck. I was standing in line at the pharmacy waiting for my prescription when I noticed one of those blood pressure cuffs on the shelf behind the counter. Just seeing the picture of the cuff reminded me of being in a doctor's office and that started the thoughts going wild. [*Until the habits of insecurity are broken, it's not unusual for a stimulus (like Liz seeing the picture of the blood pressure cuff) that was associated with past anxiety to trigger anxiety—if you allow it to! This would be a perfect time to see yourself grabbing the rip cord, changing channels, or just taking a few deep, relaxed breaths.*] I was feeling my heart beating faster, I wanted to bolt from the store, but instead, for some reason, I kind of closed my eyes for a second and saw that red emergency brake handle . . . I yanked it! I remember smiling and feeling calm. Somehow, the thoughts stopped. Maybe it was just a coincidence or maybe it was some kind of suggestion or something, but I felt better! This one instance has changed my whole attitude. I can honestly say that I'm beginning to feel that maybe I can do this!!! [*It's important to recognize what great hypnotists we are. What we tell ourselves and what we believe is what we become. Having hope opens the door to optimism. And with optimism, anything is possible.*]

Tuesday, January 31—I can't believe it, but I'm actually beginning to say no to my fictions! I can't say how this ability happened, it just seemed to happen. [*This was no accident. Liz's awareness had been steadily growing and her Self-Talk efforts are beginning to pay off.*] As soon as I become aware of feeling scared, before I actually get going with my thoughts, I find myself saying *no!* Sometimes, if the thoughts are violent, I find myself screaming the word *no* to myself. What absolutely amazes me is that now I can actually stop myself from sliding down that slippery slope. The thoughts stop for a while, but they unfortunately always come back. [*This is the very nature of any habit—they're persistent, opportunistic, and will look to reinsert themselves in your life from time to time. The fact that you're challenged again and again is not a problem, as long as you realize that breaking any habit is, in fact, a process.*] I'm hoping that as I grow stronger and more confident, this will slow down my fears. [*That is exactly what will happen. Patience, determination, and intention, will, over time, topple any habit.*] We'll see.

Sunday, February 12—Last week we talked about letting go of insecurity-thinking. I can see where that's important. Nothing's going to change unless I stop feeding the insecurity. But what was most important was that I need to learn to trust me. I know now, without any doubt, that my insecurity is because I don't trust myself. I also know that in order to trust myself, I need to risk believing I'm not going to get sick. Oh, how I want to believe this . . . I just can't seem to get there. [*If Liz were in my office telling me that she "just can't seem to get there," I would point out how this is a subtle way that insecurity is injecting a doubt. I would ask her to change her thought to a more factual "I'm not there . . . not yet!" This simple shift in perspective (fiction to fact) would prevent her from needlessly feeding her habit of insecurity while injecting a bit of determined optimism—"not yet!" When you find yourself dancing with doubts, fears, or negatives, it's always a good idea to take a look at not only what you're saying to yourself, but how you're saying it. Sometimes a simple shift in perspective is all that's needed to bring you to the next level.*]

Wednesday, March 1—Dr. Joe and I have been talking a lot about Reactive Living. I mentioned to him that I had a party to go to this weekend and was feeling squeamish because everyone seems to be coming down with the flu. I was thinking I'd be better off staying at home. We went through the Self-Talk drill and confirmed that indeed it was factual that the flu was going around, but we decided that the real reason I wanted to stay home was because I was telling myself I would definitely get the flu if I went. Rather than concede to my insecurity, I needed to consider living reactively . . . kind of letting life unfold and seeing what happens. I can do this as long as I tell myself that whatever happens, the truth is I really can handle it. So I get the flu! Why do I feel I can't . . . I'm not even sure what I can't handle. I've been sick plenty of times, I do okay . . . guess it's just my old habit trying to spook me. [*When insecurity dictates your reality, it's not uncommon to feel frozen and terrified. This was a solid attempt by Liz to separate facts from emotional fictions.*]

Friday, March 10—Party was great and no flu! [*Breaking any habit requires accumulating successes by refusing to be misled by insecurity.*] I'm so glad I went . . . met John and had a wonderful time. Reactive Living is beginning to make more sense. I've got to risk believing I can handle life, that's what frees me to not only stop worrying, but to live more . . . as doc would say, "courageously." I'm not quite there yet, but I see my path clearly laid out in front of me. My trust muscle took years to weaken and it's going to take patience for me to fully believe, but I've seen the results and I know with all my heart that I'll never go back to living like the scared rabbit that I was! [*When the clouds of insecurity begin to part and the simple truth finally reveals itself, this is a moment of sheer joy, energy, and conviction. Way to go, Liz!*]

The Last Word on Reactive Living

My friends at Alcoholics Anonymous have many clever and engaging catchphrases such as "One Day at a Time" and "KISS—Keep It Simple, Stupid." But in my estimation, none is more powerful than "Let go, Let God." I'd like to offer you a somewhat secularized version of this profound piece of wisdom.

You know how to extricate yourself from insecurity by learning to let go. And you've heard me talk about trusting that vast ocean of potentiality that is your instinctual, intuitive reservoir of survival capability. Now you have a mantra: *Let go, let God*. Specifically this means let go of the congested ego hold on your life and let God (or your instincts, intuition, or as the Swiss psychiatrist C. G. Jung referred to this part of the psyche, the "Self" with a capital "S") run your life. By insisting on controlling life in an insecurity-driven proactive way, you're choosing a life of struggle. But by handing yourself over to that in you which goes beyond the ego, you are allowing yourself to truly be reactive, spontaneous, and liberated.

11

Sketching Your Relationship Portrait

Seeing the Whole Problem

At this point we're almost ready to begin applying some long-awaited Catalytic Self-Coaching to your relationship, but before officially launching the catalytic process we need to be certain that your personal Self-Coaching/Self-Talk efforts have progressed to a place where the destructive effects of insecurity and control have been significantly reduced. Please understand that "significantly reduced" does not mean you have to be insecurity-free. Although this would be nice (and I certainly feel it needs to remain one of your goals), I can't overemphasize that your personal Self-Coaching is an ongoing process. You *do not* have to be symptom-free in order to begin the catalytic part of this program—as long as your thinking is less contaminated by insecurity's distortions.

Assessing Your Readiness

Before dismissing you from your personal training and beginning any catalytic coaching, we need to assess your overall coaching readiness. We'll determine this based on your Self-Coaching progress to date, as well as your overall psychological awareness. As I just mentioned, it's unlikely that you will have eliminated all your reflexive, controlling behavior, but this doesn't mean you're not ready to proceed. As long as you've achieved a reasonable degree of awareness—one that allows you to neutralize the behavior associated with insecurity and control—you'll be in a good position to help your relationship.

One important prerequisite is your ability to have a solid understanding of any defensive or destructive behavior that you may still display. For example, "Why did I just snap at her? All she did was to tell me I should have gone straight instead of making that turn. Guess that's my insecurity feeling challenged. My perfectionistic need to be in control didn't like being told I was wrong. I resorted to Raccoon behavior because I was angry about feeling exposed." During this final phase of your personal training, this kind of inner dialogue needs to become a routine part of your everyday effort.

Sure, it may be tedious to scrutinize your thinking and reacting all the time, but it won't be forever—only until you've extricated yourself from reflexive thinking. And please don't misunderstand, I'm not asking you to scrutinize every thought, only those defensive responses that you're now familiar with— Tiger, Turtle, Elephant, Raccoon, and Peacock. With ongoing practice, you'll find your defensiveness gradually lessening. As you replace personal insecurity and control with legitimate efforts to develop self-trust and confidence, you can expect defensive behavior to completely disappear.

Reworking Your Self-Portrait

If you recall, in chapter 7 you compiled various quiz scores and used them to sketch your Self-Portrait. At this point I'd like you to go back to chapters 6 and 7 and retake the quizzes along with recalculating your Reflexive Pattern Ratio. Once you have this data in hand, come back to this discussion.

In the diagram below, you'll see a sample comparison of one partner's *before* and *after* Self-Portraits. The *before* Self-Portrait is the same example we used in chapter 7. The *after* Self-Portrait represents a typical configuration one might expect after a period of Self-Coaching training.

Before and After Self-Portraits

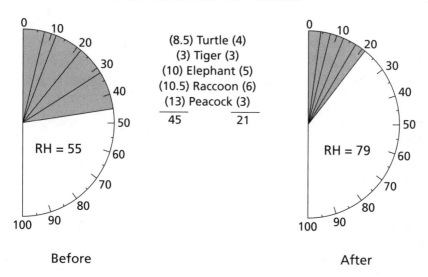

| (8.5) Turtle (4) |
| (3) Tiger (3) |
| (10) Elephant (5) |
| (10.5) Raccoon (6) |
| (13) Peacock (3) |

| 45 | 21 |

Before   After

A simple comparison of this person's Self-Portraits yields a wealth of important information. (Later in this chapter you'll see how this information is specifically used in actual case examples.) In the example above, we see that all the controlling strategies have improved, except the Tiger score, which remained the same. Turtle before score 8.5, after score 4; Tiger before 3, after 3; Elephant before 10, after 5; Raccoon before 10.5, after 6; Peacock before 13, after 3.

From this comparison you can see that this person has shown the most improvement in Turtle, Elephant, Raccoon, and Peacock tendencies. A shift such as this might, for example, suggest that this person has moved toward less obnoxious bullying, less egocentricity, less avoidance, with less complaining and snapping—overall this shift would reflect a more reasonable, sensitive, approachable partner than when previously tested. This shift is confirmed by the relationship-healthy component (RH) that can be seen by comparing the light-colored, RH portion of the before portrait with that of the RH portion of the after portrait (there is an increase from 55 to 79). A score of 79 yields a Reflexive Pattern Ratio of 3.7 (see page 97), which indicates only minimal interference from defensive, controlling behavior.

Using the example on the previous page as a guide, fill in your actual before and after Self-Coaching data below in order to make a comparison of your Self-Portraits.

Charting Your Before and After Data

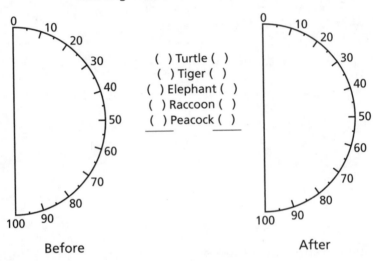

( ) Turtle ( )
( ) Tiger ( )
( ) Elephant ( )
( ) Raccoon ( )
( ) Peacock ( )

Before   After

Referring to this data, note your individual scores. Pay particular attention to any scores that have not shown much change or any scores that may have inadvertently increased. Clearly, you would want to apply any future Self-Talk efforts to these specific tendencies. I should mention that although an increase in any one defensive score is not typical, it can happen. If, for example, a Turtle-type begins to become less withdrawn and passive due to their Self-Coaching training, they may inadvertently overcompensate with a bit of Elephant bullying. "You've been telling me what to do and giving me orders for years. That's all going to change. From now on I'm going to tell *you* what to do." Usually a flip-flop like this represents only a temporary fluctuation, and as the Self-Talk continues, the scores will normalize. The goal of Self-Coaching isn't to substitute one shabby defense for another; it's to liberate you from *all* defensive behavior.

Looking at your data, what changes/improvements do you see? Using the information from your after Self-Portrait, refer to pages 98–101 to find your new Reflexive Pattern Ratio. How much of a change do you see comparing your before and after ratios? Make sure you read the ratio descriptions in chapter 7 to help you evaluate this improvement.

If you find that there hasn't been a significant change in your scores (looking at the Reflexive Pattern Ratio categories listed in chapter 7, for example, you might see that your category remains the same), give yourself more time to practice disengaging from insecurity. Continue your Self-Talk efforts with the realization that all habits are resistant to change. This is normal and not at all a problem. The best way to change your ratio is to focus your Self-Coaching awareness on those controlling strategies (Turtle, Elephant, and the like) that remain troublesome for you. You may also want to review the material in chapter 4 and see if you are inadvertently falling prey to reflexive controlling patterns such as tunnel vision, mind reading, black-and-white thinking, and so on, that may be contributing to your lack of progress.

As much as you'd like your habit of insecurity to roll over and die, it's not going to happen without your ongoing efforts to starve it. Habits oftentimes take years to form, so they will require time and patience for you to chip away at the viselike grip they can have on your life and perceptions.

The Importance of Awareness: Learning to Catch and Stop

Aside from working with the data revealed in your Self-Portrait comparison, one last measure of your readiness is your *awareness*. As I said at the beginning of this chapter, you don't have to be symptom-free to be catalytic, but in order to be catalytic, you must be *symptom-aware*. Becoming more aware of insecurity allows you to catch yourself in the heat of any defensive moment, which puts you in a position to stop reflexive, controlling behavior from persisting—catch and stop.

Your thinking might be something like, "Why was I acting like such a jerk? All she did was remind me that Saturday night we had to go to her brother's birthday party. I sure did snap. I can be such a Raccoon! Guess I want to be the one deciding how I spend my weekend—not my brother-in-law! It's so dumb. I feel like I have to protect my weekends— as if it's my last weekend on earth! Why can't I just be less rigid? I know that after I calm down, I always give in—it's never a big deal. So why do I get so negative? Guess I know why, it's my insecurity—I need to be the one calling all the shots or I feel threatened. I can be such an Elephant! Okay, let me get a grip and stop this foolishness."

This kind of catch-and-stop inner dialogue needs to be part of your ongoing everyday effort. Once this begins to happen you can begin to relax because insecurity won't be steering your life, you will be. And when self-trust rather than insecurity is behind the wheel, you'll find out very quickly how amazing the results can be.

Starting the Catalytic Process: Becoming a Student

Okay, now you're finally ready to switch gears and move from your personal Self-Coaching training to Catalytic Self-Coaching. At this point I'm going to ask you to think of yourself as a *student* of your partner. With less insecurity in your life, you can now remove yourself from your old, reflexive patterns while isolating your partner's defensive reflexes, thus learning the truth about what's been tripping up your relationship. Remember, you're the psychologist-coach now, no longer a participant in the destructive dances you once shared. If you fully accept this new role, it will help you to stay focused, motivated, and effective. "I'm the coach; I refuse to be part of the problem."

Because your Self-Coaching training is an ongoing process, from time to time you might be tempted to resort to older controlling strategies. But now you know you have a choice. No more excuses for you. Not if you're going to accept your new role of coach. If you expect to go forward from this point and become catalytic, you must—*must*—steel yourself against any unfinished areas of insecure behavior (catch and stop).

Let's begin the catalytic process with an assessment.

Combining Portraits

In chapters 6 and 7, you evaluated your control patterns and sketched a Self-Portrait. This was your *before* portrait (before any Self-Coaching training) that we discussed earlier. Now, using only your *before* Self-Portrait data, you're about to combine this information with your partner's to create a Self + Self = Us Portrait. The reason we're using your *before* data is to get an accurate snapshot of the relationship dynamic that led to your struggles (that is, before the catalytic effects of your Self-Coaching).

Now we're ready to combine your portrait with your partner's portrait. Of course it would be best if your partner would consider taking the self-quizzes in chapter 6, but at this point it isn't essential. You'll need to judge whether approaching your partner at this time will be a plus or a minus. If, for example, your partner is a highly defensive Elephant and will more than likely scoff at the notion of taking the quizzes, then it might be best to wait until you've had more of a catalytic effect on the relationship. Let's first proceed with the assumption that you have an unwilling partner, and then we'll go on to discuss a format for a willing partner.

Uncooperative partner assessment. Assuming you've evaluated the situation and have concluded that you want to reserve your best shot for when your partner will be more receptive, let's proceed (one more time) without involving your partner directly.

Since the immediate goal of Catalytic Self-Coaching is to begin to neutralize the relationship struggle, we need to establish the Self + Self = Us Portrait—ASAP. Armed with this information, you'll be able to begin shifting the center of gravity away from the typical patterns of struggle. For now, I'd like you to go back to chapter 6 and once again retake the quizzes. Only this time I don't want you to answer them for yourself, I want you to answer them for your partner.

This isn't as much of a stretch as you might think. You know from past experience how often you can predict exactly what your partner will do or say. "Oh, Bob would never, ever agree to going to counseling, he would probably say he doesn't need anyone to solve his problems." Or, "Susan would definitely not enjoy a surprise party, she always feels nervous about being the center of attention." Yes, you probably know your partner better than you think. And now, especially since you've developed enough self-trust to be able to remove yourself from your own historical insecurities, you are in a much better position to see objectively what's going on with your partner.

As you take the quizzes for your partner, all I ask is that you put yourself in your partner's shoes and answer each question as you feel he or she would. Make sure to keep very focused during each quiz. Take a minute or two between them to remind yourself that we're not interested in what *you* think is actually going on with your partner, we're interested in you answering the questions the way you think your partner would.

Cooperative partner assessment. Clearly the data derived from a cooperative partner who assures you that he or she will be as truthful as possible is the more helpful way to proceed. And don't ever underestimate the value of curiosity—you'd be surprised to find out how many uncooperative partners wind up being very curious about their own Self-Portraits. You might say something like the following: "I've been doing some reading about relationship struggle and I've come across these interesting true-false quizzes that can give you what's called a Relationship Self-Portrait. If you combine one partner's information with the other's, you can make an assessment of where the relationship stands. Let me know if you're interested in finding out more about your patterns and how these patterns combine with mine."

Once you have the data from your partner's five tests you're ready to apply this to the Self + Self = Us Portrait. Here's an example. Using the *before* scores from the figure on page 148 to describe partner A, and combining these with a fictitious set of scores to describe partner B, I'll demonstrate how to set up a Self + Self = Us Portrait.

Constructing a Sample Self + Self = Us Portrait

Controlling Patterns	Partner A Score	Partner B Score
Turtle	8.5	2
Tiger	3	18
Elephant	10	16
Raccoon	10.5	4
Peacock	+ 13	+ 10
Totals	45	50

Relationship-unhealthy (RU) score: 45 + 50 = 95
Relationship-healthy (RH) score: 200 − 95 = 105

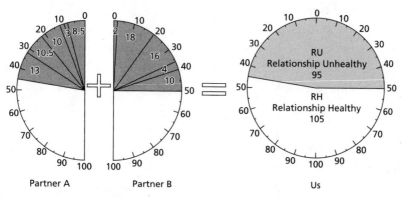

Sample Self + Self = Us Portrait

Partner A   Partner B   Us

From the figure above, you can see that combining both partners' Self-Portraits yields a wealth of significant information. By combining the two half circles into one Us-circle you wind up with a clear visual of how much is healthy and how much is unhealthy in the relationship. In this example, you can see that slightly less than half of this couple's relating is judged to be unhealthy. (Keep in mind that the goal of Catalytic Self-Coaching is to eliminate most if not all unhealthy relating.) For the moment, let's talk about how the Us-circle is derived.

Looking at the figure, note the two portions of the Us-circle. The shaded area is labeled "relationship unhealthy (RU)" with a corresponding score of 95. This score is simply the sum of all the controlling strategy scores from both partners, marked off with the corresponding number of ticks on the circle.

From this example you can see that the relationship-healthy (RH) area is the area that remains after you plot the RU score. For those who want the math: if you subtract the RU score from 200 (Since the value of each half circle is 100, the combined total for the Us-circle is 200) you will obtain the relationship-healthy score, in this case, 200 minus 95 = 105 (RH). This Us-Portrait information will be used as an eventual baseline for you and your partner to assess your overall relationship progress. As stated previously, your catalytic goal should be to minimize, if not eliminate, the unhealthy component (RU) in your relationship.

Each element of the Self + Self = Us Portrait can offer significant feedback and encouragement for your ongoing Catalytic Self-Coaching efforts. The "Us" part of the diagram provides you with an overview of the health of your relationship. Creating a visual is one way to begin not only to recognize the current status of your relationship, but also to provide a stimulus for wanting to change. As your RU/RH alignment begins to shift due to your Catalytic Self-Coaching efforts, you'll find that your improving Us-Portrait will act as a valuable source of visual feedback.

Next, by examining each partner's half-circle Self-Portrait, you will gain a more detailed view of the specific controlling behaviors that comprise the Us-Portrait. Seeing these defensive controlling patterns will help you understand—on a behavioral level—exactly what's going on. This information will assist you in your catalytic efforts to pinpoint the problem areas as you work toward removing your 50 percent contribution to the struggle.

You should be aware that some patterns can become hot buttons for conflict, especially when you have very similar defensive tendencies. For example, an Elephant and an Elephant can really lock tusks in an argument, as can a Tiger and a Tiger. A combination like this would have a high potential for violence. On the other hand, if you and your partner are very different, you might find extremes in passive versus aggressive alignments.

But instead of continuing with broad generalizations, I will present concrete Self + Self = Us data from actual case stories in the chapters that follow. Each of these examples is aimed at helping you remove any negative contributions you may be making to your own relationship struggle. The idea is for you to neutralize conflict. I'm going to introduce you to Bret and Carol and, rather than talk about the specific dynamics of their therapy, I'll just highlight their Self + Self = Us data. As you'll see, from the brief description in the next section, Bret and Carol are rather archetypal in their passive-aggressive relationship.

Bret and Carol

The first thing that impressed me about Bret and Carol when I met them was that they were polar opposites. Carol could only be described as a biting, angry bully of a wife who wanted to use the sessions to attack Bret. Bret, on the other hand, could best be described as a lump of a person who sat slumped down on the couch, expressionless, having long ago withdrawn any energy or inclination to argue with his very vocal wife.

One look at their Self-Portrait data on the next page and you'll see that Carol's Tiger (17) and Elephant (18.5) traits dominated Bret's passive, withdrawn Turtle (18) tendencies. Bret's constant refrain was, "What's the use?" "Why bother?" Or, more typically, "I just don't know what you want me to say." Carol had plenty to say: "He's a lazy slob." "You're such a moron!" "If it weren't for the kids, I'd be long gone." Take a look at Bret and Carol's Self-Portrait data, then look at their Self-Portrait diagrams, and you'll see just how important visuals can be:

Bret and Carol's Self-Portrait Data

Controlling Strategy	Bret's Score	Carol's Score
Turtle	18	5
Tiger	4	17
Elephant	3.5	18.5
Raccoon	15.5	13
Peacock	+ 3	+ 13
Totals	44	66.5

Relationship-unhealthy (RU) score: $44 + 66.5 = 110.5$
Relationship-healthy (RH) score: $200 - 144 = 89.5$

Bret and Carol

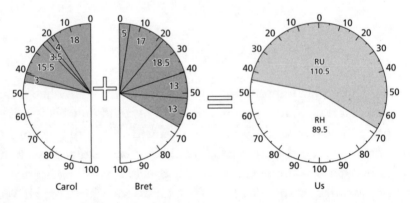

One quick look at Bret and Carol's Us-Portrait shows that unhealthy, reflexive behavior is clearly an issue: 110.5 RU versus 89.5 RH. Armed with the information from Bret and Carol's Self-Portraits, I did some individual work with them to begin recognizing and minimizing their defensive patterns. I found Carol to be receptive. (As she said, "I'll do it for the kids.") Once she was able to see and understand how her Tiger and Elephant tendencies instigated Turtle reactions in Bret, Carol began catching and stopping her verbal assaults. At first she still let the invectives fly, but she made a point to calm down and offer an apology. Bret, on the other hand, had to reckon with extreme Turtle capitulation. He was less enthusiastic than Carol because of his long-standing insecurity issues, but he nonetheless recognized the simple truth that as long as he and Carol remained deadlocked in the current alignment (Us-Portrait) nothing was going to change.

Carol, having more self-confidence, quickly became the more catalytic partner in our sessions. I could see that she was literally biting her tongue at Bret's passivity and reluctance to change. But she remained tough and determined. As she continued to withdraw her Tiger fangs and began to tone down her attacks, Bret began to relax enough to the point where he began talking more directly about his feelings rather than resorting to his old Raccoon tendency of passive-aggressively denying that he had anything to say.

Carol's response to Bret's movement was positive, albeit still somewhat sarcastic. "Finally! At least I know he's alive." I kept pointing out that Carol, since she had become the designated catalytic partner, needed to get beyond her reflexive hurt feelings and put a stop to her critical, sarcastic tone. She had to stop looking to Bret to change his shabby behavior; instead she needed to focus only on her own shabby behavior. I assured her that this would create a vacuum in the relationship and it would be filled with more appropriate responding from Bret.

This is exactly what happened. Carol began to become neutral in our sessions—no more criticism or biting remarks. She was able to talk about her issues truthfully, without any intent to inflict harm. She knew quite clearly that her Tiger-Elephant tendencies were standing in the way of her and Bret's progress. This awareness allowed her to decide to take the catalytic lead without feeling—as she initially told me—like the therapy was one-sided with her doing all the work. She managed to completely abandon her feelings of one-sidedness when she noticed that Bret was really starting to change. "He's actually talking to me at home! He still watches a lot of TV, but now we watch shows together and even wind up talking and joking around." Once Carol saw Bret poke his head out of his Turtle shell, she knew that her catalytic efforts were worthwhile. At this point she never looked back or questioned her catalytic efforts again. She didn't have to, because now she had a real partner.

PART TWO

Catalytic Self-Coaching

Working with Your Partner

12

Creating a Relationship Vacuum

Previously your relationship has been buffeted by the winds of insecurity, defensiveness, and control. But now, armed with your Self-Coaching perspective and a working knowledge of your relationship's Self + Self = Us Portrait (regardless of whether your partner participated in the self-quizzes), you're ready to initiate a catalytic effect on your relationship that will neutralize these destructive forces. Although our focus from this point on will be exclusively on your relationship, remember that your personal Self-Coaching training needs to run concurrently with your catalytic efforts. Learning to minimize your own defensive, controlling patterns is an ongoing process that will only enhance your catalytic efforts. As I've hinted at in previous chapters, Self-Coaching is your method of creating a relationship-struggle vacuum, which will then motivate your partner to change.

For now, I want you to become a student of your partner's controlling, defensive patterns. You need to study these patterns because you're about to learn a new language.

The Language of Conflict

Every relationship has its own unique language of conflict. This is not a language in the traditional sense, but more a destructive type of communication that emanates from insecurity. This language of conflict has a vocabulary derived from each partner's strategies of control. Turtles, for example, speak the language of withdrawal and passivity, Tigers of aggression, Elephants of intimidation, Raccoons of whining or aggressive snarling, and Peacocks of egocentric disregard. Becoming familiar with both your controlling patterns (which are diminishing with your ongoing Self-Coaching efforts) and your partner's is the only way to become fluent in your relationship's unique language of conflict.

As discussed in the previous chapter, your personal awareness is an essential first step if you're going to avoid the destructive habits that have historically dominated your relationship. Being aware of your insecurity-driven behavior and relying on Self-Talk to prevent you from getting hooked by your old destructive patterns is the key to becoming part of the solution rather than an ongoing part of the problem. And the biggest catalytic part of the solution is removing yourself from the senseless controlling struggles.

By removing yourself, you leave your partner disoriented and in unfamiliar surroundings. After all, for the first time, your partner has no one to defend against! The Tiger, for example, waiting for a typical response of withdrawal, may be flummoxed to find you calmly holding your ground, not participating in the chaos. The Raccoon, on the other hand, may be wondering, "What's up with her? I just threw out a guilt-bomb and he's just ignoring me!" It's this fundamental interruption and shifting of the energy that creates a receptive environment that begins to neutralize the conflict.

Keep in mind that the fuel of all struggle is control. The reason we originally designated your partner as the "reluctant" partner was because he or she is convinced that *you're* a threat. "What?" you say. "All I want is for us to be happy. How does that make *me* a threat?" To understand this seeming paradox, you must look at your partner's insecurity. And you're now in a position to do this by analyzing your partner's Self-Portrait. The individual scores (Turtle, Tiger, and so on), especially those that are the highest, will give you a snapshot of your partner's controlling patterns of defense. Behavior that was once obscure and confusing now begins to become transparent.

We acquire controlling strategies to protect us from perceived vulnerability. The operative word is *perceived*. The more insecure a person is, the more likely that they are going to perceive danger in safe places and therefore resort to defensive strategies of protection. The more secure person, on the other hand, will be more tolerant when feeling challenged and less likely to fire back a volley of defensive counterattacks. If a Raccoon, for example, feels that she is being put down and is beginning to feel threatened and vulnerable, she might reflexively snap back, "You think you're so hot. Well, let me tell you, you're not such a great lover . . ." This would be an attempt to level the playing field—if I'm out of control, then let me make you feel equally out of control. Even though two wrongs don't make a right, the second wrong sure feels good when you're feeling threatened.

Assuming your reluctant, insecure partner has routinely relied on various controlling strategies, we might safely assume that your reactions (prior to your Self-Coaching training) have been to defend yourself with some form of counterattack. If your partner is a Tiger or an Elephant, perhaps you withdrew with Turtle-shell isolation, or snapped back with Raccoon aggressiveness. Regardless of which counterattack you employed, your reactivity constituted 50 percent of the relationship struggle. This is why your Self-Coaching has been such an integral part of your training, because unless we eliminate the tit-for-tat nature of your conflicts, there's nothing to stop further erosion.

Tony and Eileen: Neutralizing the Conflict

I've found that looking at the dynamics of other couples and their struggles is the best way to demonstrate Catalytic Self-Coaching. I'm sure you've heard the expression "Unable to see the forest for the trees." When you're too close to your own problems and issues, it's hard not to get confused. Tony and Eileen's story will begin to give you an idea of how effective Self-Coaching can be when eliminating the attack-counterattack pattern within a relationship.

Tony, a mild-mannered Turtle, is married to Eileen, a relatively obnoxious Peacock. Tony and I had begun individual therapy because of his anxiety, sleeplessness, and mild depression. Before I discuss this case more thoroughly, here's the data from Tony and Eileen's Self + Self = Us Portrait:

Tony and Eileen's Self-Portrait Data

Controlling Strategy	Tony's Score	Eileen's Score
Turtle	18	3
Tiger	2	16.5
Elephant	4.5	15
Raccoon	12	8.5
Peacock	+ 2.5	+ 18
Totals	39	61

Relationship-unhealthy (RU) score: $39 + 61 = 100$
Relationship-healthy (RH) score: $200 - 100 = 100$

Tony and Eileen

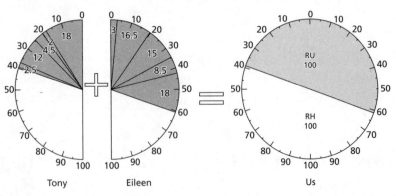

Tony   Eileen   Us

From Tony's Self-Portrait, you can see that what stands out is his Turtle defensiveness (with a secondary tendency toward Raccoon martyrdom). A Turtle score of 18 indicates a significant defense of passivity. Contrasting this with Eileen's scores, we see that what stands out is her Peacock score (along with a supporting cast of Tiger-Elephant aggressiveness). Let's take a look at how a relatively passive Tony learned to defuse a rather aggressive narcissist.

Here's a compilation of notes from Tony's earlier, individual sessions, describing his struggle with Eileen:

I really love Eileen, but she's not easy to live with. She's forty years old and insists on dressing like she's twenty. Sometimes I worry that all her primping and working out is an attempt to get more attention. Whenever we're out, she's always flirting and strutting. It bothers me . . . sometimes it bothers me a lot. But what can I do? She's attractive and she knows it. I try to tell myself that it's just a midlife thing and it will pass. I try to understand, but I just keep winding up getting depressed. What makes matters worse, she treats me like dirt . . . sometimes I think she really hates me.

The other day, she came back from the mall wearing a new coat. I was busy and didn't notice it—why would I, she shops all the time. I can't keep up with what's new and what's old. Anyway, she walks into the den, stands there and says, "Well?" I'm sitting there, confused, and say, "Well, what?" With that she storms out of the room, cursing at me and slamming the door. I went into a tailspin. I can't really explain it. I wanted to explode, scream, and cry all at once. I wound up just sitting there, pounding my fists into my head. I mean, how could this woman say these things and really love me? Maybe the truth is she doesn't. I got myself really upset. I made myself a few drinks and went to bed—at 8:30 at night!

Things have progressively gotten worse over the years. I've come to the conclusion that her good looks are her downfall. Like I said, she's always shopping, doing her nails, her hair, and now she wants plastic surgery! Don't ask me why, she says she needs an eye job. What the hell is an eye job? Her eyes are exactly the same as they always were. She's driving me crazy with her vanity, she spends hours in front of the mirror, but I can't say anything.

I guess I could manage to live with Eileen's ego, I just can't live with the way she treats me. The constant yelling, putting me down, treating me like I'm nothing more than a splinter. I don't say anything because . . . truth is, I don't know why. I guess it's because she's so overpowering. I can't honestly say I'm afraid of Eileen, but listening to myself describe what's going on, I guess it does sound like I'm a wimp. I just don't want to start a war, it's not worth it. So I wind up saying nothing and doing nothing . . . I just go off and sulk. Or pour another drink.

We haven't had sex in over a year. This is killing me. I just can't imagine approaching Eileen. I mean, why would she want to have sex with me—she hates me! I don't know what to do. I don't want to get a divorce. Underneath all this craziness, I do love her, but honestly, I don't feel this decision is in my hands.

I came to therapy because I'm drinking too much, I'm starting to get depressed, and the last thing I need right now is to go through a divorce. It would kill me.

You can see where Tony was in desperate need of some Self-Coaching. With Tony, as is the case with most Turtles, there's often a significant issue with low self-esteem and self-confidence. In our first session, after hearing Tony go on about how inadequate he felt, I asked him to tell me specifically why he wasn't "okay." As I suspected, he didn't have an answer. But after some face scrunching, he offered, "If Eileen treated me better, I'd feel better about myself."

Like so many who struggle in a relationship, he had a strong impulse to point a finger and blame his partner: "If only she/he would . . . " *If only* is a defensive trap that exonerates you from taking any responsibility by placing blame on someone or something else: on fate ("If only I got that promotion, then I would . . ."), on circumstances ("If only I didn't lose my money at the track . . ."), and of course, on your partner ("If only she would have sex with me, then I wouldn't be so aloof."). I wasn't about to let Tony get away with *if only*. It was time to teach him some Self-Talk.

Separating facts from fictions (Self-Talk, Step 1) was critical for Tony as he began to get his first glimpse that maybe there were two problems in this relationship: his insecurity/low self-esteem, and Eileen's narcissistic disregard for him. As obvious as it may appear to you reading this, Tony was shocked at the revelation that Eileen could be part of the problem. It's not that he thought Eileen was perfect; it was only that when it came to what was wrong in their marriage, Tony just reflexively felt responsible.

Why? Well, he'd probably tell you it was because of his shortcomings. As was Tony's long-standing reflex, he was first in line to assume that if there was a problem, *he* had to be to blame! He had long ago agreed with Eileen that *he* was the reason why she was so nasty, *he* was the reason why she needed to do things for herself in order to feel good, and *he* was the reason why she needed to flirt with other men. Tony's rationale was that since he didn't know how to make Eileen feel good about herself (because he wasn't a good enough husband, lover, person, and so on), he couldn't stop her from protecting herself. Talk about a catch-22.

Tony was, in fact, partially right. As I was about to find out in sessions with Eileen, she was definitely protecting herself, but not from Tony. She was running away from her own insecurity. Cloaked in her narcissistic facade of self-love was a deeper truth consisting of self-loathing and fear—coincidentally, a fear not unlike Tony's. The major difference between Tony and Eileen was that Eileen, because of her attractiveness, was able to rely on her looks to compensate for her feelings of inadequacy and shallow personality development. Tony, on the other hand, taking the opposite tack, had long ago gravitated toward insulation rather than exposure as a defense. He needed to be encouraged to poke his head out of his Turtle shell long enough to see this bigger, more accurate picture.

Tony's More Expansive View

In order to help Tony with his more expansive view, we focused his Self-Coaching training on helping him understand that his habit of insecurity wasn't anything new, it was a reflexive habit that had followed him from childhood. As a child, Tony was always shy, withdrawn, and insecure. This reflex (his emotional baggage) followed him into his marriage as Eileen's strong personality sent him quickly seeking the solace of his protective shell.

Insisting that Tony pay particular attention to his Self-Talk, we began to chip away at his insecurity by suggesting that he begin evaluating his feelings as either facts or fictions. In our sessions, if he was going to offer up a statement that he considered factual, I wanted proof. When, for example, he told me that Eileen would never respect him, I asked, "Fact or fiction?" As you might suspect, he argued with me, insisting that this was, indeed, a "fact of life." I asked him, "How is it possible that you can treat the future as a fact?" Tony conceded, but felt that I was splitting hairs. In time we overcame his baseless resistance and he came to understand that all prognostications were in fact fictions! Why? Because no one has a crystal ball, no one can see into the future. Fictions are insecurity's fabrications designed to accomplish one thing—keep you prisoner by projecting doubts, fears, and negative thoughts.

Separating facts from fictions was the key in getting Tony to begin to see the biggest of big truths—the *fact* that there was nothing wrong with him. Sure, he had some limiting habits, but as I would often point out to Tony, "You are not your habit!" Once he got used to not listening to insecurity's harangue of groundless chatter, he was in a good position to step apart and simply "let go" (Self-Talk, Steps 2 and 3). Now that his long-standing identification with insecurity was finally broken, things began to click. At this point, it didn't take long before Tony's Self-Coaching started to really pay off as he finally began to put a stop to his ruminative self-loathing. His newfound objective awareness allowed him to see that Turtle-shell living was his problem, not his solution. And certainly not his marital solution.

Now for the first time, he embraced the prospect of approaching Eileen from a place of strength rather than weakness. Tony was beginning to come alive, and perhaps for the first time in his life, he experienced a feeling of empowerment. The surge of energy that was beginning to well up was the result of toppling years of pent-up insecurity. Finally, he was able to recognize that he no longer needed to be victimized by either his reflexive fears or by Eileen's insecurity. At this point, Tony was ready to embark on some Catalytic Self-Coaching.

From Peacock to Person: Eileen's Transition

For Tony, neutralizing the relationship required that he remove his 50 percent contributions of passivity, negativity, hopelessness, and self-destructive behavior (his drinking had become a regular problem). As he threw himself into his Self-Coaching efforts, Eileen began to experience a very different Tony—a Tony who was now beginning to understand Eileen's insecurities. This awareness emboldened him to begin talking directly to her from a place of power rather than impotence. He wasn't afraid to ask her how she felt about him, about life, or about growing older. He talked to her openly and freely about her fears and doubts. As you can imagine, this wasn't easy. Eileen's knee-jerk reflex toward Tony was to dismiss him outright, but Tony wasn't about to be deterred. And once Eileen began to open up, things began to flow very nicely.

Since Tony wasn't cowering or retreating from Eileen's Tiger-Elephant aggressiveness, Eileen at first found herself confused. She even asked him at one point, "I don't understand. After what I just said, why are you so calm?" She was definitely off balance. No longer getting Tony's typical response of withdrawal from her aggressiveness, unsure-Eileen began to tone down her assaults. You might be wondering why Eileen was so quick to abandon her aggression. This is a critical question. When controlling strategies work, such as was the case with Eileen's Peacock-Tiger-Elephant defense, there's no problem. But when a controlling strategy begins to crumble, there's nothing left in its place. And when stripped of one's usual facade, what's left is vulnerability. It's this vulnerability that becomes your catalytic goal—to break down the controlling defense long enough to encourage legitimate and healthy change.

Catalytic Self-Coaching Tip
The goal of Catalytic Self-Coaching is to break down your partner's defense long enough to create a constructive environment of emotional vulnerability.

Whenever Eileen tried to intimidate him, Tony would now calmly wait until she was finished, at which point he would reflect on what was "factually" going on, and then with awareness, he would respond, "There's no need to be angry with me. What's really bothering you?" Eileen wasn't at all comfortable with exchanges like this—they were, to say the least, disorienting. Although she quickly began to feel more uncomfortable with Tony, she also recognized that she was feeling less sure of herself. Her traditional defenses had always given her a sense of control over the relationship, but now she was feeling anything but control. And she didn't like it!

Since her Tiger-Elephant aggressiveness wasn't cutting it, Eileen began to rely more on her Peacock defenses to save the day. She became more aloof and detached, insisting that the marriage was only an impediment to her real need, to be admired, wanted, and sought after by others. Once again, Tony, in spite of this new challenge, was able to remain neutral, continuing to create a vacuum. Once, Eileen would have rationalized her flirtatious ways like this: "Tony's inadequate, and since I'm in a nowhere relationship, I need to feel better about me. The hell with him." Now that Tony was acting . . . well, "adequate," the rationalization no longer worked. Actually, Tony was acting more than adequate; he was acting like someone with confidence and power. No longer was he a punching bag, now he was becoming a real person who couldn't be pushed around or taken for granted.

Eileen, in spite of her Peacock-Tiger-Elephant reflexes, was beginning to respond to Tony's metamorphosis. She wouldn't admit it at first—actually, she couldn't, because for years she had been building her own insulation, just waiting for the right man to come along so she could slam the emotional door shut on the marriage while arranging to live safely and happily in romantic bliss. But now something was different. It wasn't as easy to dismiss Tony. In fact, at first she resented having *any* positive feelings for him. Keep in mind that Eileen's whole protective program depended on her minimizing her feelings for him. Tony's Catalytic Self-Coaching turned her world upside down. And this is *exactly* what a catalytic partner needs to accomplish.

Tony took away Eileen's raison d'être: he stripped her of her distorted fears about relating. And he opened her eyes to the fact that she was running, not so much from him, but from her own emotional baggage. It was at this point that Tony told me that Eileen was worried and asked if she could talk to me. She had seen how much Tony had progressed and improved and was beginning to feel like she was "missing something."

What's a Peacock without Feathers?

Eileen was indeed in a subdued panic when I met with her. She acknowledged that she was now seeing Tony as the strong one in the relationship and that she was becoming the weak, neurotic one. One thing I learned from these sessions with Eileen (although this wasn't obvious to her) was that deep down, she never intended to leave Tony. What she was really doing was setting up a cake-and-eat-it scenario. She wanted to have the stability of her long-term marriage, house, two dogs, one cat, and the financial ease of Tony's lucrative hardware business while keeping a lover/flirtation on the side. She had herself convinced that she could have it all, if only she could find a discreet lover who wouldn't upset the status quo. "If only . . ."

As you can see, Eileen's ultimate neurotic vision of stability depended on Tony never changing. Inspired by his growth, she was now convinced to begin her own Self-Coaching. She did this with more enthusiasm than Tony expected. This is the best possible outcome of Catalytic Self-Coaching. As the catalytic partner begins to become less defensive and more constructive, modeling appropriate and healthy behavior, the reluctant partner then starts to abandon reflexive doubt and hesitation. At this point things begin to soar. Just as each partner fed negatively off each other, now, once the catalytic wheels of progress engage, each partner encourages the other toward a more healthy relationship and connection to life.

13

Working with
Self + Self = Us Portraits

Before moving on to the next chapter, which officially represents the end of your solo catalytic work and initiates a shift to a joint catalytic effort between you and your partner, it's important for you to realize the adaptability of Catalytic Self-Coaching to any situation—most importantly, to your situation. Using a case story where two Elephants collide, I'll show you that regardless of the unique Self + Self = Us Portrait, the catalytic process remains essentially the same.

The goal in this chapter is to show you how easily you can adapt Catalytic Self-Coaching to fit any Self + Self = Us configuration, including yours.

The following is a distillation of the catalytic process:

- Using Self-Coaching, you, the problem-solving partner, work to minimize and eliminate your own insecurity-driven, controlling habits.

- By eliminating your controlling habits, you create a relationship vacuum, making it unnecessary for your partner to maintain his or her defensive posture.

- Once the motivation for defensive relating is eliminated, the reluctant partner is enlisted as a co-catalytic partner to work mutually toward relationship success.

Different or Similar, Conflict Is Conflict

In the last chapter you read about Tony and Eileen, a couple who gave you a glimpse of a Turtle-versus-Peacock struggle. Their particular Self + Self = Us Portrait represented a kind of oil-and-water alignment, in which their differences were a major source of conflict. Although oil-and-water relationship struggles tend to be more common—the old notion that opposites attract—it's not at all unusual for certain struggles to possess very similar controlling alignments (Raccoon versus Raccoon, Peacock versus Peacock, and so on). When this happens, then like magnets of the same polarity, you wind up with a repelling situation that can lead to some very intense struggles. If you've never seen the classic 1989 movie *The War of the Roses*, I highly recommend that you rent it and see what happens when two Tigers get divorced.

Whether Self-Portraits are different or similar, conflict is conflict and, either way, it's going to be bad for the relationship. Fortunately for you, it doesn't matter what your Self-Portrait alignments are—similar or different. The process of applying Catalytic Self-Coaching remains the same.

When Elephants Collide

I'd like to introduce you to Jason and Maryann, two pachyderms who couldn't avoid each other's swinging trunks. Jason's a dot-com salesman who knows how to schmooze people. He's a fast talker, adept at changing directions on a dime and keeping you off balance. He's been called a control freak by most who know him, and he doesn't disagree. He's gotten into trouble more than once because he doesn't know how to keep his mouth shut. Most recently, after being stopped by a policeman for not having an appropriate inspection sticker on his windshield, Jason was almost arrested because of his insulting remarks. Jason isn't someone you want to argue with—he's a know-it-all who feels he's never wrong.

Maryann is no different. She is an office manager for a dentist. She runs the office with an iron fist. If you have a problem paying your bill, if you happen to show up late, or you're calling at the last minute to cancel an appointment, you'd better watch out, because Maryann will let you know that your behavior will not be tolerated. Although her boss has asked her to tone down her Elephant ways, he, being of the Elephant persuasion himself, has kept her employed for twelve years, obviously appreciating the tight ship she runs. When his patients complain, he just says, "Oh, that's just Maryann, don't take it personally." Unfortunately, since both Maryann and Jason are know-it-alls, you can imagine what happens when they disagree.

Let's look at Jason and Maryann's Self + Self = Us Portrait:

Jason and Maryann's Self-Portrait Data

Controlling Strategy	Jason's Score	Maryann's Score
Turtle	3	2
Tiger	9	8
Elephant	16	15
Raccoon	4	5
Peacock	+ 2	+ 4
Totals	34	34

Jason and Maryann

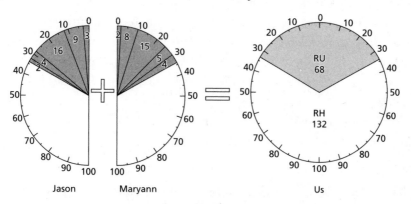

Jason and Maryann's arguments had reached critical mass over where to go on vacation. Jason dug his heels in, insisting that a cruise in the

Caribbean was the only thing that made sense. As he put it, "It's time for a real vacation. I need something to look forward to. And besides, any idiot would realize that a cruise is a more exciting vacation than being stuck at the Jersey shore." Maryann, equally dug in, argued, "You're such a drag on vacations. I'd rather be at the shore where I at least have my sister to keep me company. Why would I want to be stuck in one of those coffin-sized cabins fighting with you for a week? You've got to be kidding, right?" After a solid week of berating each other, mocking, insulting, and threatening, things came to a head when Jason left the house, announcing that he was going to a motel. Maryann slammed the door behind him.

After Jason had lived in a motel for a week, Maryann e-mailed him suggesting that they either go for counseling or get divorced. Uncharacteristically, Jason agreed. As I later found out, he saw therapy as his opportunity to finally prove Maryann wrong. He felt that any intelligent person (a.k.a. yours truly) would certainly agree with his logic. After all, as Jason told me, "How can you compare going down the shore with going on a cruise?" In Jason's Elephant world, everything was crystal clear, Jason crystal clear. He had no reason to believe I wouldn't do "the right thing" and agree that Maryann was wrong.

Regardless of *why* they wound up in my office, or what Jason's agenda was, it was still a good thing that they found their way into counseling. Maryann showed up separately from Jason, carrying a tape recorder. She said, "I want proof of what we talk about, so he doesn't try to twist what goes on here." Jason, showing up ten minutes late for the session, immediately asked about the tape recorder. I explained Maryann's request, and for the second time in one week, he agreed with his wife. "Now, that's a good idea. You'll finally be able to hear how ignorant you sound."

So it was that we began to compile tapes of each of our sessions. I had absolutely no problem with objective data, and certainly with this couple, from the outset I had a strong intuition that both Jason and Maryann could profit from "rewinding the tape." The following are excerpts from our initial sessions:

Jason [*glaring at Maryann*]: Okay, I guess you want me to start. For years, I've wanted to go on a cruise. A programmer I work with has been telling me about a deal he got with one of the cruise lines and I decided that, damn it, I deserve to do what I want once in a while. The problem is my wife. Every year we wind up going down the shore. Our rental house becomes a hotel for Maryann's family and any strays who wander by. She winds up cooking every night, while I'm out on the deck entertaining her brother-in-law, who does nothing but yell at his kids. It's awful. And you know what? I'm just not going to give in this year!

Maryann: Every year I ask you what you want to do for vacation and you usually shrug your shoulders and tell me, "Whatever." You're being such a jerk, making it sound like you're such a martyr. You go fishing, crabbing, to the boardwalk . . . you're such a damn liar! When I mentioned going down the shore this year, you didn't say anything—as usual—so I made the plans with my sister.

Jason: You're calling me a liar? You gotta be kidding, right? You never asked me about this summer. You're delusional. I never agreed to anything! I know this for a fact, because I decided a long time ago that last year was my last shore vacation. You know I've always hated the beach. I can't just sit there listening to your sister whine hour after hour. After all these years, I deserve to have one chance to decide where *I* want to go.

Maryann: Don't tell me I didn't ask you about the shore! I did! If you're deaf, that's your problem. You know damn well I asked you. I guess you must be deaf *and* stupid! So what do you want me to do now? You can't expect me to tell everyone last-minute that we're not going. You know my sister counts on us to split the house rental. I won't do that to her. If you're so hell-bent on a cruise, go ahead, knock yourself out. You'll be very happy with yourself. That's if you can fit that thick head of yours in the cabin door.

Jason [*reddening*]: You know what, this isn't getting anywhere. Doc, would you tell her that I deserve a turn! What's fair is fair!

Maryann [*before I could respond*]: Okay, you know what, I agree you deserve a turn, but *not* this year! Plans have already been made and people are counting on us.

Jason: Screw other people! Why should I be the one who loses? It doesn't make any sense. You know what [*raising his voice*], I really don't give a s*** anymore!

Phew! This volatile exchange was followed by Jason seemingly doing an about-face: "Fine, you want to go down the shore, then we'll go." Neither Maryann nor I felt comforted by his capitulation—it clearly sounded like a threat. Maryann, regardless of the strings that might be attached to Jason's apparent surrender, decided that it was good enough for her—she just wanted to protect her sister from embarrassment. She didn't argue.

The next session brought out the price that Jason planned to extract for missing out on his cruise.

Jason: I have nothing to say tonight.

Maryann: He's been like this all week. Obnoxious, mean, actually wicked. He insults me, puts me down, and refuses to talk about the vacation.

Jason: No offense, doc, but this [therapy] is a waste of money. [*I was being punished now for not agreeing with Jason's need for a cruise.*] Maryann got her way . . . and I lost. That's it. Case closed. There's nothing left to talk about. [*Looking at Maryann*] I'm going to sit in the car, come out when you're done. [*Jason gets up and storms out of the office.*]

Maryann, red-faced, sat there looking at me for direction. It was time for me to introduce Self-Coaching. Maryann was definitely less defensive and willing to explore the situation. She said, "I know I'm a pain in the ass, everyone tells me. It's just the way I am. But as you can see, Jason's no bargain; guess we're just too similar. I know he's not wrong about going down the shore, but bailing out now wouldn't be the right thing to do—not with everyone committed. He's just so pigheaded, it seems like all we do is fight."

I explained to Maryann that unless Jason would agree to come back to our sessions, the only viable option would be for her to do some catalytic coaching. She knew from past experience that once Jason decided to teach her a lesson, there was no hope of changing his mind. She and I decided that she would invite Jason to come back, but that if he refused, she and I would continue with some Catalytic Self-Coaching.

Catalytically Respecting

The next week, as expected, Maryann showed up—alone. She mentioned that Jason said he wasn't going to waste his money arguing with her—he could do that at home for free. I had instructed Maryann that we were going to take the first catalytic step by her calmly telling Jason that he was welcome to join her for our next session. I impressed upon her that the most important, catalytic thing she could do was not to argue this point. Whatever his reaction, she was to catalytically respect it—"respect" meaning that Jason was entitled to his decision and perception. It's inappropriate for us to tell anyone they are not entitled to their view of the world. Catalytically respecting Jason's view meant that there would be no arguing. Maryann didn't argue; she forced herself to be respectful: "I could see that Jason was expecting me to fire back at him when he told me he wasn't coming to therapy, but I just told myself that he was entitled to his point of view—however ass-backwards it was—and then I just calmly told him that that was fine with me and I would be going by myself. He was speechless!"

Learning to catalytically respect is a fundamental component to your Catalytic Self-Coaching work. Please note that "respecting" doesn't mean you're happy with your partner's behavior, it's simply the realization that you're not going to insist on changing your partner—your partner needs to do that. If, instead, you are nonaccepting and disrespectful, then you automatically remain a threat and the cycle of defensive struggle will be reinforced.

A cautionary note regarding abuse. Obviously, catalytically respecting any kind of Tiger abuse *does not* mean that you allow yourself to be abused—it only means that you respect the fact that your partner has a significant problem that he or she must deal with. In an abusive situation, before any Catalytic Self-Coaching takes place, you must first remove and protect yourself from harm. There is no exception to this rule!

When dealing with an abusive relationship, Self-Coaching, by teaching you to break your habits of insecurity, empowers you to do what's necessary to protect yourself. And be clear about this: protecting yourself is catalytic! By not participating or otherwise enabling your partner's abuse, you create the necessary vacuum for change.

From what you've seen, Maryann and Jason's fundamental Elephant problem was lack of respect and lack of acceptance for any view other than their own. As you begin to initiate your catalytic efforts with your partner, simply insist on reminding yourself: *respect.* You'll find that catalytically respecting will also put you in the right frame of mind for enhancing your Self-Coaching efforts.

The Child-Reflex

In my previous books, I've discussed a type of reflexive thinking whose origins are established during our early developmental years. This type of thinking describes ingrained, childlike thinking habits that are insecurity-driven and destructive. This childlike component of reflexive thinking I refer to as your Child-Reflex. When a Child-Reflex is allowed to steer your thinking and reacting, you suffer. Why? Because the Child-Reflex has only one perception of the world, the primitive, distorted, out-of-date perception that was established when you were struggling as a child to feel less vulnerable. As adults, it's essential to learn to separate from the child's reflexive view of the world. Maryann and Jason's story is an example of Child-Reflexes gone wild.

Realizing the childlike quality of our first session, we played back a few minutes of our tape recording. After listening, I asked Maryann to describe how she thought she and Jason came across in their exchange. She responded, "We sound like two children." Bingo. I told her that that was exactly how it sounded, explaining that oftentimes Elephant-type arguing takes on a childlike flavor because we default back to older, primitive habits of defense—Child-Reflexes. Maryann had no trouble understanding that her contribution to the argument was just as childlike and primitive as Jason's. She said, "Now that you mention it, that's exactly how I would fight with my sisters when I was a kid. Guess not much has changed with me."

Catalytic Self-Coaching Reflection
Awareness facilitates change.

I explained to Maryann that Elephant behavior is a childlike attempt to control someone by bullying them. Elephants bully because Elephants have never progressed to a more mature, trusting way to handle life and situations. Instead, they rely on pushing people around in order to feel more in control. This may work if their partner is submissive, but as you've seen, when two people are pushing simultaneously, nothing productive can possibly happen.

With adequate self-trust you learn to handle any struggle in a nondefensive way. Catalytically respecting is a technique for realizing that you don't have to participate in any Elephant trunk swinging, Tiger clawing, Turtle fleeing, Peacock preening, or Raccoon snarling in order to take care of yourself. In Maryann's case, she didn't succeed in getting Jason to come to the session, true, but had she tried to intimidate or bully Jason, what would she have accomplished? Nothing other than to perpetuate the cycle of struggle. Instead, by catalytically respecting, Maryann took a major step not only in neutralizing the perennial struggle between her and Jason, but also in beginning to create an uncomfortable vacuum for Jason to wallow in. And when it comes to relationship dynamics, discomfort can be very motivating.

I asked Maryann what she felt when she told Jason that with or without him, she was going to come to our session. Scrunching up her brow for a second, then smiling, she said, "I felt really strong! You're right, I see what you're saying. I felt like no matter what Jason did, he couldn't threaten me because . . . I was steering. No matter what he said, I didn't have to argue. I respected his negativity and accepted it without trying to change him." Here she smiled. "If he wants to be a horse's ass, he's allowed to be one. It felt great not to have to battle him! For the first time I realized that changing Jason wasn't my responsibility." This was a big step for Maryann, and it set the tone for the Self-Coaching that followed. She was able to experience firsthand a more mature, empowered way of taking care of herself.

Maryann progressed with her Self-Talk, and as you might expect, Jason became more and more disoriented. Having nothing to swing his trunk at, "trunk swinging" became superfluous and Jason slowly began to tone down his trunk-swinging Child-Reflex. Although Jason never returned to our sessions, Maryann's catalytic efforts were not only paying off, they were producing unexpected benefits in the area of intimacy, communication, and trust.

So, you might ask, what happened with the shore house? The solution just seemed to evolve with the positive energy that was erupting in the relationship. Maryann and Jason went to a travel agent, took home a bunch of brochures, and selected the cruise that they would go on—the following year. As far as Jason was concerned, feeling that his needs were embraced by Maryann allowed him to start looking forward to the warm waters of the Caribbean and to lighten up enough to admit that regarding this year's excursion to the shore, "Well, I guess I do enjoy surf fishing at the shore."

When You're the Problem

Until now, we've been dealing exclusively with reluctant partners (problem avoiders) who contribute more to the relationship unhappiness than the problem-solver partner. Although not as common, one last scenario needs to be mentioned. This would be the seemingly paradoxical situation where the problem-solving partner is in fact the more destructive partner. Note that I said *seemingly* paradoxical. From the outset, I've described the problem-solver partner not necessarily as the one with the fewest problems, but the one who wants to do something to initiate change. If your Self-Portrait reveals that you are indeed more of a problem to the relationship struggle, then you should rejoice!

That's right, rejoice in the fact that since you're the problem-solver partner, you are actually in a better position to eliminate the caustic elements of your relationship. In a relationship where the reluctant partner is the bigger contributor, the problem solver is one step removed from directly eliminating these problems. But the reverse is true for you. And just because you may have a partner with fewer controlling problems (a better Self-Portrait profile than you), that doesn't necessarily mean they are more inclined to work at saving the relationship—they're still reluctant.

Perhaps your reluctant partner has slammed the door shut because he or she has become convinced that because of your destructive, controlling tendencies, there's just no hope, so why bother. If, for example, you were a violent, abusive Tiger, we can clearly understand why a partner would become reluctant to believe that things could be different. Or safe. Or perhaps a reluctant partner may have given up if you are a completely entrenched Turtle who refuses to leave your shell long enough to have a legitimate relationship. If you're the bigger contributor to the relationship struggle, don't confuse your partner's reluctance with neurosis. More likely it's their understandable defensive posture to protect themselves from *you*.

If you are the major problem, then your training will naturally focus on the Self-Coaching portion of this program. Although the catalytic process remains the same, you can expect that your Self-Coaching efforts will yield a very receptive catalytic response from your partner. In contrast, in a relationship where your partner is the designated reluctant partner *with* the bigger problem, the goal is to create a vacuum by removing yourself from the conflict equation. This vacuum generates a discomfort. If you recall from our example in this chapter, Jason, finding out that there was no incentive for any ongoing trunk swinging, began to feel a discomfort that led to his abandoning his defensive Elephant posture. In the case where you, not your reluctant partner, are the major problem, by using Self-Coaching to develop your own sense of security and self-trust, you too will be creating a vacuum. The only difference is that you will not be creating a vacuum of discomfort for your partner. You will be creating a positive relationship vacuum, a vacuum that will be catalytic for positive change.

14

Coaching Each Other
Risking Trust

The final step in Catalytic Self-Coaching is for each partner to learn to coach the other. In order to assess whether you're ready to proceed, please review the following checklist:

- [ ] You've retaken the insecurity quiz from chapter 4, as well as the five reflexive pattern quizzes in chapter 5. Your retest results should confirm that you've progressed significantly with your Self-Coaching training.

- [ ] You've made a preliminary assessment (with or without any input from your partner) of the Self + Self = Us Portrait and have been working with these results.

- [ ] You've been using your Self-Talk to substantially neutralize the relationship conflict and thereby have begun to create a relationship vacuum.

- [ ] Your reluctant partner, due to your neutralizing efforts, shows a willingness to work with you, or at the very least shows an interest in your coaching efforts.

It's important to achieve these goals before engaging your partner more directly. Without a proper foundation, your efforts will be for naught. You've been putting up with struggle for a while and you've come this far, so a little delay should not matter. What's another day, or week, or even another month? You may in fact be a lot closer than you realize. Imagine that you've been chipping away at a stone wall of your conflict, seeking your ultimate liberation. Self-Coaching has been your chisel and hammer as you've created a significant hole in the wall (you've begun to neutralize the conflict). At this point you assess your efforts; unfortunately all you see is more wall in front of you. Now is not the time to be discouraged. It may feel discouraging, but you honestly can't know if just one more chip might break you through to the sunshine and liberation that wait for you on the other side of the wall (relationship bliss). So if you need more work before proceeding, now is the time to refortify your resolve and prepare to finish the work you started—one chip at a time.

Partner Time: Coach-Coach Mode

If you've checked all the criteria in the list on page 185, then it's time to approach your partner directly. Since your Self-Coaching efforts have begun to reduce your partner's defensiveness, this would be the perfect time to discuss your training. I suggest that you have a general discussion about Catalytic Self-Coaching, emphasizing that the "Self" component is what you've been working on. This will let your partner know that you haven't been plotting or planning to manipulate him or her, but rather have been focusing on what *you* could do to improve the relationship.

Remember, most unenlightened, reluctant partners invariably feel that *you* (certainly not they) are the source of the relationship struggle. You can circumvent this tunnel-vision problem by agreeing that you indeed have been working to be more effective in the relationship. You might ask, "Haven't you noticed that we've been getting along better these past few weeks?" You need to stress that you've taken your training seriously and that you've reached a point where, in order to take this further, you need your partner's help. "I'd like you to consider helping me go forward with this program. I think it could make a big difference in our relationship."

At this point, if you haven't already, it's time to share this book with your partner, pointing out one or two of the Self + Self = Us Portraits in the book while explaining how it's possible to create a visual representation of what's going on in a relationship. Further explain how the profiles in the diagrams are based on the results of the five reflexive relating quizzes.

Such a conversation might go like this: "I took these quizzes to determine my relationship personality profile. Here's a copy of my initial Self-Portrait. What it shows are my reflexive tendencies." This would be a good point to briefly explain your Turtle, Tiger, Elephant, Raccoon, and Peacock descriptions, while inviting discussion. "I've come to realize how these tendencies are contributing to our struggle. I'd like you to take the same quizzes so that we can compare and combine our profiles in order to get a picture of where we stand as a couple. We could use our relationship portrait to show us what we both need to do to improve our situation."

Here are a few important points to consider when approaching your partner:

Don't try to control the situation. Be willing to accept a less than enthusiastic response or even a rejection of your proposal. Often, especially with Tigers, Elephants, and Peacocks, their knee-jerk reaction to anything is to say no—relationship struggle is all about control, and saying no is a way of controlling a situation. If this is the case, then simply let your partner know that you understand his or her hesitations, but would like your partner to think it over. Leave the book for him or her, bookmarked at chapter 5's quizzes. Wait a day or two and then reintroduce the proposal.

Although we aren't anticipating a rejection at this time, should it happen, you must resort back to your Self-Coaching efforts and do a bit of relationship jujitsu—keep yielding while continuing to neutralize. Eventually, even the most stubborn of partners will recognize the importance of joining you. After all, now that you are practicing Self-Talk techniques, your partner will no longer feel the need to protect him or herself from you.

Remember what was said earlier—most people are curious to know about themselves. Leaving the quizzes for your partner to consider will tempt him or her to assuage curiosity as well as save face and not capitulate too readily to your request. You may offer one last bit of temptation: "When you've taken the quizzes, we can compare our scores and see where we are similar and where we differ." Once again, you're letting your partner know that you've taken the step—you've taken the quizzes—and since you've already done this, you clearly are not asking him or her to do anything that you haven't done. As you'll see in upcoming chapters, a strategy of fairness represents everything that will follow in your catalytic training.

No finger-pointing. Perhaps the worst thing you could say to your partner would be, "I've done my training, now it's your turn." You've come a long way with your Self-Coaching training, and now is not the time to get uppity or defensive. Your approach must be genuinely humble and encouraging. "I've taken these quizzes and I've come to realize some interesting things about myself and how I relate. I'd love for you to consider taking them as well. We could use the information to help us understand why we've had so many difficulties in the past."

Be a resource. You might begin by talking about your Self-Coaching approach, especially how you've been applying Self-Talk to help you become less defensive and more secure. If your partner is showing interest, you might discuss how the Self + Self = Us Portraits are assessed. You could demonstrate this by sketching a rudimentary diagram showing how each Self-Portrait is combined to yield an "Us" assessment of the relationship status. Again, depending on your partner's receptivity, you could produce your actual Self + Self = Us sketch that you've been working with.

I recommend using actual data only when you detect significant interest. If you feel like you're pulling teeth, be satisfied with patiently laying more of a catalytic foundation with your ongoing efforts to neutralize and create a vacuum. This is especially true if you compiled your partner's Self-Portrait using your estimates as to how he or she would have responded to the quizzes. In which case, make it very clear that you were only guessing at your partner's responses in order to try to make a rough estimate of the relationship struggle. Follow up with, "Clearly, having you make a more accurate assessment will give us a more realistic 'Us' result."

Also, be sure to inform your partner that you made your Self-Portrait prior to any Self-Coaching training, so therefore it represents how you were when things were more chaotic. Use this discussion as a natural opportunity to talk a bit about Self-Coaching and the three steps of Self-Talk.

Take a look at Doug and Tracy, a newlywed couple who are a good example of how Catalytic Self-Coaching gets launched into the coach-coach mode.

Doug and Tracy

Doug was a twenty-seven-year-old entrepreneur whose Internet sports memorabilia business had finally begun to take off. His wife of six months, Tracy, also twenty-seven, was a high school English teacher. From the beginning of their courtship two years ago, Doug and Tracy struggled. From all outward appearances, it seemed that it was Tracy who was struggling with Doug's Peacock-Elephant tendencies. Against the advice of her parents and her friends, and with her own reservations, Tracy agreed to marry Doug, hoping that once he settled down he would become less selfish and more sensitive to her needs.

Tracy was predominately a Turtle who occasionally showed a few Raccoon, martyr tendencies—not the snarling, more aggressive side that Raccoons are prone to, but a more weepy, feel-sorry-for-me withdrawal from any conflict. Here is the data from their Self + Self = Us Portrait:

Doug and Tracy's Self-Portrait Data

Controlling Strategy	Doug's Score	Tracy's Score
Turtle	2	17
Tiger	6	3
Elephant	11	3
Raccoon	3	10
Peacock	+ 17	+ 4
Totals	39	37

Doug and Tracy

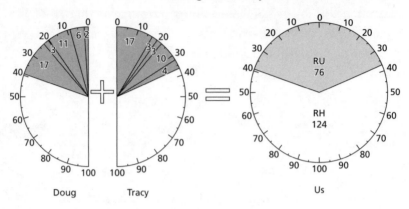

Doug   Tracy   Us

Tracy came into counseling feeling mildly depressed following an incident where she and Doug had been to a holiday party. She said:

> We were at a lovely party at my girlfriend's house. It started out great,
> we were having so much fun, laughing, teasing, and joking around.
> But then after a few beers Doug got to talking about his business.
> Unfortunately, whenever we're out and Doug starts talking about
> business, he just drones on and on. I know that once he gets into
> what's going on at work, that's usually the end of anything that's going
> on with me. I called this one right. After about a half hour of nonstop
> shop talk with my girlfriend's husband, I decided that I might as well
> go and find someone else to sit with. Doug's selfish, I've always known
> that. I know he's not trying to be rude or uncaring, it's just who he is.
> He's still a great guy in so many ways, but it's always about him.
>
> Anyway, we're at the party and Doug's going on and on about his
> plans for the business while completely ignoring me. It wasn't like I
> didn't have my friends to talk to, it's just that I didn't have Doug to
> talk to, know what I mean? After about an hour or so, I noticed that
> Doug wasn't around. After a bit of exploring, I found him sleeping
> on a couch in the den. I woke him up and asked what was going on;
> he told me he was tired. Tired? I told him that it was rude of him to
> just disappear. He quickly became defensive, telling me he was up
> late the other night working and he needed a quick nap. I couldn't
> make him understand that his behavior was just plain selfish.

On the way home, he was angry with me! He was telling me that I was being ridiculous and that no one cared that he wasn't around for twenty minutes. I tried to explain how uncomfortable I felt not knowing where he was or what happened. I begged him to just admit that he was wrong. I started to cry. Doug, rather than comforting me, exploded. Then he tells me he just doesn't want to talk about it anymore and proceeds to turn up the volume on the radio. This is when I began to feel out of control, shaky. I tried to get him to talk, but he wouldn't budge. He just ignored me.

That night I kept hearing my parents' warnings: "Please don't jump into this marriage, Doug's a great guy, but he's so selfish . . . are you sure you want to do this?" It hit me that maybe I had been wrong, that things weren't going to change, that Doug was only going to become more self-centered and I was going to be left more and more alone in a marriage that was one-sided.

Tracy was a Turtle-Raccoon victim, feeling powerless and victimized by the relationship. It was this loss of control that led to her anxiety and mild depression. It was imperative for Tracy to realize that Doug was only half the problem and that her passivity and insecurity was the other half, allowing and enabling him to indulge his Peacock-Elephant behavior.

At first, Tracy was confused. "How could I be half of the problem? Doug's been selfish all his life. I didn't make him selfish!" No, Tracy didn't make Doug selfish, but she wasn't doing anything to encourage him to become unselfish. In fact, what she was doing was allowing him to get away with a type of selfishness that bordered on relationship abuse.

Tracy was quick to pick up the essence of Self-Coaching as she started to recognize that it was her insecurity and passivity that enabled Doug to dictate the course of the marriage—right into a brick wall. She understood that the only way Doug was going to change was if she took *her* life back from reflexive insecurity. Fortified with this understanding, she methodically began starving her habit of insecurity by using her Self-Talk training to risk stepping apart from her Turtle-shell fears.

Now armed with a Self-Coaching capacity for self-trust and a burgeoning sense of self-confidence, Tracy refused to allow herself to succumb to her reflexive feeling of being intimidated by Doug. She saw that her habit of Turtle intimidation was nothing more than a Child-Reflex, long ago established and never challenged. All that changed as she began to insist on more appropriate, here-and-now, factual living (rather then the fictional fears instigated by her Turtle defense). For example, she allowed one simple, here-and-now *fact* to guide her: she deserved to be loved adequately. Period.

Tracy, now with a reconstituted trust muscle, was able to respond to Doug nondefensively while still catalytically respecting his Pea-cock-Elephant view of the world. If you recall from our discussion in the last chapter, catalytically respecting means that everyone is entitled—right or wrong—to their own decisions and perceptions of the world. Going back to the holiday party incident, for example, Doug was entitled to think his nap was not a big deal. It was critically important for Tracy to understand that catalytically respecting Doug's behavior *only* meant that there would be no arguing. It did *not* mean she needed to approve, condone, agree with, or embrace his shabby, egocentric behavior.

After all, who are we to say that someone isn't entitled to be neu-rotic? Yes, your partner is entitled to be neurotic, but in a partnership, where your partner's neurosis contributes to your unhappiness, you too have rights. It reminds me of the argument against smokers' rights. Sure, someone has the right to smoke, but when that secondary smoke wafts over to me and fills my lungs—that right stops there. In a restau-rant where smoking is permitted you have two choices: you have the right to do nothing or you have the right to leave. In a relationship, you have a third option: you have the right to catalytically change the relationship. Once Tracy understood that catalytically respecting Doug's Peacock-Elephant behavior was a form of relationship jujitsu, she began to feel that this was her best strategy for implementing change.

Self-Coaching Reflection
Challenging your partner is a strategy that will generate defensiveness. Catalytically respecting your partner is a strategy for eliminating defensiveness.

Tracy let Doug know that she couldn't change his behavior or his view of the world—that was his job. In the past, where she would retreat into her shell and sulk, she now began to speak up. "I can't tell you that your way of treating me is right or wrong. I'm not going to battle with you any longer. But what I can tell you is that the way you treat me creates friction for me. It makes me angry and resentful. You need to decide if you want to be in a relationship where your partner sees you as being unfair and at times abusive." There was no more demanding or insisting that Doug change. If you recall, it was on the ride home that Tracy tried to get him to admit he was wrong. Remember what happened? Doug exploded.

As it turned out, Doug was very coachable. His behavior wasn't about lack of love, and as strange as it may sound considering his shabby behavior toward Tracy, it really wasn't about a lack of respect. It was nothing more than a misguided, long-standing Peacock-Elephant reflex. (If you recall from earlier chapters, reflexive behavior is automatic, unconscious, knee-jerk reacting.) At first he was upset hearing that his wife resented him; he definitely wasn't happy knowing that she saw him negatively. He always thought (as you might expect from a Peacock) that she looked up to him and admired him, which is why I call it a misguided reflex. Since he never paid much attention to Tracy or to what she would say to him, he got away with believing the myth—are you ready for this?—that Tracy was a lucky woman. He was understandably shocked to find out that just the opposite was true. Confronted with the truth (and embracing it), he *knew* he didn't want Tracy to think of him negatively, but he had a hard time translating this into change.

As Tracy grew more secure, becoming, in her words, "less mousy," Doug was beginning to get a Catalytic Self-Coaching education. Rather than running away from struggle, Tracy would now calmly assert her point of view. If Doug was unable to respond appropriately, Tracy would find a way to take better care of her own needs. For example, she told Doug that he was entitled to forget about her in social situations, and that she couldn't make him change. But since this was humiliating and embarrassing to her, she wasn't sure she wanted to accept any future invitations to attend parties with him.

At home, if Doug would become impatient with Tracy when she wanted to tell him about an incident that day with her teaching, she would immediately stop the conversation, telling him, "That's okay, I don't need to tell you about my day." At this point she would remove herself from the discussion and pursue any non-Doug activity. As much as it saddened her, she catalytically respected that fact that Doug was still too egocentric to care about her day. It was up to him to change that behavior, not her. By terminating the conversation, Tracy was creating yet one more vacuum for Doug to begin to see the bigger picture. Through all of her catalytic efforts, she remained confident, knowing that it wasn't a matter of Doug not loving her, it was only a matter of his love being eclipsed by his habits of insecurity.

As you can see from this case history, Tracy's interventions were done very respectfully, creating an encouraging, constructive environment for Doug to begin to see the bigger picture.

Catalytic Self-Coaching Mantra
Encourage rather than discourage.

Following Tracy's catalytic efforts, Doug began to feel the ongoing sting of the vacuum that was created and readily understood the need for change. He said, "We can't go on like this!" It was at this point that Tracy approached him with the concept of creating a relationship portrait. Doug, who happened to be a visual person, jumped at the chance to *see* what was going on. He welcomed the opportunity to take the five tests listed in chapter 5 (on handouts I had given Tracy), then he and Tracy plotted their Self + Self = Us Portrait. Once he saw the dominance of his Peacock-Elephant tendencies (followed up by some reading from the text and lots of discussions with Tracy), he felt he had a real handle on what he needed to work on. Keep in mind that since Tracy was able to share her own previous Self-Coaching efforts, Doug felt no hesitation in, as he put it, "anteing up" and doing his share.

At first this was a welcome respite for Tracy, but clearly it was going to be a process for Doug—a process where Tracy was ready and willing to assume her more active role as coach. Tracy left the handouts I had given her with Doug to review, which he did with surprising intensity. As she told him, "More than anything else, your taking this seriously has convinced me how much you do love me." Doug, with Tracy's ongoing feedback and coaching, progressed rapidly with his own Self-Coaching efforts.

Catalytic Self-Coaching Reflection
THE FOREST-FOR-THE-TREES BENEFIT

When you reach the point where you and your partner are both engaged in your personal Self-Coaching efforts, it's critical to understand the forest-for-the-trees benefit of coaching each other. Since we all tend to become less objective when we're too close to an issue, there's enormous value in acquiring a one-partner-removed, objective view.

As your catalytic coaching efforts begin to reduce the overall level of defensiveness in the relationship, recognize that anything that promotes objectivity is going to further facilitate your progress. Look to each other for feedback, impressions, intuitions, even hunches, and don't be afraid to embrace all that you're hearing. Be confident in the knowledge that any half-baked impressions will wither away, while those with relevance and truth will endure. Now's the time to realize that you're both coaches, so begin coaching!

Tracy and Doug's coaching provided mirrors for each to reflect back the objective truth, as in, "Come on, Tracy, you're pulling away, don't do that. Tell me what's bothering you." Or, "Doug, I sense you're not listening to me. Am I right?" Whether you see yourself as a coach, a therapist, or a mirror, when each partner begins to work to facilitate a nondefensive, trusting relationship, everything begins to move along at a breakneck pace.

The Essence of Mutual Coaching

When both partner-coaches begin to offer encouragement, objectivity, support, and, at times, a needed kick in the butt, the relationship will inevitably begin to reflect these efforts. Rather than fighting the same old battles, each partner now becomes capable of understanding conflict from the new perspective: insecurity and control. Now, for the first time, both partners are able to look at conflict not with confusion or frustration, but with a simple format for understanding. Instead of reacting with, "I'll show him, he's not going to get away with treating me like that!" they can look for the underlying truth. "He's yelling at me. What's he trying to control? Why is he feeling so insecure right now?" Catalytic coaching provides a plan for understanding struggle and promotes a willingness to risk trust.

Catalytic Self-Coaching Tip

Whenever in doubt about any destructive behavior from your partner, ask the question "What is he/she trying to control?" If you understand control, you will understand all neurotic, destructive, or inappropriate behavior.

15

Putting It All Together
Follow-Through

Through the many years I've been in practice, I've found myself repeating certain words over and over again with my patients. You've heard me mention two of these words throughout the preceding chapters: *insecurity* and *control*. As you've seen, an understanding of insecurity and control is essential to all your Catalytic Self-Coaching efforts. I hope I've convinced you that if we eliminate or at least minimize insecurity in you and your partner, then the controlling behavior (Tiger, Turtle, Elephant, Raccoon, or Peacock) that fuels your struggle will begin to diminish. At this point in your coach-coach mode of training I'd like to double your catalytic vocabulary by adding two more equally critical words: *fairness* and *respect*. Fairness and respect are both components of what I call relationship follow-through.

Relationship Follow-Through

Once the toxic behavior has been removed or at least minimized in your relationship, then it's time for *follow-through*. In athletics, whether it's swinging a golf club, hitting a baseball, or kicking a soccer ball, you don't stop your motion once you've made contact and whacked the ball—you continue the motion beyond the point of contact. The same holds true for Catalytic Self-Coaching: you need to follow through and continue your motion (efforts) beyond the point where you "whacked" insecurity and controlling behavior out of your relationship. Following through is your insurance that your efforts will continue to make your relationship healthy.

Fairness and Respect

As the saying goes, "what's fair is fair." In other words, fairness isn't something that's negotiable; it's either fair or it's unfair. Right? This is often true, but not always. Unfortunately, one person's idea of fairness may not agree with another's. Issues of fairness are often the root of many relationship frustrations and therefore deserve our special attention.

Let's start out by recognizing that *fairness* is a relative term. In Iraq, for example, it's culturally acceptable for rural Kurdish women to mingle with males, but they're not allowed to make their own decisions regarding sexuality or husbands. If a Kurdish male were to date an American woman, you can imagine the conflicts that would ensue over issues of fairness. Just as different cultural views can clash, each partner's "cultural" view regarding issues of fairness may conflict with the other's.

I was recently working with a couple where the wife, coming from a family of six siblings, wanted to have a third child. The husband, an only child, was insisting that two children needed to be the limit. The husband's lament: "She's not being fair; I don't want a large family." The wife's lament: "He's not being fair; I want a large family." Two perceptions of fairness: neither is right or wrong, but both are problematic. As you can see from this example, each partner's personal view of fairness is a reflection of their history—experience, values (cultural view), and intellectual conclusions.

The ultimate success of any relationship, especially when dealing with issues of fairness, depends on each partner being able to use Self-Coaching to step apart from personal limitations in order to objectively assess the relative fairness or unfairness of any given situation.

Catalytic Self-Coaching Reflection
You can assess the fairness of an argument only if you're not
mired in reflexive thinking. Reflexive thinking limits you to
one view—your own!

When my wife tells me she's been cleaning all day and doesn't feel I've contributed enough, my first reaction might be a surge of defensiveness. "What do you mean, not contributing? That's not fair! I've been work-ing on my book . . . I was too busy." My first reaction might be that my wife is being unfair, but, being an ardent student of Self-Coaching, I understand that from time to time my older reflexes will try to surface and influence my perceptions of fairness. Now, being much too savvy to allow insecurity to dupe me, I'm able to do a bit of reflection: "From my wife's perspective, she's been working all day getting ready for the party while I've been sitting at my computer. I can understand why she feels abandoned by me. Although I don't think I've done anything wrong, her criticism of me is a fair one."

After this scrutiny, I'm in a position to make a judgment. For example I might reflect, "I knew the party was tonight, it really wasn't fair for me to leave the burden of preparation to my wife." This realization leads me to make some mental adjustments. As a matter of fact, I'm about to stop writing this chapter because yesterday was cleaning day and I wasn't being "fair." In a couple of minutes I'll turn off the computer and do my "fair" share of helping with the post-party cleanup.

This scenario is rather straightforward, but what if I had had a dif-ferent view of fairness? Let's say I had a deadline from my publisher that I told my wife about. Knowing this, she still decided to have a party in spite of my literary demands. In this case I might have responded to her accusation as follows: "You knew about my deadline. I'm sorry I couldn't help out, but it just wasn't possible. I feel you're the one who's being unfair." This would represent an example where the two partners are on different sides of the fairness fence. In such a situation, the eventual resolution comes not from trying to decide who's being more fair and who's being less fair—it comes from recognizing that neither one of you is trying to be unfair. And this is the key.

It may feel that your partner's being "unfair," but now, knowing that you're both adhering to responsible, coach-coach relating, you need to make every attempt to embrace your partner's frame of reference. In the above skirmish, I might begin to defuse the situation by reflecting, "I know my wife and I discussed my writing deadline, but I'm sure she thought I could take some time away from writing. I know she respects my need to work; obviously she was just frustrated and tired when she accused me of not helping out." Once you embrace your partner's frame of reference, you can begin to see that their perception of fairness isn't an attempt to bully, manipulate, or hurt you—it's simply another view, other than yours, of a given situation. It's this objective understanding that will allow you to negotiate a successful resolution without resorting to older, insecurity-driven habits.

The Fair-Minded Solution

When confronted with a fairness conflict, you and your partner, to the best of your ability, need to rely on your Self-Coaching training to make every attempt to separate the facts, not only from the fictions, but from any strong knee-jerk emotions. You're not about to embrace your partner's frame of reference if you're too busy firing back a volley of it's-not-me-it's-you-who's-being-unfair accusations. First follow any necessary Self-Talk efforts to diffuse your reactivity. Then try to understand why your partner's view of fairness is different from yours.

You'll need to step into your partner's shoes, metaphorically speaking, and experience his or her view of the world. To do this you're going to have to see what your partner sees. Trust that if your partner is seeing something as "fair," and you happen to think this view is foolish, then in fact you're *not* seeing your partner's view clearly enough. You need to work harder.

How do you know when you're seeing clearly enough? When, standing in your partner's shoes, you see *why* your partner's perception seems fair to him or her. You don't have to agree with your partner's perception, just understand it. Only when each partner appreciates the other's perceptions will you be in a position to resolve, compromise, or work toward a mutual solution to any struggle. Why is this? Because once you know that your partner is being *fair-minded*, then you can trust that your struggle is based on legitimate differences and not on defensive, egocentric demands. It's at this point that you're willing to drop the word *fair* from your dialogue. Because now you're convinced that if two loving partners are acting with a mutual perception of fairness, you don't have to feel that your partner has any intention of being "unfair." With this assurance (trust) you're able to approach any disagreement as nothing more than a difference of opinion—instead of thinking that you're being abused or manipulated.

Catalytic Self-Coaching Reflection

Being fair-minded is an attitude of success. In order to become fair-minded, you need to rely on your Self-Coaching training to minimize your own defensiveness.

Respect

I confess that I don't share my wife's inclination for maintaining a meticulously clean house. I'm simply not a detail person. But I don't have to share her views or her inclinations in order to respect them. Don't confuse *follow-through* respect with what you've learned in the last two chapters about *catalytically respecting* your partner's insecurity-driven, reflexive point of view. There's a subtle but important difference between the two. The intention of catalytically respecting your partner's defensive behavior is to create a vacuum in the relationship by reducing the unnecessary friction caused by battling each other. When, on the other hand, you use respect as a form of follow-through, we're talking about respecting and *valuing* each other's differences. Rather than just reflexively accepting, you are working to value, embrace, and recognize the legitimacy of your partner's differences.

Without Self-Coaching, a controlling person is prone to demand only his or her own view in a relationship. A healthy, Self-Coached person, on the other hand, recognizes that there needs to be room in a relationship for differences. When your partner says, "I think pomegranate red would be a perfect color for the living room. What do you think?" you need to realize that even though you feel that a pomegranate red living room might make you nauseous, it's not a good idea to say, "You're kidding, right? That's the ugliest color I've ever seen!" This insulting response would be telling your partner that he or she has terrible taste; how dare your partner suggest something that doesn't appeal to you! And once you respond in such a primitive, selfish, controlling manner, you've inadvertently subtracted from the relationship balance. The right (fair and respectful) response would be, "I'm afraid that color just isn't to my taste. Can we explore some other options?"

Realistic Expectations

The ability to follow through with fairness and respect is dependent on both you and your partner's Self-Coaching efforts. Obviously, you're not going to be able to muster up the needed objectivity and compassion necessary to be fair and respectful if you're busy defending your own psychological turf. If you're finding yourself struggling with being fair and respectful, then you're not quite where you need to be—not yet.

In order to get beyond the last remnants of your insecurity and control habits, you need to recognize that reflexive behavior can't always be completely extinguished. Remember when I told you how I began to bristle when my wife criticized me for not contributing to her pre-party cleaning? The truth is that all your habits of insecurity do *not* have to be extinguished—not completely—they only need to be neutralized. That's where your ongoing Self-Talk efforts pay off.

In my example, I was quickly able to see my old reflex of insecurity trying to influence me. Once I recognized that defensiveness beginning to well up, I was able to stop it and let it go. It was that easy. This is the ongoing objective of Self-Coaching: first you develop and fine-tune your awareness of your reflexive, controlling patterns (Tiger, Turtle, and so on), then you neutralize them, and then you let them go. You strive to continually replace reflexiveness with fairness and respect.

Now that you and your partner are in the coach-coach mode, you're in an offensive position where insecurity can be attacked and neutralized. And keep in mind, you don't have to be 100 percent reflex-free to neutralize anything that insecurity throws at you, you just need to remain smart. Smart enough to know the difference between facts and fictions, between fairness and unfairness, and between respect and disrespect.

Communication Skills: They're Not Rocket Science

I've waited until now to introduce the concept of communication. Poor communication can be a symptom of insecurity and control, but it can also be nothing more than ignorance, faulty technique, or just plain laziness. Improving your communication skills at this point in your Catalytic Self-Coaching training is a win-win proposition, often requiring little more than a commonsense understanding of the dynamics involved. Until now, most of your efforts to improve communication probably fell by the wayside, sabotaged by an undercurrent of insecurity and control. But now, having eliminated defensiveness, you're ready to fight the final battle: eliminating the misunderstandings, misperceptions, and misinterpretations that have crippled your relationship.

In the coach-coach mode, you've been working on establishing a firm foundation of trust in your relationship. It's trust (both in yourself and in your partner) that will enable and embolden you to become an effective communicator. Let's face it, trying to understand your relationship struggles without effective communication would be like trying to figure out your new DVD player with the wrong set of directions packed in the box. In a foreign language. Clearly, whether it's a DVD player with the wrong directions or a relationship going in a wrong direction, without healthy communication, you're headed for chaos.

The Do's and Don'ts of Successful Follow-Through in Communication

Your follow-through efforts aren't limited to an awareness of fairness and respect. The final challenge is becoming a better and more responsible communicator, a true team player who's willing to give as well as take, to make adjustments, and, most importantly, to be able to evolve and change according to the ongoing challenges that you and your partner face over time. This is the core of your follow-through work along with your continued efforts to build and strengthen your trust muscle. Once liberated from the haze of insecurity, you're in a position to make some straightforward adjustments to your behavior. Take a look at the following communication do's and don'ts, keeping in mind that at this point in your training, you're ready to insist on becoming not only a good partner, but a great one.

Separate facts from fictions. In your Self-Coaching training, you were taught to separate facts from fictions (Self-Talk, Step 1). Now, rather than focusing on your own thoughts, you're going to apply the same principle to any relationship struggle. It's always dangerous to assume, speculate, or otherwise guess what's going on in your partner's mind—especially if negative emotions are involved. When in doubt, ask. I can't tell you how many misinterpretations wind up as relationship catastrophes. "I didn't mean I can't stand *you*, I really meant that I can't stand the way you act when we're with your brother." Or, "I wasn't mad at you, my sister got me upset this afternoon and I was feeling really depressed."

Catalytic Self-Coaching Reflection
Until you've learned your partner's factual intent, you are
not allowed to assume. When in doubt, ask.

Fred, a forty-two-year-old man I worked with recently, suffered from a profound fear of emotional intimacy. He was a rather intellectualized, controlled Turtle whose reflexive habit of withdrawal wasn't sitting well with him or his partner, Ralph. He deeply loved Ralph, but his fears of vulnerability were more powerful than his desire to love openly. Ralph, without any significant communication, had long ago concluded that he just wasn't attractive enough for Fred, and had begun to pull away from the relationship in an attempt to protect himself. We began couples counseling and within fifteen minutes of the first session, Ralph finally knew the truth. All it took was an open, honest communication.

But why, until our session, was this simple communication avoided? It was avoided because insecurity oftentimes creates a reflexive pattern of avoidance. We go on doing the same-old-same-old because . . . well, because we do. As I've said so often in previous chapters, human beings are creatures of habit. On some primitive, reflexive level Fred was victimized by the fictional notion that he couldn't possibly expose himself by being honest. Insecurity will do that; it will convince you that you *can't* handle certain aspects of life. And this is always a fiction. Habits of insecurity seem to prefer the dark; once exposed they begin to wilt. Without the truth, this couple was headed for ruin, but once facts were separated from fictions, the healing began in earnest.

Listen with *at*tention, not *in*tention. Becoming an effective listener begins with an attitude of receptivity. In order to be an effective listener and communicator you can't have a hidden agenda. A good example of this is *yes, but-ing.* "*Yes*, I should help out more with the chores, *but* you don't understand what I'm going through." *Yes, but-ing* is listening with the intent of furthering your own—hidden—agenda. In a sense, it's a kind of half-listening, listening only to launch your own agenda.

Your Self-Coaching training is essential if you're going to listen to your partner with attention and without intention (or hidden agenda). Egocentric needs, which are typically behind most struggles, need to be challenged directly. What's needed is true understanding of the value of mutuality. You need to see yourself as part of a team. And a team relies on a mutual team effort to function. Coach Greg Schiano of the Rutgers University football team said something recently that I thought was catchy. He said that if you don't take care of your "one-eleventh," then you're not doing your part to trust that the other ten guys will do what they're supposed to do. That's what good football teams do. On a football team if you think you have more than a one-eleventh amount of importance, then you're diminishing the value of your team. The same holds true in a relationship. If you think your needs are more important than your partner's, then you're diminishing the likelihood of mutuality and increasing the probability of struggle.

Use affirmations. One of the simplest ways to improve a struggling relationship is often the most overlooked—affirming your partner.

Often, in longer-term relationships, you wind up with a kind of relationship laziness. For example: "You never tell me I look good." To which the response might be, "If I didn't think that dress looked good on you, I would have said something." Everyone needs to feel valued and worthwhile. I've often asked why such a simple contribution to the relationship dynamic becomes so absent. The only answer I've come up with is that we become relationship-lethargic. So lethargic that we feel we don't need to say certain things. We say, "Why do I have to tell you I love you? You know I do." For whatever reason, it becomes too much effort to repeat what you have already said in the past. From a Self-Coaching perspective, I have only one piece of advice: *get over it*. If you feel or think something, find the energy to say it.

Laziness can be symptomatic of a general apathy that can erode your relationship. And don't be sitting there thinking, "My partner never tells me anything good about me, so why should I say nice things about her?" You now know enough about Self-Coaching to realize that you change your relationship by changing yourself. It's up to *you* to change the status quo; don't worry about your partner. Focus on what you can do to be a better, more effective part of the solution. Just remind yourself that thinking something positive about your partner does nothing for the relationship. Saying something positive does.

Develop an Us-first attitude. Ask the simple question, "What serves this relationship and what hurts it?" This is one way to nurture your relationship. An even better way is to start thinking in terms of what serves *us*, instead of what serves *me*. Once again, you can see where a shift of focus from egocentricity to mutuality brings into play the fundamental team aspect of your relationship—you depend on each other for happiness, therefore you have a vested interest in all Us-related issues.

Insecurity promotes egocentric, me-first thinking, which is why partners become polarized in their struggles. By embracing an Us-first attitude, each partner begins to understand his or her role and responsibility within the context of the relationship. It's a simple shift in thinking, but essential if you're going to start recognizing that a relationship is where two people combine to form a third "Us" entity. (Remember your Self + Self = Us Portrait.) You have a vested, 50 percent interest in preserving, protecting, and nurturing the "Us" component of your relationship. After all, it's only common sense.

Compromise, take turns, and agree to disagree. In a successful relationship, it's important to learn what to do with normal, unavoidable differences. Let's face it, not all conflict can be resolved—at least not in a mutually satisfying way. But with a burgeoning capacity for fairness, respect, and understanding, along with an Us-first attitude, you will discover that every conflict and every friction can be resolved. Sometimes the answer will be an obvious compromise. "I'll do the cooking if you'll do the dishes." Other times, where compromise is not possible—"We went to Florida last year, I want to go to Maine this year"—the solution has to do with understanding the value of fairness (don't forget respect) and the willingness to take turns. "Okay, I got my way last year, this year it's your turn." And sometimes there are issues that defy solution: "I can't believe you're going to vote for a Republican!" Sometimes it's just a matter of respect and agreeing to disagree: "Guess we have to accept that we see things differently."

Solving problems isn't a one-size-fits-all method. It requires that you be flexible and willing to recognize that every problem can be resolved without friction and relationship erosion. Self-Coaching, by reducing your insecurity and need for control, is an essential component in helping you navigate through the potholes of disagreement. Understand that the Us-component of your relationship is both fluid and flexible—so don't become frozen and inflexible! Which brings us back to the question "What serves our relationship (Us-component), and what hurts it?"

Always encourage. Everyone needs hope, encouragement, and a pat on the back—it's motivating. And it's smart! During the coach-coach mode of catalytic training, don't hesitate to reward and reinforce positive effort. And don't let any historical skepticism, hesitation, or doubt deter you from uttering a well-deserved "Atta-boy" or "You go, girl." Human beings can do extraordinary things if the motivation is strong enough—why wouldn't you want to encourage and rev up your partner's motor? As the kids say, "Duh."

Be curious. When you experience a regression or a transgression—it happens to the best of us—your goal is to find out how insecurity and control might be contaminating what's going on with your partner (or yourself). One way to step apart from your emotions is simply to be curious. Rather than getting defensive, get curious. A curious inquiry might sound like this: "After all our coaching efforts, I don't understand why you would insult me like that. *I'm curious*; could you help me understand your behavior?" Being curious keeps you in the right frame of mind so as to not get snagged by your own defensiveness.

Risk trust. Trust, both personal self-trust and relationship trust, is defined as willingness to believe. When working together, both you and your partner must be willing to take that risk. If both of you have done your Self-Coaching and have successfully entered the coach-coach mode of catalytic training, then it's time to take the brakes off your own hesitations about trusting. Ask yourself, what do you have to lose? If you're wrong and you get burnt, it won't be the end of the world. But if you're right, it could be the creation of a brave new world—one where you don't have to risk *believing* that you can trust, you'll *know* you can.

Connect rather than disconnect. From our discussion earlier about respect, you now understand that respecting your partner means stepping out of any egocentric tendencies that you might be prone to and valuing your partner as a person. This begins by valuing what your partner has to say. If, in a discussion, you find yourself bored, distracted, or uninterested with your partner, it's probably because you've disconnected and have drifted into your own self-centered thoughts. In order to really find value and stimulation in your partner, you need to connect. You do this by becoming an active listener—one who listens with intent and enthusiasm. You refuse to permit drifting—especially any controlling tendencies that insist you have to be the center of attention. Don't be afraid to practice listening; it's worth the effort. Being a great listener goes hand in hand with being a great partner.

One technique I learned a long time ago is called "parroting." It's an exercise that's guaranteed to cure inattentiveness. Let's say you and your partner are in a conversation. Your partner starts off by telling you about her day. Before you're allowed to respond with any reaction, you must first repeat (parrot) back what you just heard your partner say. This may be a tedious exercise, but it will force you to pay more attention. Bottom line: the more you value your partner, the more you'll value what your partner says.

Give support. Give and ye shall receive. Helping your partner deal with insecurity, control, awareness, or motivation is a way of helping and solidifying your own evolution. Remember, this is a team effort. You may, for example, have different and important insights from your own Self-Coaching training efforts that could be valuable for your partner. You might say, "I know when I get anxious, it helps me to visualize being in a safe place." Offering support, empathy, understanding, or compassion to your partner is not only in his or her best interest, it's in yours as well.

Change. Ask not what your partner needs to be doing to change—ask what you need to do. Go back to Self-Coaching 101 and remember that if each of you takes personal responsibility for change, success is all but guaranteed. Accept the fact that your finger-pointing days are over. Take your personal responsibility very seriously by asking what you can do each day to progress as a person and as a partner.

Reject conflict. When it comes to any conflict, remind yourself that there are always choices. You can contribute to the conflict and become part of the problem, or you can use your Catalytic Self-Coaching to become part of the solution. If you think any conflict can't be resolved—you're wrong.

Here are some of the wrong techniques we use to relate. These will all sabotage your efforts to reconnect with your partner.

Don't use guilt. Avoid relying on guilt to motivate your partner. "You're a terrible husband, you're the reason I have these headaches." Guilt is a primitive mechanism of coercion, and although it might achieve the desired results, it will also produce a lasting resentment in your partner. It's manipulative, controlling, and driven by insecurity.

If you catch yourself attempting to instill guilt on your partner—stop! Go back over your Self-Coaching training and realize that guilt is an attempt to take a relationship shortcut: rather than taking healthy responsibility for working out a problem, you're just trying to get the results you want.

Don't use shame. Like guilt, shame can easily backfire when your partner begins to see you as a finger-wagging parent. "And you call yourself a man? Look at how weak and helpless you are!" Shame and guilt are feeble attempts to throw your partner off balance by creating a psychological disturbance strong enough to get them to comply with your wishes. But by this point in your training you probably realize that *what goes around comes around*—you might win the battle, but you've just fueled the war.

Don't use coercion or threats. Forcing your partner to relate or respond is a dangerous ploy. "If you don't have sex with me, I'm going to find it somewhere else." Becoming a relationship bully is one of the last things you want to allow. Sure, bullies tend to get compliance, but it instills an anger and rage that will come out either directly or indirectly. Once again, if you see your Elephant or Tiger emerging, get back to your Self-Coaching work. Your goal isn't to subdue your partner, it's to find mutual solutions to your needs and your partner's needs.

Don't manipulate. "Do this for me and we can have sex." Think about it, do you want your partner to be working for a payoff, or working to be fair and respectful of your needs? Manipulation may get results, but it doesn't teach anything—at least nothing useful. At its worst, manipulation can be a form of control, and if you've learned anything from Catalytic Self-Coaching, you know that anything that controls your partner will come back to haunt you—in spades.

Don't make idle promises. "Give me time, I'll get to it. Maybe I'll do it tomorrow." Remember the boy who cried wolf? If you're prone to idle promises as a means of escaping relationship responsibility, be aware that your credibility may be on the line. "I said I'd do it tomorrow. I don't understand, why won't you believe me?" Idle promising is a form of procrastination and it's insulting to your partner. If a request is fair, then rouse yourself and do the right thing. Stop controlling the situation by either avoiding the effort or doing it when you're "good and ready." Control is *never* good for you, nor is it good for your relationship.

So what technique *should* you use to relate to your partner? I've saved the most important for last.

Honesty. As you know from previous chapters, the essential healing principle of both Catalytic Self-Coaching and your own Self-Coaching is the development of trust. Trust is the slayer of insecurity and control and ultimately the source and fuel of all love. Trust is synonymous with honesty. Without legitimate, ongoing honesty, trust will remain elusive. Because of your Self-Coaching, you should be in a position to stand up to any habit of insecurity and risk being who you are. Sure, it takes courage to be forthright and up-front with your partner, but it's your insecurity that will convince you that you can't be "too open." After all, some things need to be protected. Poppycock! The only thing that needs to be protected is the integrity of your relationship. Starting right now, realize that honesty is a choice. So is having a wonderful, trusting, loving relationship. It's up to you.

16

Love, Infatuation, and Infidelity

Up to this point in your training, eliminating the struggle in your relationship has been the main goal of Catalytic Self-Coaching; now it's time to raise your expectations to a higher level. Eliminating the struggle is only the beginning. It can be the prelude to igniting a true and lasting experience of love between you and your partner.

Love? What exactly is love? I'm sure if you ask ten people you'll get eleven different interpretations, with little if any consensus. Considering that we've come to rely on Hollywood to provide us with an archetype for what love is and what it isn't, it's no wonder there's confusion.

The blockbuster romantic movies show us love as a fierce, overpowering, rapturous force that transcends all worldly demands. We see our romantic heroes and heroines enduring pain, suffering, quitting jobs, flying to the ends of the earth, and risking life and limb to be united. This powerful, compulsive force is what we tend to idealize as love. Regrettably, real life can't compare with what we see on the silver screen. No wonder many people begin to question, if not the legitimacy, at least the intensity of what they think they *should* be feeling in their relationships. But what exactly is love? If there was a one-size-fits-all explanation of love, Hallmark would already own the patent on it. Perhaps the best we can do is to construct a grounded understanding and conceptualization of love—at least from a Catalytic Self-Coaching perspective.

Why Romeo and Juliet Had to Die

Arguably, the most famous of all love stories comes not from Hollywood, but from William Shakespeare's tragedy *Romeo and Juliet*. Would it surprise you if I told you that this remarkable play had nothing to do with love? But how can this be? How could such a grand passion, expressed by these "star-cross'd lovers," not represent the highest, purest expression of love? After all, who, like Romeo, hasn't at one time in their lives been touched by a similar agonizing longing?

> See, how she leans her cheek upon her hand!
> O, that I were a glove upon that hand,
> That I might touch that cheek.

The fact is, Romeo did not love Juliet. He was infatuated with her. Infatuation, like love, is another, often confused emotional experience. Conceptually, most people caught up in the intense feelings associated with infatuation are not likely to see it is *just* an infatuation. They'll argue tooth and nail to explain how what they're feeling is the quintessential expression of love. But when it comes to knowing what you need in your relationship, you'd better understand the difference.

But before explaining the difference between infatuation and love, let me ask a question. From a literary standpoint, why do you think it was imperative for Romeo and Juliet to die? From a poetic standpoint, you might be inclined to say that their tragic double suicide was the highest demonstration of their love. But from a psychological standpoint, it's because infatuation cannot be restricted by earthly forces. An infatuation cannot be tethered to mundane reality; it belongs to the celestial spheres. Romeo and Juliet's deaths represent that which cannot endure—an infatuation. All infatuations must one day end.

Infatuation

Infatuation is what we call a state of projection. Just as a projector projects an image onto a screen, so too does infatuation project the longings of our soul onto another person. Plato, in his *Symposium,* described this powerful process in a very compelling way. According to Plato, at the beginning of time there were no men and women, only what he called primal androgynes—large round figures possessing both male and female attributes. Because the androgynes were growing in power, Zeus became apprehensive. He eventually settled on a plan. He decided to split the androgynes in half, thus creating a separate male and female, and thereby halving their power.

As time went on, whenever a male half (former androgyne) met a female half and joined together, this consummation led to a powerful, evocative experience, reminiscent of the original state of wholeness that now resided only in the memories of each male and female. The *Symposium* serves as an adequate metaphor for the profound evocative experience of reconnecting with the transcendent aspect of our own nature that longs for wholeness and completeness. Only by looking at this union in an almost mythical way can you begin to understand the compelling forces involved in an infatuation. We can use the same Self + Self = Us template to show this union:

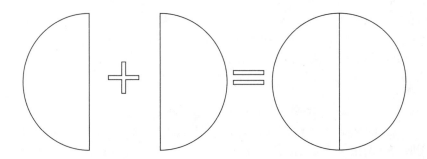

I marvel at Plato's conceptualization. As I see it, we humans are hard-wired both to experience and seek this primal state of union, which can best be described as the combining of opposites in order to achieve a state of "completeness." From a psychological standpoint, experiencing this ecstatic state of wholeness is truly a riveting, transcendent feeling that releases us from our material existence.

In order to gain more perspective on this concept of infatuation, we need to move from the poetry of Shakespeare and the mythology of Plato and look to the biology of Charles Darwin for a clue. From an evolutionary perspective, as our species evolved, it would have been a biological imperative for a mechanism such as infatuation to become an integral component in our genetic survival. Thus from a Darwinian sense, we could say that the aim of infatuation is sexual union. And from a purely biological perspective, procreation is the determining criterion of success for any species. We can therefore postulate that the biological mechanism that drives this infatuated union with its associated urge for sex (procreation) was combined with and facilitated by a psychological experience that we call ecstasy.

Are You Sure This Isn't True Love?

Ecstasy is the psychological experience of both infatuation and orgasm. Both represent major chemical shifts in the brain. (Some have compared this shift to the powerful effects of heroin.) To say that an infatuation (or an orgasm) is "just" another emotion would truly be comparing a lightning bug to lightning. Ecstasy is that feet-off-the-ground component of infatuation (as well as the experience of orgasm) that replaces reality with a surreal rush of biological-psychological bliss.

Let's take a look at Linda's infatuation experience with Kevin. You can get a taste for the compulsive, driven, ecstatic emotions that, tsunami-like, can sweep you off your feet:

> I met Kevin on spring break. I was driving to South Beach from Virginia with my girlfriend, who told me that her friend Kevin was looking for a ride and that he would split the expenses. We picked Kevin up the morning of the trip, and from the moment we met, we just seemed to click.
>
> The trip to Florida flew by as we laughed and joked the whole way. We just hit it off. I know it was fast, but I knew within hours that Kevin was everything I ever wanted in a man. He was

handsome, intelligent, funny, and very sensitive . . . in kind of a puppy dog way. When we got to Florida, we wound up spending all our time together. It was like I wanted to devour him; I just couldn't let him go. I know he felt the same way, I could see it in the way he looked at me—it was obvious. What a whirlwind experience! I honestly don't think either of us slept the entire weekend. I was so high; it felt like I was drugged.

It was almost spooky how we both loved the same music, the same movies, we both wanted to have a large family—there was nothing we disagreed about. He seemed absolutely perfect! When we got back to school, we began to sleep together. Kevin was so romantic. Every weekend, he'd bring me a rose and a love poem. I'm telling you, this guy was too good to be true.

I not only found it hard to study, I found it impossible to do anything without Kevin. He and I became inseparable. I'd be walking out of a class and he'd just be standing there, smiling. One night I was studying late at the library and he showed up with a coffee for me. He was such a sweetie. It was uncanny; he seemed to know what I needed before I knew it! I remember one time I was sick with a flu and out of a deep sleep I opened my eyes and there sitting on my night table was a container of chicken soup, a bottle of cough syrup, and a get-well card. I didn't just think he was perfect, he *was* perfect!

The intensity of the love I felt for Kevin felt . . . almost painful. I just couldn't bear not to be with him. The absolute worst moments came after making love, when he would need to leave and go to class. I found those moments as he walked out the door so difficult, so unbearable.

To say that everything in my life was different would be a gross understatement. I mean everything—the music, the sunshine, even my outlook on life—was different. It's like my life prior to Kevin was monochromatic and now it was all vivid color. Until Kevin I was never a morning person, now I found myself leaping out of bed each morning, singing in the shower, and almost skipping off to class. I wanted to hold on to this experience forever—it was just too good to be true. With Kevin I would have the life I always dreamed of. After all, I knew that anything this perfect had to last. I mean, why wouldn't it? We were just meant for each other.

Don't get me wrong, when I say Kevin was perfect, I don't mean that he had no flaws. He did. He told me that before he met me he suffered from anxiety, and in his freshman year even had a panic attack that landed him in the emergency room of the hospital. I already knew he liked to drink, but it seemed to loosen him up, and I didn't see this or his anxieties as a big problem.

Then a few months ago, things began to change. I noticed that Kevin was starting to drink more heavily every time we were together. He became more quiet and withdrawn. I kept asking him what was wrong and he would only get agitated and tell me, "Nothing." Instead of us spending every day together, Kevin began to pull away, telling me he needed to study or to get more sleep. Sure, I was disappointed, but I didn't think much of it. I just assumed he was struggling with his studies. I loved Kevin and I knew he needed some space. I never thought he'd lie to me.

In time I couldn't avoid the realization that what Kevin and I had had together was vanishing. I began to become frantic with worry. It was about that time that I got a call from a Stephanie, a former sorority sister of mine, asking if I was still going out with Kevin. Surprised, I told her yes and asked why she was asking. There was a long silence on the phone. Finally, Stephanie told me that she had met a rather drunk Kevin at a frat party the night before and he asked her out. She told Kevin she'd think about it and get back to him. She told me she wasn't about to go out with him until she talked to me first and made sure I had no objections. I never answered, I just hung up and began sobbing.

Linda, as you can imagine, was devastated. She felt disoriented and wound up dropping out of school for the semester. It was at this point that she came to see me for therapy. Although there were a few clues in her relationship with Kevin, Linda had paid no attention to these red flags. After all, how could anything that felt so perfect be . . . not so perfect?

As it turned out, Kevin was an infatuation junkie. After Linda broke up with him, she began to hear other tales of how he would start similar highly charged, infatuated relationships, where he would promise the world, grow bored, and move on. Linda, unfortunately, had inadvertently become part of Kevin's rather predictable pattern of love 'em and leave 'em.

Reading this, you're probably feeling that Kevin was nothing more than a user and an abuser. Although I never met or spoke with him, I'd venture to guess that he wasn't either—at least not intentionally. The way I see it, he was victimized by his own infatuation. But how could Kevin possibly ignore his history of frequently falling in and out of love, and think that this time he had found true love? The answer isn't complicated: emotions are shortsighted.

Even though the relationship turned out to be nothing more than Kevin's infatuation du jour, he nonetheless was able to convince himself that surely, this was the one! Finally, he had found the perfect person. Bottom line: his infatuation was real and it was steering his life just as it was steering Linda's. But for Kevin, as the infatuation experience began to yield to a more earthly, grounded relationship—where his projections of perfection could no longer be sustained—reality set in and he lost his ecstatic high.

The truth, unbeknownst to Kevin, was that he wasn't looking for legitimate love or relationship. He might have thought he was, but because of his insecurities, what he was actually looking to accomplish was to step out of his anxiety-riddled life (after the breakup, Linda found out that Kevin had been hospitalized the previous summer because of intense anxiety and depression) by sidestepping life entirely through infatuation. Like his drinking, infatuation was an intoxicant that alleviated his suffering. He was quite literally an infatuation junkie.

Infatuation: A Perspective

Now, in retrospect, it's easy to see that what Linda and Kevin shared together wasn't love; it was a facsimile called infatuation. How do I know this? Because in an infatuation, you're not relating to the actual other person, you're relating to the longings of your own soul—that which you perceive will complete you. These longings are projected onto your lover. In a very real and literal sense, you're not relating to the other person—you're relating to a skeleton of the other person who is fleshed out with your longings, desires, hopes, and dreams. To say it differently, you're relating to your own soul-image of romantic perfection, which is why we often describe a romantic partner as a "soul mate."

This is why infatuation has nothing to do with love, because you're not really relating to the other person. Mostly, you're relating to your own intoxicated feeling of being whole, invulnerable, and totally secure. Only when an infatuation begins to wane, and you begin to relate to the actual, earthbound, flesh-and-blood other person, can true love evolve— or infatuated love dissolve.

As I mentioned earlier, it helps to see infatuation as a possible prelude to true love, but at best it is nothing more than a hit-or-miss proposition. An infatuation isn't meant to be an accurate predictor of true love, it's only meant to draw two people together for the possibility of, as the sociologists call it, pair bonding. But as is often the case, when an infatuation dies, you wake up one morning with the feeling, "What in the world did I see in him/her?" Ever hear the expression "love is blind"? This should be changed to "infatuation is blind."

Two Reasons Why You Need to Understand Infatuation

I've spent a good deal of time explaining infatuation for two reasons. The first has to do with helping you understand that both you and your partner need to be clear on how you define the love that you seek. If either of you is looking back over your shoulder, lamenting, "I'm not feeling the high I once felt, there are no more fireworks when we kiss," then you very well may be missing the point—infatuation may still be your goal. If your relationship seems devoid of the old bells and whistles, then find solace in the notion that at least you are in a position for true love to take root, which can't happen if you're floating up in some infatuated stratosphere amid the cacophony of bell-ringing and whistle-blowing!

The second reason you need to know about infatuation is because of the inexcusable possibility of infidelity. Whether it's a midlife eruption, an office dalliance, or seduction by a neighbor, if you're receptive to trading struggle for a blissful intoxication, you are vulnerable to infatuation.

It doesn't even matter that you've been a straight arrow in your relationship until now. If you're unhappy, if you're somewhat depressed and struggling with anxiety, if you feel neglected and unloved, or if you're just plain bored with the mundane same-old-same-old, you can't eliminate the possibility that you could be susceptible to infatuation's promise to rescue you from your unhappiness.

Since all infatuations are time-limited (as is the case with any intoxicant), eventually, like Romeo and Juliet, the feeling must die. When this happens, then the enormity of the infatuated indiscretions begins to sink in. I can't tell you how many patients I've treated over the years who've come into therapy shocked and appalled, saying, "What have I done? I've ruined my marriage! How could I have thrown everything away for that awful person? How could I have been so unconscious? My life is ruined!" How? Easy, you were swept off your feet by an infatuation.

Now for the really big question. How can we predict who, in a committed relationship, is susceptible to the intoxications of an infatuation? Could it be you? Your partner? You may not want to know this, but the answer is that potentially anyone who is ruled by insecurity is at risk. Which is why I've insisted on a thorough and ongoing Self-Coaching format for you and your partner. Only by liberating yourself from your habits of insecurity can you be assured that your world will remain safe from the impulses associated with infatuation.

Let me offer an example. I started working with Gary, an emotionally inhibited, mildly depressed, compulsive forty-five-year-old husband and father who never mentioned to me in our initial sessions that he had become thunderstruck by an equally receptive coworker. This was his secret. Fast-forward a few months. After a clandestine afternoon sexual encounter at a local motel, our inhibited, restricted Gary found himself blurting out, "I love you" to his paramour. All of a sudden his emotional restrictions were gone, all hesitations and fears—*gone*. For the first time he told me he felt free and open, liberated—*finally*. It was at this point that we can say that Gary, our husband and father, was no longer in control of his life. Infatuation was.

Prior to being bitten by his infatuation, Gary had been struggling with relationship dissatisfaction. He had told me, "I'm just not turned on anymore. I know I'd be able to perform if I could just feel more excited."

Gary had long ago convinced himself that there was nothing he could do to change the situation, and for the most part tried not to dwell on his unhappiness. So here was the kindling for infatuation's fire: a mildly depressed, inhibited guy who had been bailing out of his relationship for almost a year. Gary had turned himself over to insecurity and had become a true Turtle-victim. When infatuation came knocking, he was happy to open the door.

When insecurity goes unchecked it can, as in Gary's case, create receptivity for a quick fix. Let's face it, anything that can take a struggling life of malaise and unhappiness and turn it into an ecstatic world of bliss is going to get your attention. This is the work of insecurity—only insecurity is able to be this shortsighted and attracted to such obviously destructive solutions. But as obvious and destructive as the path of infidelity may be, most people suffering from insecurity remain easy prey. Only by eliminating the insecurity and catalytically recreating a true and lasting experience of love in your relationship can you be assured that you will never be surprised by infidelity.

When I Cheated It Felt Like the Real Me

One question that often comes up is, "How come I was able to be so free and open with my lover? With my partner I've never been able to experience that kind of liberation and excitement." The answer has to do, once again, with insecurity. In a grounded, legitimate relationship, you're dealing with reality. In an infatuation, you're dealing with fantasy—projected longings and intoxication. Since an infatuation is a kind of fairy-tale romance, you—the real you—are never exposed. And since there's no danger of real exposure, you're free to be anyone you want. It's almost like being anonymous—you don't have to worry about your old insecurities because that was your *old* reality, which has been replaced by this new surreal relationship. Since all infatuations always come back to earth, eventually you'll lose your romantic persona and wind up where you left off, with all your old Turtle, Tiger, Elephant, Raccoon, or Peacock traits firmly back in place. Alas, in life and in infatuations, there are no free lunches.

The Midlife Crisis

Keep in mind that insecurity isn't only connected to what's going on in your relationship; it's more often driven by personal shortcomings and vulnerabilities. This is particularly true of the dreaded midlife crisis. From my experience the term is a misnomer. It has nothing to do with a chronological point in one's life. "Midlife crisis" is a relative term that affects anyone who, because of insecurity, has been living an ostrichlike life filled with regrets, misgivings, or doubts that have been smoldering unnoticed in the recesses of their unconscious. For a relationship that isn't in sync, this smoldering can take place over years, if not decades. But at some point, a person begins to realize that time is running out. This could be at thirty, forty, fifty, or even sixty years old. It's a point where someone feels they need to challenge their unhappiness.

This challenge may not result in infidelity; it could take the form of other distractions like a new Porsche or a tummy tuck. But it can also start out as an innocent flirtation whose underlying destructiveness is often minimized with, "We're just friends. We only text each other. I wouldn't let this get out of hand." Or, "As long as I don't cross the line and have sex, what's the harm?" Famous last words. I've been asked many times, "What's the harm in having a little fun? Surely there's nothing wrong with that." My standard answer is, "If you'll go home and share this with your partner, then you're probably right, there's nothing wrong with it. But if you insist on keeping this a secret, then you can bet your boots there's something wrong with it."

I'm sure it will come as no shock to you that most midlife affairs wind up crashing and burning. As you've seen, the success of any infatuation is always a flip of the coin. When an infatuation occurs within the context of a relationship, then no matter what side of the coin turns up, you lose. Ever hear of a geographic fix? It's when you decide to sell the house and move across the country to solve your problems, saying, "I just need to get out of this town and start over." A geographic fix isn't a fix at all—your problems will migrate with you. Wherever you go, there you are. Having an affair is an infatuation fix—sooner or later, the same problems you're trying to run away from now will crop up again in your infatuated relationship. Insecurity is like a tail dragging behind you: eventually it catches up to you.

Looking Ahead to True and Lasting Love

I hope your Catalytic Self-Coaching training has now convinced you that infatuation isn't the goal of true and lasting love. We've spent a good deal of time discussing what love isn't; now it's time to discuss what it is. In the next chapter I hope to present a concise, workable definition of true love—one that can serve as a motivational tool to assist you and your partner in your Catalytic Self-Coaching follow-through efforts.

17

True Love, Great Sex
A Self-Coaching Understanding

When Mamtaz Mahal died, her husband, Shah Jahan, cried out with grief, "like an ocean raging with storm." He refused to appear in public or transact any affairs. From his constant weeping he was forced to use spectacles. His hair turned gray. Adhering to his dying wife's request to build a memorial to their love, Shah Jahan spent the next twenty years of his life constructing an appropriate tribute to the loving memory of his wife. Today, we call Shah Jahan's tribute the Taj Mahal.

The Taj Mahal's stunning beauty defies description, particularly at dawn and sunset or under a full moon when the onion-shaped white marble central dome—sometimes referred to as a tear on the face of humanity—appears to glow with a transcendent eeriness. Clearly, the Taj Mahal was an expression of Shah Jahan's eternal grief, but more importantly, it was also an expression of his eternal love. Love is never an easy emotion to describe, but Shah Jahan came pretty close.

True Love

Whether it's through architecture, poetry, or even psychology, I doubt anyone will ever be able to explain that love is this or love is that. Instead of attempting to define love, I offer you a couple of Catalytic Self-Coaching insights that may help you get a handle on this indescribable emotion.

True Love Begins When Infatuation Ends

Let's begin with something you learned in the last chapter: true love can begin only when infatuation ends. Perhaps you've come to agree with me that infatuation is merely a prelude to love, but if you're in a relatively new relationship, how exactly do you know when your infatuation has ended? One way is to realize that being infatuated causes both an emotional and a chemical high. As with any chemical high—alcohol, cocaine, caffeine, and so on—you're able to anesthetize yourself from life's problems while enjoying a drug-induced euphoria.

An infatuation is over (or diminishing) when you begin to return to your previous, nonintoxicated existence—your mundane reality of job, pressures, anxieties, stress, all of which were minimized and eclipsed by your infatuated experience. Although you're no longer infatuated, you may still feel your relationship is totally right and wonderful. But now, without the anesthetic of infatuation, you begin to realize that your relationship is no longer insulating you from the normal stressors of your life.

It's at this point that you and your partner can begin to build a life based on each other's *factual* uniqueness rather than on infatuation's *fictional* projections. What's critically important is that you realize that losing an infatuation is *not* a bad thing. If true and legitimate love is what you're really after, then giving up an infatuation is not only a good thing, it's an essential thing.

Unfortunately, if you've been brainwashed by the popular media into thinking that when you're in love you're *supposed* to be high, then a receding infatuation will leave you disappointed and questioning the value of the relationship—you'll see this as a bad thing. You simply need a bit of education to recognize that infatuation isn't an ending, it's a beginning.

A more serious problem arises when you're an infatuation junkie. You may recall Kevin in the last chapter, who was a serial infatuation addict. If you fall into this category, insecurity is driving you to sidestep your personal struggles by using infatuation to self-medicate. When you need to stay high at any cost, a fading infatuation is indeed cause for concern as old, nagging anxieties and insecurities begin to emerge once again.

Infatuation can be wonderful—who doesn't like fireworks?—but I hope I've been able to convince you that it is never the goal of true relating.

True Love Depends on Extinguishing Insecurity

The capacity for true love depends on minimizing or extinguishing insecurity. Throughout this book, you've learned that insecurity can cause havoc in any relationship:

- A jealous, insecure husband can't trust his wife around other men and therefore isn't going to risk opening up to love.

- An insecure Turtle wife may have so little self-respect that she just can't believe her husband could possibly love her. In fact, she may get angry at him for "lying" when he tells her he thinks she's wonderful.

- A depressed woman (remember, from a Self-Coaching standpoint, depression is a symptom of the depletion caused by insecurity) is unable to relate in a healthy way. Instead she begins to insulate herself by avoiding intimacy.

- An emotionally restricted, insecure Elephant partner may only be able to relate intellectually, never getting too close or exposing true emotions (other than hostility). It's just not his habit.

Any of these scenarios, if left unchecked, is capable of preventing the evolution of true love. This is why I spent so much of this book talking about Self-Coaching. Unless you are able to extricate yourself from the shackles of insecurity, your capacity to give and receive love will suffer. Only by removing the interfering effects of insecurity will you begin to open yourself up to true and lasting love.

Acorns and Insecurity

It's time for another visual. Imagine the potential for true love as an acorn that has recently been covered over by a freshly laid sidewalk. Surely, in this situation, the acorn's plight would be daunting, if not impossible. Desperately, the acorn would work tirelessly, trying to find a crack from which to send its shoot upward toward the light. Without the necessary nutrients from the sun, the best our frustrated acorn might do is to send a feeble, contorted stalk through one of the small cracks in the sidewalk.

Insecurity, sidewalklike, is an overlay to your personality, preventing your innate potential for love to evolve. Self-Coaching is the jackhammer you use to chip away at the habits of insecurity, thus allowing your instinctual potential for love to emerge and grow. And when love—and acorns—are allowed to grow unrestrained, the outcome is truly awe-inspiring.

Biology's Two Gears

Whenever I try to understand the psychology of who we are and why we do what we do, I ask: what is the evolutionary, adaptive advantage of such and such a behavior? Clearly genetic mutations (accidents) either cause an adaptive advantage or they don't. Over the millions of years that we were becoming "human," those traits that were adaptive to the ever-changing environment had a higher chance of survival (and therefore breeding), while those that offered no distinct advantage wound up as evolutionary dead ends. From an evolutionary perspective, a mechanism such as infatuation that brings two strangers together as a prelude to sex (procreation) seems rather obvious. The more intriguing, less obvious question is why staying in love *after* conception would create a survival advantage.

From a strictly biological-evolutionary standpoint, for our species to be successful, there needed to be two "love gears." The first gear was the falling-in-love gear, and the second was the staying-in-love gear. We've been talking extensively about the falling-in-love gear (infatuation) as the biological mechanism that brings two strangers together with the potential for procreation. So how do we explain the second gear, staying in love?

Let's travel back in time to the origins of our species. At the dawn of our evolution in the dangerous African wilderness, if a father wasn't tethered to the mother and child, the survival chances of a mother burdened with childbirth and childrearing would be slim. Assuming that our species evolved as hunter-gatherers, a mother with child would be limited in her ability to provide food, shelter, and protection from the brutal environmental challenges. If, however, there were a psychological mechanism that predisposed a father to stay with mother and child, then the chances of survival would be significantly improved. Without such a mechanism for keeping the father tethered to the mother and child, males would become infatuated, sow their seed, and move on. In which case, I probably wouldn't have written this book.

In order for our species to endure, some inclination toward what sociologists call pair bonding must have become part of our hardwiring. Such a pair-bonding instinct would ensure that as a team, a husband, wife, and child would greatly improve their odds of survival in the wilderness. And for pair bonding to become solidified, there needed to be a corresponding psychological mechanism to ensure it. This mechanism is the psychological experience we call love. Love is the glue, the bonding impulse, and the capacity for commitment—all of which come into play to ensure our survival. I know I'm reducing the sublimely beautiful experience of love into a genetic propensity for survival, but on the other hand, it's important to know that the force behind love is as powerful as life itself, which would not exist if it weren't for our capacity for love.

Self + Self = Us = Potential for Love

So now you know the rest of the story, at least from an evolutionary perspective. Infatuation is the initial force that brings two people together with the express underlying biological drive toward intercourse. Following infatuation, a second force begins to kick in, ostensibly for the purpose of childrearing, a force that attempts to bind two infatuated strangers together for life. But like all things instinctual, these forces must contend with environmental realities. The potential for a life of lasting love depends on many things, foremost of which is the level of insecurity in one or both partners. Bottom line: insecurity can interfere with, if not mute, a propensity for love.

Okay, so we know that love's two stages are an integral, compelling component in what makes us human—and what makes Hallmark successful. But we're still no closer to conceptualizing the loving experience in which two people become one, yet remain two. (This is not to be confused with the infatuated experience in which two people, based on mutual projections, experience only a facsimile of this experience of "oneness.") If you think back to our Self + Self = Us Portraits, you saw that partner A combined with partner B formed an "Us." But what exactly is an "Us"?

The Relationship Us

Just as the chromosomes from two parents combine to form a child, in a comparable way, true love can be seen as the Us-child created by the *psychological* blending of two partners. And like the uniqueness of a child, the Us-component of your relationship is something unique on this planet. From a psychological perspective, the Us is nothing less than a new and separate personality. No longer does each partner think exclusively in terms of "I." He or she now has a different viewpoint. "What will *we* do if I don't get the job?" "Don't worry, *we'll* manage to get through this."

As you've seen from your work with your Self + Self = Us Portraits, insecurity can contaminate a relationship, resulting in an unhealthy Us-Portrait (refer back to your original Self + Self = Us Portrait). But once insecurity is minimized or removed, what remains is a healthy expression of the Us-component. In attempting to understand the Us-component of a *healthy* relationship (that is, one catalytically engineered), you're actually beginning to create your own working definition of true love.

Catalytic Self-Coaching Reflection
Once insecurity is removed, the Us-Portrait of a relationship
is an adequate measure of the true love that exists.

If you could define true love, you would simultaneously be defining the Us-component of an insecurity-free relationship. Let me offer a few Catalytic Self-Coaching insights:

True love means true solace. As children we grow with an innate anticipation of the "other" (refer back to our discussion of Plato's *Symposium*). It's our instinctual "incompleteness" that propels us to seek the permanence of a partner. Infatuation starts the process of aligning ourselves with another person, and true love is the force that binds us. From the Us-experience, we derive a profound sense of solace, completeness, and resonance.

True love is enduring and progressive. When insecurity is reduced or eliminated from your life, true love is able to grow and mature. A stagnant relationship is a relationship suffering from insecurity—stagnation does not occur in a liberated, secure relationship. True love, like fine wine, must develop over time to reach its full maturity. The road toward mature love is often fraught with bumps and challenges, but with the right amount of self-awareness and trust, the bumps and challenges wind up helping rather than hindering.

True love changes your perception from "I" to "we." Until and unless we discover true love, we walk through life as relatively isolated, autonomous beings. I don't mean that love of friends, family, and pets isn't important or significant—clearly this isn't the case. I mean that the love between two life partners is indeed a unique and special experience. With true love there is a diminishing of ego boundaries as we begin to discover the "we-ness" of our new lives. The amount of unity that a couple possesses directly correlates to the love that exists, and is inversely proportional to the amount of insecurity existing in the relationship. Ego blending doesn't eliminate personal differences, it embraces them. The Us-component of a relationship brings you into a greater appreciation of your expanded relationship personality—one with twice the potential.

True love offers stability, comfort, and numerous other benefits. If you need proof that we as a species profit from being in a committed, loving relationship, you'll find plenty of data demonstrating that couples live longer, enjoy life more, are healthier, less depressed, and less anxious. The only variable to all the good news is how much of the contaminating effect of insecurity you can eliminate from your relationship. A struggling relationship negates all the potential benefits of a true and loving relationship.

True love is liberating and more efficient. I have a few single friends. The amount of energy, time, and resources that go into their pursuit of a partner is astounding to me. In contrast, being in a true and loving relationship frees you from the burden of "searching." You don't have to pursue love; you are free to pursue other pleasures like hobbies and interests, or simply stay home and read a good book or watch a TV show without feeling pressured.

True love offers a perception of permanence. One of the most difficult challenges of being on this earth is dealing with the impermanence of life. Change is not a bad thing, but ultimately a world of constant change leaves us feeling out of control and ungrounded. A stable loving relationship allows you to embrace and trust that there is one profound, permanent truth to your life—your partner. The words "Till death do us part" are indeed profound. Amid the turmoil and upheaval inherent in everyone's life, the knowledge that there is one enduring life component that you can count on and trust, *till death do us part*, not only offers solace to our chaotic existence, but more importantly offers us the opportunity to live our lives more courageously.

True love isn't something you find—it finds you. Throughout this book we've been focused on eliminating the influences of insecurity and liberating your capacity for true love. It's important that you don't overthink the issue of trying to find true love; this can actually impede your progress and experience. A better approach is to focus on removing any and all obstacles, trusting that love will occur naturally when there is no longer a perception of danger. As the saying goes, let go, let God. Let go of intellectualizing and let the instinctual, natural forces emerge.

The Role of Sexuality in True Love

How do you know you have a problem with sex?

- If your sexual experience is rigid, mechanical, and lacking in emotion, there's a problem.
- If you find yourself avoiding sex, there's a problem.
- If you find yourself repelled by sex or sexual adventurousness, there's a problem.
- If you aren't turned on by your partner, there's a problem.
- If you feel ashamed or guilty after sex, there's a problem.
- If you find sex boring, there's a problem.
- If you're not having sex, there's a problem.

For many, sexuality can be the source of intense relationship struggle. How can something so natural, so instinctual wind up becoming so difficult? From all that you've read to this point, you probably can anticipate where I'm going to point my finger: sexual struggle is highly correlated with insecurity. Like love, sexuality isn't something you need to study, practice, or rehearse; it's something you need to release. Saying this differently, get out of your head and what follows is an innate capacity for sexual fulfillment—whether you're a Turtle, Tiger, Elephant, Raccoon, or Peacock. I'm not saying you can't improve your technique or your approach, but before resorting to more intellectual pursuits, when it comes to reviving or salvaging a waning sexual experience, nothing is more important than eliminating insecurity.

Sexual dysfunction has many guises. Take Cory, an overly intellectualized, I'm-in-charge Elephant, whose attitude toward sex was shaped by his need to control. "I need my wife to know that I'm in charge. You know, I need to be in control of what happens. That's why the other night when I had difficulty getting . . . you know . . . an erection, I didn't want her to notice. I just got up and told her that her perfume was killing me. I don't think she knew what happened. Since then I've been avoiding sex. How do I know it won't happen again?" Cory's excessive need for control was now being tested as he began to spiral downward, ruminating incessantly about "not performing."

Cory had long ago created his I'm-in-charge Elephant persona. He wasn't about to risk being vulnerable. For him, not being able to perform sexually was terrifying. After all, his carefully crafted, macho image was at stake. Little did he understand that his insistence on sexual potency was the reason for his sexual impotency—he was trying too hard to be in control. His insecurity was about to create a sexual roadblock—more than Cory wanted to have sex, he wanted to avoid being exposed as having a weakness. Especially a sexual weakness.

In contrast to Cory's dilemma, Pat, an insulated Turtle I was working with, presented a somewhat different scenario. "Gary's always complaining about our sex. He says I'm like a dishrag, just lying there. He wants me to get into it. I can't say he's wrong, but sex has always made me uncomfortable. Recently, Gary brought home a porn video that he wanted me to watch. He felt it would help loosen me up. There's no way I was going to watch that trash! I can't explain it, I just can't. Watching a video of other people having sex is . . . disgusting. If I were completely honest, I'd be happy if Gary and I didn't have sex. It's the only thing we fight about."

Pat's hesitations, along with her emotional baggage about sexual morality, along with her overly defensive sexual posture, were creating a formidable wall, preventing a natural, more liberated experience to emerge. The culprit, as in all relationship struggles, begins and ends with insecurity. In Pat's case, it turned out to be her historical habit of keeping her emotions in check—especially intense emotions connected to her suppressed sexuality. Letting go to sexuality requires an abandonment of the ego, a letting loose of very strong instinctual forces. For Pat, who had long ago convinced herself that she needed to keep her emotional world in check, the ecstatic possibilities of sexuality were much too threatening.

Cory and Pat represent two variations of how insecurity can infiltrate and undermine sexuality, even in a loving relationship. I'm not saying that other problems don't contribute to sexual struggle, but as you're about to see, it's not the real-world problems that lead to sexual difficulty; it's *how* these challenges are dealt with. Let's take a look at some legitimate relationship realities that contribute to sexual struggle.

Physical Problems

Whether it's diabetes, irritable bowel syndrome, premenstrual syndrome, chronic fatigue syndrome, thyroid or adrenal dysfunction, hypertension, obesity, or other physical conditions, these are real problems that can have profound effects on your sexuality. Medications such as cold remedies, antidepressants, antihypertensives, and diuretics can also contribute to physical challenges. We should include in this list drugs such as alcohol, nicotine, stimulants, marijuana, and so on. Physical challenges can also include chronic or acute stress, fatigue, anxiety, or depression, all of which can affect the physical receptivity of you or your partner.

The best advice I can give you for handling physical problems comes from my grandmother, who was fond of saying, "One door closes, another opens." Alan, a fifty-five-year-old patient whose prostate surgery left him impotent, sums this up rather succinctly:

> Jean and I avoided sex. We didn't even talk about it in those months following my surgery. I guess we were both driven by fear. Fear in admitting that unless I wanted to consider surgical implants, or penile injections, we were never going to have normal sex again. I can't tell you exactly what I was feeling. Just kind of overloaded with emotions, regrets, anger, even resentment toward Jean. Don't ask me why I resented her, maybe because she was a constant reminder of what was wrong with me. Regardless of how I tried, I kept coming back to the fact that I was no longer a man. Those were dark days.
>
> Perhaps the darkest day was when I went to Jean and told her that I would understand if she wanted to leave me. Jean started crying. I thought she was crying because I had guessed her true desires, but what I later found out was that she was crying because she loved me and her heart was breaking because she knew that I was struggling with all this. That was the turning point. That was when we began to talk.
>
> I found that Jean was just as fearful as I was about approaching the subject—she, because she didn't want to upset or depress me, and me, because I was feeling that I was cheating her out of the life she deserved. We talked about sex and intimacy. I knew that without an erection, I could still have an orgasm, not the same as before, and there were a few complications with my incontinence, but nevertheless, there were options. What we decided to do was not to figure things out. We more or less agreed to throw out our old notions of sex and kind of see what happened.

It was awkward, but it was nice. From the very first try, we cuddled, stroked, kissed. You might think I'm rationalizing, but I must tell you, I've never had better, more enjoyable, more loving sex in my life! Jean and I have become very adventurous, and the more involved I become in wanting to explore our newfound openness, the more truly excited I feel about where we're going. Before I started counseling, I always thought the most sensitive male organ was the penis; I've come to realize I was wrong. It's my mind.

As I said, one door closes, another opens.

Attitudes and Beliefs

Physical problems are objective realities, but equally challenging are the attitudes and beliefs that we drag along in life, allowing them to enter our bedrooms. Toxic attitudes such as, "I was always taught that sex was dirty"; "Sex is exploitative—I need to stay in control"; "I can't let her think I'm not a man, I've got to dominate." Attitudes, especially those based in insecurity, are learned. When it comes to challenging an attitude, nothing is more important than bringing it out into the cold light of day and scrutinizing it. Attitudes, especially reflexive attitudes that are unspoken, may go unnoticed—unnoticed, but definitely experienced as they constantly undermine normal sexuality.

Typically, all that's needed with repressive attitudes is an open mind and a bit of education—both of which will not happen if insecurity dominates. If you recall the example of Pat earlier in this chapter, you can see that becoming receptive to a more natural, instinctual sexuality requires the capacity for opening your mind and learning to risk trusting. Sure, stepping apart from any long-standing habit is going to feel unnatural at first, and that's okay. Just because it feels unnatural doesn't mean it is unnatural. Your Self-Coaching training can help you step apart from reflexive thinking and become more open to your capacity for sexual ecstasy. Not only is it not dangerous, it can be fulfilling, relationship-nurturing, and well worth any initial discomfort you may feel.

The Psychology of Sexual Resistance

We've discussed physical limitations and attitudinal resistances. Lastly we come to psychological problems and issues related to sexuality. Good sex requires stepping out of your ego and letting go. Sexuality is a visceral experience—*not* an intellectual one. Insecurity will keep you in your head, spinning thoughts, judging your performance, and destroying any possibility of getting turned on. Once again, it's insecurity that insists that we control sex. And by its very nature, sexuality is not meant to be controlled.

Here's where your Self-Coaching needs to be put to the test. In order to experience ecstasy, you must be willing to let go . . . to risk being vulnerable and, in a very real sense, handing yourself over to a powerful force that lies beyond ego consciousness. If you're holding on to a need to control sex, your sexuality will remain mechanical, nothing more than a physical release, or expressed in various deflections like porn addiction, excessive masturbation, or fetish compulsions. Only by letting go of control will you be allowing yourself to experience one of life's most gratifying pleasures. Actually, I'd go as far as to suggest that the sexual, orgasmic moment is the closest we humans come to our own transcendency—the timeless, boundless nature of our beings.

Here are a few do's and don'ts to keep in mind as you work through your sexual resistance:

Do learn to see sexuality through the eyes of your partner. As you've seen throughout this book, whenever I try to understand psychology, I turn toward our evolutionary past for clues. In a strictly biological sense, sperm is cheap and eggs are valuable. Men have the luxury of wasting millions of sperm without consequence, whereas for a woman, a fertilized egg is a totally different story. This biological difference produces accompanying psychological components. Men are more driven to pursue sex—sometimes quite compulsively. Women, on the other hand, are more driven to protect their eggs. In evolutionary times long past, it would have been disastrous for a woman to be less than selective by choosing a deadbeat father to mate with. Therefore, women are more tuned in to deeper emotional aspects of relating and sexuality—aspects that instinctually confirm for her that her guy is a secure bet to hang around for the long term.

I would sum this up by suggesting that men are inclined to seek sex in order to confirm love, while women are more inclined to confirm love before pursuing sex. I recognize the sexist connotations to this overgeneralized argument, but from personal and professional experience, this seems to be the case more so than not. I can't tell you how many times I hear these comments:

Typical male: I just want to have sex. The way I see it, it doesn't matter what's going on, once you engage in sex, nothing else matters. Sex gets you in the mood for sex.

Typical female: He doesn't get it. Unless we have some experiences like communicating, relaxing, and cuddling, I just don't get in the mood for sex. When I feel close and loved, I feel sexy.

You should see the wide-eyed stares I get when I tell couples struggling with this problem that a woman needs twenty-four hours of foreplay prior to sex. I of course clarify this by saying that, in my opinion, sexual foreplay for a woman has to do with the total relationship milieu that leads up to the bedroom. I encourage couples to take some Us-time during the day: a cup of coffee together, a walk, something that affirms the bond of intimacy that exists. This is what makes for great sex.

Don't hold back to protect yourself from your insecurity. Protecting yourself by avoiding sex is counterproductive—it creates problems. In order to let go, you need to risk. How? Well, for starters, stop expecting your partner to make the first move. Take responsibility and initiate. Your partner, because of his or her hesitations, may not be in tune with your desire to break the negative patterns, so it's up to you to take the lead. And expect to feel a bit of anxiety about breaking your own reflexive insulation or avoidance. Some anxiety is both normal and expected. Safety, security, and comfort come *after* you've had a bit of experience with your new sexual interactions and have begun to incorporate them into your relationship.

Do communicate. Reminds me of a joke I heard recently: "I came home the other day and my wife greeted me dressed in some sexy underwear. 'Tie me up,' she purred, 'and you can do anything you want.' So I tied her up and went fishing!" You can't expect your partner to be on the same page if you're only hinting at your needs. Sure, it may feel risky, even frightening, but once you take the first step, it becomes not only easy, but natural.

What you're really after in your relationship is a reactive sexual experience. Once you step apart from your congested thinking, you can allow yourself just to react. Remember, it's that other, nonintellectual part of your being that allows you to fully participate in all this—if you let it. Reacting to sexual urges without conscious contemplation or reservation means you're headed for ecstatic bliss. Such a state cannot be experienced if you're clinging to thoughts—any thoughts.

Sex is a shared pleasure that not only affirms and confirms the love you feel, but deepens and reinforces the intimacy that needs to grow throughout your relationship and your life. And as a valuable side effect, sexuality will reduce your tension and stress, allowing you to be more effective not only in your relationship, but in your day-to-day activity. Sex can give your life perspective like no other experience. It can teach you that problems, stressors, and challenges are transient . . . love is enduring. Sex, with its capacity for confirming your love, allows you to participate in something profoundly transcendent and timeless.

Catalytic Self-Coaching Reflection

Think of your sexual experience as a mirror reflecting the quality of your relationship. If the reflection is a mechanical, lifeless orgasm, then you are still caught up in control. If the reflection is a selfish or one-sided attempt to meet your own needs, then you are detached from your partner. If, on the other hand, your reflection reveals connectedness, adventurousness, excitement, and emotional abandonment, then you are allowing love to steer your experience. In which case, congratulations!

18

The Ten Essential Principles of Successful Relating

Every summer I go to the local nursery and buy a dozen tomato plants. I carefully prepare the soil with humus and fertilizer, spacing the plants evenly apart in small shallow "dishes" made of mounded dirt to hold enough water for the fledgling plants. As the plants grow, I continue to fertilize, water, prune, stake, support, and offer protection from a few wandering deer (I just found a nifty motion sensor that squirts a spray of water at any would-be intruder). Eventually I'm rewarded with the best beefsteak tomatoes this side of the Hudson River.

My point is that revitalizing a relationship requires more than planting a few strategies and positive affirmations. In order to reach the fruit of your Catalytic Self-Coaching efforts, you'll need to realize that reading this book is just a beginning—the fertilizer and humus part. Now it's time to nurture, support, and protect your efforts. Just as you can't expect tomatoes to grow on immature vines, you must allow your efforts to ripen and mature. With patience, intention, and attention, you will be richly rewarded.

Ten Ways to Ensure Success

You now have the necessary foundation to undo the habits and patterns of insecurity that have been holding you back from the relationship you want and deserve. Before officially discharging you from this phase of your training, I'd like to list for you what I feel are ten essential principles that comprise the ongoing catalytic efforts necessary to ensure success.

1. Trust

As you continue to eliminate insecurity, you will become more objective, rational, and clear about your life. You will develop both self-trust and relationship trust. Your Catalytic Self-Coaching training will allow you to see through any remaining reflexive distortions and patterns—Elephant, Tiger, and so on—of insecurity. Now is the time to recognize the ongoing need to fine-tune your awareness. Awareness of the need for ongoing positive change is the first step, embracing and trusting these changes is the final step in reaching your ultimate goal of relationship trust.

In relationships where trust has been damaged by insecurity, you may have an understandable hesitation about taking the necessary leap of faith required for trusting. You or your partner may need to be convinced, which is why patience is important. Keep in mind that positive change, in order to last, must be consistent over time. Remember:

> Consistent, positive, loving behavior over time + your willingness to risk = trust

Sometimes progress will be obvious from your partner's accountability, reliability, fidelity, or actions, but oftentimes trust is something you'll need to infer from the total relationship experience. In this case your feelings should confirm what you're seeing. And if what you're seeing and feeling becomes consistently positive, then at some point you need to encourage yourself to lower any remaining defenses and take that leap of faith. Bottom line: trust is nothing more than a willingness to believe. Nothing more, nothing less.

2. Responsibility

A relationship is a team (Us) effort. If your team is to be balanced and effective, then you and your partner must share the responsibility fairly.

Responsibility in a relationship covers a lot of ground, everything from grocery shopping and household chores to communication, honesty, fidelity, and, as is the case with Catalytic Self-Coaching, mutual effort. If your relationship is unbalanced and one partner winds up handling more than his or her fair share of the responsibility, make no mistake, there will be friction.

In order to accurately assess what's "fair," each partner must be liberated from insecurity. Since insecurity will distort your perception of fairness, it's important for you and your partner to use Self-Coaching to reach a level of objectivity that will allow you to know whether or not you're being fair in any given situation. Once your insecurity is gone, it takes only a moment to ask yourself, "Am I really being fair?" Honest self-scrutiny remains the single best way to becoming a responsible partner.

3. Personal Awareness

Personal awareness is something you cultivate. To do this, I encourage you to keep a journal. Your journal should include all your Self-Coaching efforts, paying particular attention to any lingering controlling behaviors along with a list of any ruminative doubts, fears, or negatives. Putting your experiences on paper removes them from the thinking part of your brain and places them in a more visual part. Sometimes the awakening that ensues is startling. If you've never tried to use a journal, you might be amazed at the insights that come from this simple practice.

Another great source of personal awareness can come from your partner. Get in the habit of asking your partner for feedback. Since you and your partner are practicing Self-Coaching, you can begin to trust that what they tell you is truly valuable information. Although you may feel a bit hesitant, I heartily recommend sharing your journal with your partner. This is a courageous step in liberating yourself from any lingering insecurity that may be keeping you from truly letting go and experiencing a frictionless relationship. And think about the practicality of this suggestion. Who is in a better position to give you accurate, insightful feedback than your partner? Trust me on this, a liberated partner can rival the best psychologist in helping you to see yourself accurately.

4. Partner Awareness

Personal awareness is only 50 percent of what's necessary for success in your relationship. The other 50 percent is partner awareness. Since your relationship was struggling, there's a high probability that, back in those dark days, you developed some distorted perceptions of your partner. Be aware that perceptions that have become habituated are slow to change. In couples counseling, I hear it all the time. "What? You say I'm always yelling! Haven't you noticed that I haven't raised my voice in six months?" We all have a tendency to keep "seeing" old behaviors long after they've been removed. I refer to this tendency as having "reflexive perceptions." This is critically important, since clinging to old, outdated perceptions will interfere with the Self-Coaching task of learning to put your guard down and risk trusting.

Gaining a more accurate partner awareness oftentimes requires nothing more than careful and objective scrutiny. You can cut right to the chase by discussing with your partner ways that they feel they have changed or ways that your partner feels you haven't. It's important for each of you to be engaged in here-and-now reality, assessing rather than permitting old, reflexive perceptions to linger. There's nothing more discouraging to your partner than for you to fail to notice positive change.

5. Maturity

I often point out to battling partners how childlike their exchanges become when one or both is engaged in defensive interacting. This is particularly true when awareness and trust are absent. Before there can be relationship maturity, there must first be personal maturity. What's maturity? For starters, it's acting like an adult rather than a child. You know yourself (if you're honest) when you're acting childish. "No, I said no! I'm not going to go to your mother's!" "Oh yeah, you think I'm being rude? Well, look who's talking. You're being a jerk!" Go to a playground and observe children in conflict. It will help sensitize you to inappropriate, immature behavior.

It's a good practice to observe and listen to yourself whenever you feel threatened. At first most people feel that they can do this only in retrospect. Only after a flare-up can they look back and realize, "Guess I really lost it there." This kind of immediate in-the-moment self-scrutiny is definitely a skill. But with the right attitude, patience, and practice you can acquire it. Don't give yourself a pass on this one. Make this skill happen.

I should point out that immaturity is so prevalent in struggling relationships because insecurity is a primitive defense whose origins were laid down in your childhood. When you regress to this level of insecurity, you're abandoning your maturity and replacing it with old, childlike defensiveness. You are actually acting as you did when you were a child. Not very attractive, huh?

6. Fidelity, Loyalty, and Commitment

We live in a world of temptation. Choosing to remain faithful, involved, and committed to the evolution of your relationship isn't an option; it's a requirement. Insecurity and immaturity go hand in hand when it comes to indiscretions. Cheating comes in many guises these days, especially with the ease and anonymity of the Internet. Anyone can be tempted. But a secure, mature person knows that such impulses are transient vestiges from older, neurotic needs. An insecure partner, on the other hand, can't readily distinguish an adolescent or neurotic urge from reality; fragmented egos can't resist the temptation to seek infatuation's hypnotic spell.

If you find yourself capable of drifting, you need to do something now. *Today.* You can begin by spending more time on your Self-Coaching. Go back and read chapter 16 on love, infatuation, and infidelity, or better yet, check in with a psychologist and get some perspective. As you read in chapter 16, being seduced by an infatuation may have absolutely nothing to do with your partner or your relationship's ultimate potential for success—it has everything to do with your own insecurity. What may seem innocent one day could wind up innocently ruining your relationship the next. It happens all the time.

7. Friendship and Companionship

Friendship and companionship are two qualities that you might assume are inherent in every loving relationship. This isn't always the case—but it can be. I was recently told by a young wife, "I really love my husband, but we're just not good friends. We really have nothing in common." Learning to enjoy each other's company requires stepping apart from your egocentric world and embracing your partner's uniqueness. When, because of egocentricity and insecurity, you're only interested in selfish things, you will quickly become bored with your partner. This is one more reason why your Self-Coaching training is so valuable—you need to open your eyes and your heart to the full potential of your relationship.

If you find that you don't look forward to seeing or being with your partner, then recognize that it's time for some effort. You've got to get creative. Find mutuality, explore novel possibilities, but most importantly, take the time to really explore your partner's personality. I recall an oil painting class I took in college. We were instructed to observe an egg for at least five minutes and then paint it. After a couple of minutes, what started out as just an egg surprisingly began to yield its more intricate texture, shading, and complexity. When you look—really look—at something carefully, you begin to see endless possibilities and discoveries. Don't let habituated patterns—"Oh, he's just a stick in the mud"; "She does her thing, I do mine"—stop you from challenging the status quo. Refuse to let old habits dictate the optimism you're beginning to cultivate. Remember my egg.

8. Sense of Humor and Playfulness

Remember Step 3 of Self-Talk, letting go? If you want to enjoy your relationship, you can't get bogged down with insecurity's gnawing, congested thinking. Letting go and having some fun is a terrific way to inject energy and vitality into your relationship. And when insecurity is removed, you'll find that humor is a natural, spontaneous occurrence. From a therapeutic standpoint, I'm always more concerned about a couple who sit across from me humorless and grim than I am about a couple who have still retained the capacity for interactive humor.

If you find that you're too rigid, too grim, or somber in your relationship, then you must question your level of insecurity. The main reason you get like this is because your spontaneity is being stifled by insecurity and control. Don't get me wrong, I'm not saying you need to walk in the door each night and do five minutes of your best stuff. But I am saying that everyone likes to have fun—except if you're too busy protecting yourself from insecurity's doubts, fears, and negatives. Letting go, enjoying a bit of playfulness, letting that happy childlike spontaneity find expression is a sure prescription to enhancing the desire to be with each other. And wanting to be with each other is a testimony to the fact that you're truly connecting to your relationship center.

9. Effort

As obvious as it seems, having a great relationship requires an investment of energy. Often, relationship stagnation reflects years of apathy and lethargy. Bad habits, nothing more. In order to ignite the energy inherent in your relationship, you're going to have to agree to try . . . and try . . . and try. Whatever it takes, you must infuse your relationship with the vitality and energy it needs to grow and mature. Whether it's going dancing or to the gym together, taking a walk, or playing tennis, you need to be willing to invest the physical energy required. But not just the physical energy, the psychological effort will also require effort—oftentimes more than the physical. Psychological effort means becoming a better listener, connecting more to your partner's world, and embracing, with interest, your partner's point of view. If you don't have the energy for your relationship—find it!

10. Risking Love

Lastly, we come to the heart of Catalytic Self-Coaching. Everything you've learned has been moving toward this one central component, the need to risk loving your partner. Insecurity will always want you to love with a one-foot-in, one-foot-out hesitation. No one wants to get hurt, rejected, or burnt in a relationship. This makes sense when you're beginning a relationship or healing from a broken one, but ultimately you need to abandon all fear, all hesitation, all doubt, and take the plunge. You need to risk being vulnerable.

What do you have to lose? You've come this far. You've both been working to shed the effects of insecurity—why hold back now on this very last challenge? It makes no sense. Perhaps before you both began to shed insecurity and were mired in destructive, spiraling conflict, that was a point where self-protection made sense. But now, with awareness and a liberated capacity for openness, there is no more reason—at least no more legitimate reason. I can't tell you it's time—only you can. I can only ask: if not now, when?

Eric and Robin: Vive la Différence

I conclude this book with a discussion of how long-standing problems can easily be resolved once the Catalytic Self-Coaching process is employed. As you read Eric and Robin's story in the following pages, keep in mind that they had successfully gone through their own Self-Coaching efforts and were at the point in their counseling where their individual insecurities were reasonably neutralized. This story picks up at a point where both partners had become equal participants in the healing process. And it was at this point that Eric and Robin were feeling a great deal of satisfaction and relief knowing that their once faltering relationship was now on rock-steady ground. Steady with one exception: their sex life.

Eric's a thirty-four-year-old computer programmer. Robin, a year younger, is employed as a teacher's aide. They've been married for five years. Eric was a bit of a know-it-all—a highly intellectualized Elephant with leanings toward Peacock arrogance. Robin had both Turtle tendencies as well as a bit of a Raccoon's penchant for being the martyr. Initially their problems had to do with lack of effective communication, chronic friction, arguing, general unhappiness, and relationship malaise. It was Robin who arranged for counseling and it was she who was initially the more motivated partner.

Because of Eric's rather strong Elephant defensiveness, Robin had to be more proactive with her own Self-Coaching in order to create the necessary vacuum to encourage Eric to stop swinging his trunk around (and begin his own Self-Coaching exploration). Once he began to back off his defensiveness though, progress was swift—with one exception. The issue of sex. According to Eric: "Not enough sex!" According to Robin: "Oh, please! That's all Eric thinks about."

Here's what Eric had to say about wanting more sex:

We're doing much better in so many ways, but nothing has changed in the bedroom. Robin is always too busy, too tired, or too distracted. I try, but I get very discouraged. Sometimes I get angry. It's really not fair. Robin has no idea how hard it is for a man to go weeks without sex. I start to think about it all the time and the more I think about it, the angrier I get at Robin. I don't want this frustration to undermine the progress we've made, but something has to be done. Soon!

I asked Robin to give me her perspective on this situation. She replied:

For the record, we rarely go weeks without sex. But that's exactly what I'm talking about—Eric distorts the facts. One thing's for sure, Eric has a one-track mind! He drives me cuckoo. I mean, I could be folding the laundry and he gets excited. Sometimes I stay up late so I don't have to be harassed every time I go to bed. It's not like I don't enjoy sex. I have absolutely no problem. But I don't have the same compulsive drive that Eric does.

Fortunately, Eric and Robin had progressed in their counseling beyond their personal insecurities and could now take this problem and deal with it in a mature, direct way. I asked, "Can we all agree that when it comes to sexual preferences, we're not dealing with facts, we're dealing with each other's perceptions? You've learned that moralizing, judging, or name-calling is nothing more than an attempt to control a situation. Right now, I'm going to ask each of you to step into each other's 'psychological shoes' and become your partner. Eric, I want you to imagine you're Robin, and tell us not how *you* think, but how you think Robin thinks about this problem. Robin, I'm going to ask you the same thing. You're Eric. I want you to tell us how Eric thinks. Okay, Eric, tell us what Robin thinks the sexual problem is:

Eric [*role-playing Robin*]: I wish Eric wouldn't think of sex all the time. He makes me feel so trapped. Sometimes I just want to hide. I can't help it if I don't have a big sex drive.

Robin [*role-playing Eric*]: I need to have a release. This is so frustrating. Why won't she just relax and enjoy . . . why does she have to fight it? I really think there's something wrong with her chemically. It's not normal to not want sex.

And there it was. From the above exchange you can see one major theme: both Eric and Robin were assuming that Robin was having a problem (psychologically or physically) with her sex drive. If you recall, Robin was prone to Turtle-martyr avoidance and guilt. It's reflexive for her to feel like she's wrong when in conflict. The fiction that fuels this problem can be summed up as Robin thinking that Eric feels there's something wrong with her: "there's something wrong with her chemically." And Eric believes that Robin admits the same problem: "I don't have a big sex drive."

I asked Eric and Robin to try the same exercise again, only not to assume the premise that there was anything wrong with Robin or her sex drive.

Eric [*role-playing Robin*]: I wish Eric wouldn't take it so personally when we don't have sex. It's not that I don't want him to be happy. I'm just not into it as much as him. Maybe there's a compromise?

Robin [*role-playing Eric*]: This is very frustrating, but I understand that we're different people. Somehow we need to go forward without ignoring my needs, but also not ignoring Robin's differences.

Bingo. If you recall the metaphor I used in chapter 4, sometimes the key is simply realizing that if you start off with a bent coin in the stack, everything that follows will tilt. Eric and Robin recognized that the problem—the real problem—wasn't with Robin. It was in their failure to understand each other's differences. It was this straightforward realization that put them in a position to seek a solution.

Catalytic Self-Coaching Reflection

Can you respect that you and your partner have legitimate differences, or are you like Eric, insisting that your partner agree with your view of the world?

Of course, if Robin had been less of a Turtle, she might have been more likely to respect her own sexual preferences rather than agree with Eric that she was the "defective" partner. As a rule of thumb, watch out for old reflexes of insecurity that put you on the defensive, and in any conflict, always begin with curiosity—*never* guilt. Had Robin been curious instead of guilty, she might have been willing to explore the facts and fictions of Eric's allegations more carefully. "Eric's correct, I don't share his sexual appetite, but who's to say he's right and I'm wrong?"

As you progress with your own relationship, every once in a while you'll encounter leftover reflexes that need to be challenged. At this point in your training don't feel this is a big deal. You have all the tools, the awareness, and the trust to undo any emotional baggage that persists or that revisits your relationship. Just stay curious rather than defensive and you'll be in the best possible position to unravel the thorniest of problems.

In Robin and Eric's relationship, they were both perpetuating the "defective" partner perception, and all it took was a bit of Catalytic Self-Coaching to topple this myth. The only hint I gave Robin and Eric once they began to see the bigger picture was to recognize that this wasn't a Robin problem, but was instead a relationship problem. The issue—the real issue—that had to be addressed was, "What can *we* do about this?" This was their homework, and it only took a week before they came in with what Robin referred to as their plan:

> First, I want to mention that Eric and I decided to pay more attention to each other. What was hurting us was allowing our own insecurity to see things in a one-sided way. The role-playing we did opened our eyes and we've been using that to help us continue to tune in to each other's perspective. I know for me, I have a much deeper appreciation of not only the physical pressure Eric feels when it comes to wanting sex, but also the emotional connections he has to it. And I feel confident that Eric understands that my needs are different—not better and certainly not worse than his. So, based on our newfound awareness, here's what we came up with.
>
> We both agreed that we would be patient with each other and rather than trying to contrive *when* we were going to have sex, we

would both take a risk and trust that we'd be better off letting the opportunity for sex come to us when the time was right. We agreed not to think about when or how and simply go back to our Self-Talk training and *let it go.* I remember you telling us how when the pupil is ready the teacher appears. This is the attitude we decided to embrace. It did take a bit of convincing before Eric was willing to risk believing that I really was "receptive" and not just making excuses. (It didn't hurt that we took a ride to Victoria's Secret after dinner the other night and selected a few naughty outfits for me.) We agreed that we were just going to wait and see what happened.

Well, I'm glad to report that we did have a wonderful experience the other night, and I must tell you, it was absolutely perfect. It just happened, like we predicted. Sure, we had been talking about it and all and it was in the air, but the other night we were kind of joking around and feeling giddy. Eric just kind of reached over and gave me a meaningful peck of a kiss . . . nothing dramatic, but a kiss that sent electricity through both of us. I've never felt so sexual in my life. It found us.

Congratulations

Eric and Robin's story is a good place to end this book. Building trust in a relationship is the endgame; it's the way all good things will find you. Don't neglect the foundational work that needs to be done, and then be willing to come back to center anytime you're blown off course. There's a Zen adage that says, "Seven times down, eight times up." If you and your partner are willing to outlast any insecurity or defensiveness you will be guaranteeing success. As Eric and Robin found out, then *it* will find you.

This is all I have to say. It's all I need to say. You have everything you need to ensure that your relationship can break the shackles of insecurity and soar to the limitless opportunities that love offers. If I had one wish, it would be for every couple to realize just how simple and effortless true loving really is. It has never been that complicated. It only felt that way because of insecurity's distortions. All that's changed now.

Index

253

love (*continued*)
  infatuation and, 214–224,
    226–227
  insecurity and, 228
  as risk, 247–248
  sexuality and, 233–236
  sexual resistance and, 237–239
  Us-Portrait and, 229–232
loyalty, 245

Mahal, Mamtaz, 225
manipulation, 73–74, 210. *See also*
  Raccoons
maturity, 244–245
medical problems, sexuality and,
  234–236
meditation, 135–136
mental illness, 120–121
midlife crisis, 223
"mind-reading" control pattern, 62
Moro reflex, 7

"name-calling" control pattern, 63
narcissism, 75–76. *See also* Peacocks

Occam's razor, 38
orgasm, 216–217

pain, in relationships, 3–6
pair bonding, 229
panic ("grabbing the rip cord"),
  122–124, 141
parroting, 208–209
partner awareness, 244
passive-aggressive avoidance, 30
Peacocks, 59
  defined, 75–76
  examples, 164–171, 189–195,
    248–252
  self-quiz for, 91–92
  See also reflexive personality patterns
perception, 69–70

of "defective" partner, 251–252
insecurity and, 163
point of view of each partner, 8–9
Reactive Living and, 138–139
of sexuality, 236
See also reflexive personality patterns
personal responsibility,
  105, 243
physical problems, sexuality and,
  234–236
Plato, 215–216
playfulness, 246–247
pornography, 83
primal androgynes, 215–216
problem avoiders. *See* avoidance;
  reluctant partners
procreation, love and, 228–229,
  237–238
projection, 137, 215–220, 219–220. *See*
  also fiction, separating fact from

Raccoons, 59
  defined, 73–74
  examples, 109–111
  self-quiz for, 90–91
  See also reflexive personality patterns
Reactive Living, 54, 134–135,
  136–139, 142
Reflections/Tips
  on coaching each other, 192, 194,
    195, 196
  on follow-through, 199, 201, 204
  on insecurity, 36, 37, 43, 50
  on love, 230, 250
  on love and sexuality, 239
  on reflexive personality patterns, 76
  on relationship struggle, 23, 31, 33
  on relationship-struggle
    "vacuum," 169
  on Self-Talk, 104, 111, 112, 115, 119,
    126–127, 132, 133
  on Us-Portrait, 181